The Education System
since 1944

The Education System since 1944

PETER GOSDEN

Martin Robertson · Oxford

First published in 1983 by Martin Robertson & Company
Ltd., 108 Cowley Road, Oxford OX4 1JF.

British Library Cataloguing in Publication Data

Gosden, P.H.J.H.
    The education system since 1944
    1. Education—Great Britain—History—
20th century
    1. Title
    370'941 LA632

ISBN 0–85520–280–7

Typeset at the Spartan Press Ltd, Lymington, Hants
Printed and bound in Great Britain by
Billing and Sons Ltd., Worcester

Contents

List of Tables

List of Abbreviations

ACC	Association of County Councils
ACSET	Advisory Council on the Supply and Education of Teachers
ACTST	Advisory Council on the Training and Supply of Teachers
AEC	Association of Education Committees
AMA	Association of Metropolitan Authorities
AMC	Association of Municipal Corporations
ATCDE	Association of Teachers in Colleges and Departments of Education
ATO	Area Training Organization
ATTI	Association of Teachers in Technical Institutions
BEC	Business Education Council
CAT	College of Advanced Technology
CCA	County Councils Association
CNAA	Council for National Academic Awards
CEE	Certificate of Extended Education
CSE	Certificate of Secondary Education
CVCP	Committee of Vice-Chancellors and Principals
DES	Department of Education and Science
GCE	General Certificate of Education
GLC	Greater London Council
HMI	Her Majesty's Inspector
HNC	Higher National Certificate
HORSA	Hutting Operation for the Raising of the School Leaving Age
ILEA	Inner London Education Authority

Joint Four	Joint Four Secondary Teachers' Association
LCC	London County Council
LEA	Local Education Authority
NACEIC	National Advisory Council on Education for Industry and Commerce
NACTST	National Advisory Council on the Training and Supply of Teachers
NADEE	National Association of Divisional Executives for Education
NCTA	National Council for Technological Awards
NUT	National Union of Teachers
ONC	Ordinary National Certificate
RSA	Royal Society of Arts
RSLA	Raising of the School Leaving Age
SFORSA	School Furniture Operation for the Raising of the School Leaving Age
SSEC	Secondary School Examinations Council
UGC	University Grants Committee

Preface

In a lecture which he gave in 1979 on 'Government, Parliament and the Robbins Report', Lord Boyle pointed out that the first conclusion which followed from his lecture was that as material became available, the history of English education since the war would need to be studied by historians trained in the discipline of weighing evidence, and not simply by social scientists. He added that

Education history is not only about the interplay of interest groups, or about the way educational systems display a tension between continuity and change. It is also the story of struggles for influence within the Department, of the ability of individual ministers to impress their colleagues in Cabinet, and of the readiness or otherwise of experienced advisers to show themselves adaptable in the light of altered circumstances.

Policy turns largely on the decisions and attitudes of individuals and a fuller understanding can come through the historical study of the records.

In 1977 the Association of Education Cpmmittees closed down. Its records were given to Leeds University and in due course became available for research. Constant and intimate contact with the Ministry of Education – from 1964 the Department of Education and Science – by Lord Alexander, the General Secretary of the Association, has meant that this very large collection of files contains important evidence for historians which will not become available through the central government's records until the next century under the 30 years rule.

Having completed *Education in the Second World War* and

having therefore been immersed in the plans for the reconstruction of the education system which lay behind the Butler Act of
1944, I had hoped in due course to examine the impact of that
measure and of the reconstruction during the following quarter
of a century. The opening of the AEC archive has made it
possible to undertake this study much earlier than would
otherwise have been the case.

I would like to record my thanks to Lord Alexander for
proposing and to the late Vice-Chancellor of Leeds University,
Lord Boyle, for facilitating the deposit of the AEC papers. I am
grateful to Leeds University for promptly financing the necessary listing and classification of the papers and to the University School of Education for research support. I am grateful for
the help which colleagues in the Brotherton Library have given
me, particularly for assistance from Dennis Cox, Vivian
Johnston and Peter Morrish.

I owe much to colleagues and to research students with
whom many of the matters covered in this book have been
discussed. David Leadbetter, who was head of Schools Branch
before he retired in 1968, has been kind enough to read the
section of the text relating to schools and his comments have
been most helpful. Finally I would like to thank David Garner
who has worked with me as research assistant and has
undertaken the exploration of many more files than I could
possibly have surveyed alone in the time available. I must add
that the opinions expressed and any errors are my own.

CHAPTER 1

Pupils and Schools

At the end of the Second World War there were not quite five million pupils in maintained schools in England and Wales. By the 1970s there were nine million. In 1945 there were about half a million pupils in secondary schools. Thirty years later there were four million. In other words, there were not only more children but the school system itself had undergone a fundamental reform and had been remodelled in order to ensure that every child would go to a secondary school – perhaps the main achievment of the Education Act of 1944.

But the process of legislating is often much less difficult and less complicated than the process of achieving in every day practice the legislative ideal. Thus it was only after 20 years of struggle that enough secondary school places had been provided to put an end to the all-age school. The achievement was due above all else to the sustaining of the political will to reconstruct the school system during the two decades following the war. The sheer physical difficulties which confronted the reconstruction were immense. The facilities and resources were much more readily available between the wars – but at that time the political will was lacking. Parliament had enacted measures in 1918, 1921 and 1936 providing for the raising of the school leaving age, but these had all come to nothing. It can be argued that it was a direct consequence of the impact of war on society that the political will of the community came to insist on the reconstruction of the school system actually being carried out in spite of adverse circumstances.

IMMEDIATE POST-WAR ISSUES

By the time the war ended there was an acute shortage of housing. Virtually no private houses had been built for six years. Moreover aerial bombardment had led to more than

1

three million dwelling houses being destroyed or damaged according to the War Damage Commission. The damage to other types of property was equally severe. Of the 24,000 schools that had existed in 1939, about 5,000 were destroyed or seriously damaged while another 3,000 had suffered some form of lesser damage. The problem of dealing with this situation was aggravated by the weakened condition of the national economy and the shortages of building materials. In 1939 about a million employees worked in the building industry, by June 1945 this figure had fallen to 550,00.[1]

The enormous demand for housing and the need which any government would feel to concentrate all its resources on meeting it led to considerable anxiety over school building in the Ministry of Education during the latter part of the war. A Cabinet memorandum of 1944 on post-war building made no mention of the need for schools. The Minister, R. A. Butler, put in a further memorandum himself to the Cabinet describing this as 'an extraordinary omission'. He argued that parents with children would be unable to occupy houses provided on the new estates if there were no schools for their children to attend and proposed that school and house building should be granted an equal degree of priority.[2] This was a very strong claim. It brought the need for a high priority for school building to the notice of the Cabinet which instructed the Minister of Reconstruction and the Minister of Works to give further consideration to priorities bearing in mind the case for school building.[3] The measure of priority given to school building was to continue to cause difficulty as long as the controls over building and building materials persisted and the matter was raised both in Parliament and in the newspapers from time to time. There was particular disappointment at the apparent slowness of the first post-war government in launching a worthwhile building programme. *The Economist* was not far from the mark in 1946 when it suggested that the delays sprang from two sources. The Attlee Cabinet regarded its housing drive as of such pre-eminent political importance that little other building could make headway. Moreover, 'the engines which should be fuelling the 1944 Education Act along are either too old or too tired to do their job properly'.[4] There was some truth in the second of these assertions as well as the first.

Following the traditional framework for the administration of education, the central government decided national policy while the local education authorities were to provide the schools. In an effort to adapt the administrative machinery and to make it respond more readily to the building programme which was now needed, the Ministry set up a working party of its own and LEA officials to review the existing machinery. The greatest amount of capital expenditure ever previously approved in one year was £16 million in 1938 when the machine was working at full pressure. The new target was to complete £1,000 million of schemes in 15 years. Thus the officials reported in 1946 that 'the normal procedure with its careful provision of checks and counterchecks' needed to be replaced and new methods would have to be adopted. In particular they recommended that planning and site acquisition procedures should be speeded up, that the principles of school construction should be re-examined and that more technical and administrative staff should be employed by both the Ministry and the Local Education Authorities (LEAs).[5] Reorganization of the administrative machinery on these lines was bound to take some time since even the pre-war organization had ceased to operate.

But the first political crisis point was disturbingly close. In response to public pressure the wartime all-party Coalition Government had given an undertaking that the school-leaving age would be raised from 14 to 15 no later than 1 April 1947. This would increase the number of pupils in the schools by about 400,000. If sufficient accommodation was to be provided the central government would have to act directly and the Ministry of Works would need to build the additional classrooms on behalf of the local authorities. In May 1945 – after victory in Europe but while war continued against Japan – the Ministry asked LEAs to complete returns not later than 14 July showing the minimum additional accommodation they would need for the additional age group.[6]

The general election of 1945 meant that action on the returns became the responsibility of the Attlee Government whose new Minister of Education was Ellen Wilkinson. Standardized, prefabricated units were to be provided and erected by the Ministry of Works, often on the playgrounds of existing schools. The LEAs were to be charged 8 per cent per annum of the total cost either until the prefabricated building ceased to be used or when the total original cost had been met. LEAs generally accepted the scheme as the best that could be hoped for in the circumstances, but there were some objections to the use of prefabricated buildings. One objector, Northumberland, did not send in a return of its needs. The Ministry therefore made an estimate and wrote telling the authorities what figures had been put in on its behalf.[7]

A more difficult point was raised by some other LEAs, including Wiltshire, which wanted to have the prefabricated buildings erected on the sites of modern schools so as to use them to facilitate reorganization rather than at the existing all-age schools which the pupils were currently attending. The Ministry had already considered this possibility and believed that the additional planning dimension involved would wreck any chance of providing the new accommodation on time. The thinking behind the Hutting Operation for the Raising of the School Age (HORSA) scheme was set out by the Permanent Secretary, John Maud, in a letter to the Association of Education Committees (AEC) and other associations. Resources being as limited as they would be up to 1947, the Ministry had had to consider whether to go for a slow advance on a wide front of educational reform, 'beginning in particular the reorganization of schools and the reduction in the size of classes and concurrently beginning the provision of the new accommodation needed for the raising of the compulsory school age'. This would have meant the indefinite postponement of the date for raising the leaving age. The alternative was to concentrate all resources on attaining the short-term objective, raising the leaving age on 1 April 1947. Maud recalled that priorities had been discussed in the debates on the Education Act and the Government had decided on the intensive emergency programme so as to finally realize 'the long desired and long deferred reform of raising the school age'. Reorganization was a much bigger problem. In Wiltshire alone it would not only require provision for 1,300 pupils of 14 to 15 but also for 4,000 aged 11 to 14. 'Multiply these by the corresponding requirements of other counties and one must see that the building programme involved would be totally out of scale with the practical possibilities . . .'.[8] In a speech at Oxford at about this time the Minister described the decision to accommodate the extra year group by 1947 as 'an act of faith rather than an act of wisdom'.

Maintaining the aim and finally attaining it in time was a considerable administrative and technical achievement. The last serious attempt to bring about postponement was made by the Treasury in January 1947 through the recommendation of a Cabinet committee. Rumours that the date might be postponed began to circulate in the second week of the new year. On 16 January the AEC Executive held a special meeting and sent a telegram to the Prime Minister urging the Government to stand by its pledge.[9] The telegram was well timed for at 9 p.m. the Cabinet met to consider the recommendations of its committee on economic planning one of which was 'that the raising of the school-leaving age should be postponed from 1 April to 1 September 1947'. In the Cabinet Ellen Wilkinson argued strongly against this pointing out that it would deprive 150,000 children of a whole year's education. These would be mainly working-class children whose education had already suffered because of the war. Moreover LEAs had been given a definite date and if the Government went back on this now, 'the success of any future efforts by other departments to get local authorities to complete tasks by a given date would be gravely prejudiced'. A number of other ministers supported Miss Wilkinson's argument so that 'Finally it was felt that the political disadvantage of breaking the pledges which had been given to Parliament outbalanced the economic benefits which would be derived from the proposal'. The Chancellor of the Exchequer, Dr Dalton, said that in view of the general attitude he would not press the proposal but it was now even more important that the Cabinet should accept other proposals which he would bring forward to meet the grave economic situation.[10] This was the last major battle that Ellen Wilkinson was to fight for education in the Cabinet for she died on 6 February 1947 at the age of 56.

The shortage of labour and materials led to a good deal of delay in executing the HORSA programme. Building contractors took up to twice the estimated time to erect the buildings. the number of rooms completed by the end of

December 1947 amounted to 42 per cent of the total which
LEAs had said they would need for the previous September.
But it should be borne in mind that some authorities certainly
overestimated, fearing delays would develop. By 1949 the
scheme was completed. 4,162 classrooms and 2,195 practical
rooms had been provided. Of a total of 363,000 additional
places provided in maintained schools between the end of the
war and 1949, 153,000 had been built under this scheme. The
abysmal shortage of school furniture was overcome through a
parallel scheme SFORSA (School Furniture Operation for the
Raising of the School Age). Under this scheme the Board of
trade arranged for the manufacture and supply of a special
range of utility furniture to meet the demands of the additional
pupils. Under this scheme 252,000 chairs and 227,000 desks
were provided.[11]

In spite of delays, enough places were provided in time to
prevent any children from being excluded from school. This
was due to the practice of pupils leaving school at the end of the
term in which they attained the minimum leaving age. Most of
those who attained the age of 14 just before 1 April 1947 left
school at Easter since LEAs had been asked by the Ministry to
ensure that the school term should end on or before the last day
of March so as to make certain that this group of pupils would
not be required to stay longer.[12]

The situation in 1947 was also eased by the fluctuations in
the birth rate. There were 5,004,211 pupils in maintained
schools on 1 January 1947. This was half a million fewer than in
1938 and proved to be the low point in total numbers – thus
technically 1947 was the best year in which to raise the leaving
age. During the 1930s the number of live births had sunk lower
than it had been for many decades. the year with fewest births
was 1941 when there were only 579,000. A marked increase in
the number of births began in 1942 with 652,000. Immediately
after the war there was, of course, a peak with 881,000 in 1947.
It was thought that the pattern would then follow that after the
Great War and decline to a lower level. This appeared to be
happening with a steady fall to 668,000 in 1955. School
building plans then had to be adjusted upwards again to meet a
rise which continued until 1964 with a peak of 876,000 only to
be followed by a decline to 569,000 live births in 1977. Since

that year the figure has been increasing again. Thus even in a society where other factors were constant – no movement of population to the suburbs, no increase in the average length of school life and no forms of school reorganization – the demographic factor alone would ensure that at different times there was pressure for more school places while at other times some school buildings were underused.

Immediately after 1947 the number of pupils in the schools began to rise rapidly – as may be seen from Table 1.1 Quite

Table 1.1.

Pupils in maintained primary and secondary schools, 1947–79

1947	5,034,275	1965	7,092,155
1949	5,528,776	1967	7,328,110
1951	5,737,698	1969	7,748,282
1953	6,205,988	1971	8,165,472
1955	6,515,676	1973	8,511,519
1957	6,776,549	1975	8,923,975
1959	6,901,187	1977	8,979,130
1961	6,961,517	1979	8,924,658
1963	6,925,328		

apart from the reconstruction aim of providing a place in a secondary school for every child over the age of eleven the most urgent need for the next four years would be to concentrate on providing additional places for the swelling younger age groups in the primary schools. The overall strategy became one of providing new places for these larger age groups as they moved up through the system and using the opportunity this afforded to reorganize into secondary schools provision for senior pupils. Thus providing for the 'bulge' in the birth-rate and fulfilling the main reform of the Butler Act of 1944 coalesced.

SECONDARY PLACES FOR ALL: 1950 TO THE GOLDEN YEARS

One of the main ways in which the legislation of 1944 sought to secure active implementation was through development plans. Every LEA was to prepare a development plan in which it would indicate how it proposed to meet the needs of its area in terms of the new requirements. The Ministry asked that development plans should be submitted by 1 April 1946 but it proved to be impractical to prepare them so soon. By 1948 only about 20 plans had received the approval of the Minister. The intention had been for the Minister to issue a local education order to give statutory force to the development plan once it was approved. Any variation after approval was to require an amending order. This machinery proved in practice to be very time consuming and clumsy, the shortage of manpower and materials in the early post-war years was not foreseen and this aggravated the very complicated issues involved in planning a new secondary system designed to cover the whole of the senior age groups. In some districts it proved to be difficult to reach agreement with the various interests involved on the future status of voluntary schools and much negotiation was needed to bring together the representatives of the churches and the locality so as to find a pattern of school provision which would match the aspirations and the resources of the different parties.

In 1949 the Ministry first sought to simplify formal planning arrangements while continuing to conform with the requirements of the Act and circulated its suggestions to the local authority associations. The associations felt that these did not go far enough and that something more drastic was required. Apart from the burdensomeness of applying for, preparing and issuing amending orders each time a development plan was modified, the Ministry as well as LEAs found this mechanism restrictive on its own freedom to adjust to new circumstances.[13] The issuing of amending local statutory orders was therefore dropped in practice even though LEAs still had to indicate the relationship of each building proposal to the development plan. This requirement eventually vanished as a formal requirement in 1967 when the Government was seeking to bring about a rapid spread of comprehensive reorganization. It was hardly in the interests of this policy to ask LEAs to relate their comprehensive proposals to development plans dating from the tripartite era. Moreover the conception of relying on development plans was more suited to a society which had a more settled demographic pattern and was less mobile than it in fact proved to be.

The attainment of the necessary momentum for the school building programme depended upon a close working relationship between the Ministry and the local authorities. The success of the arrangements for building came to depend on three factors. Each local authority needed to have as much notice as possible of the projects which it would be permitted to undertake each year and the Ministry tried to meet this requirement by announcing building programmes for each year as a whole and as early as possible. Secondly, authorities needed to know in advance what the Ministry would require in respect of each school building so as to avoid endless passing back and forth and alterations to building plans. Thirdly, experience soon showed that local authorities also needed to have in advance some idea of the costs which the Ministry would find acceptable. The system based on these three points was later described by the Association of Chief Education Officers as not only necessary but as good as could have been devised to deal with the immense problems which the building programme raised.[14]

As so often is the case, the formulation and application of each of these elements depended on achieving a balance between what was ideally desirable and what could be achieved in practice. According to the Act the Minister was to prescribe through regulations what standards of accommodation the Government would require in respect of each school building. It was thought in the Ministry that these should be issued as soon as possible after the passage of the Act. There was some delay in issuing the regulations since 'bombing, pressure of work and other troubles have simply thrown our plans out of gear' as the head of the Ministry's secondary branch put it. But the new regulations appeared in draft in November 1944 and they became definitive from 1 April 1945.[15] There was some criticism of the high standard which the Regulations set and that both the minimum standards of accommodation and the minimum sites for playing fields were too lavish. But initially the Ministry was very conscious that it was going to build for the long term and it did not want new schools to emerge from the reconstruction which would appear to be quite inadequate once the difficult conditions of the war and immediate post-war years were over. Thus in 1946 a memorandum was sent to inspectors 'in words which the Minister directed should be underlined, that it cannot "be too strongly emphasized that the Building Regulations have statutory sanction and are minimum requirements rather than maximum standard" '.[16]

The attempt to enforce these standards in the face of the endless economic difficulties which confronted the country in the early post-war years contributed to the slow progress made by school building outside the HORSA arrangements. Very wide variations in costs for similar buildings under different LEAs became increasingly difficult even to understand, let alone to justify, at the national level. In 1948, for example, Anthony Part, who was handling this matter in the Ministry, found that of new schools built for 250 to 320 children, the cost per pupil place (excluding playing fields) varied from £123 to £349, the average cost being £197.[17] The financial crisis of that time culminated in the largest ever single devaluation of the pound sterling and the retrenchment in public spending which followed made it look as though there would have to be a reduction in school building. In fact the pressure of these events led to the introduction of national cost limits per pupil place and a major review of the 1945 Building Regulations in order to preserve the possibility of undertaking the necessary school building.

In 1949 the Ministry introduced cost limits of £170 per place in new primary schools and £290 in secondary schools. The financial situation led to a reduction in these limits to £140 and £240 per place for projects included in the 1951 building programme. These were the lowest nominal figures achieved since the relentless pressure of inflation led to a slight increase in the permitted cost figures from 1953. The major review of the Building Regulations led to the withdrawal of requirements for various ancillary facilities in schools. New schools no longer needed to provide cloakrooms for pupils' outdoor clothing. As a cheaper alternative fittings for hanging coats were to be placed along corridors although the Ministry sounded a note of caution in that 'the appearance of the corridors seen from either end must not be rendered unduly depressing by an unbroken line of hanging coats and hats'.[18] The number of lavatories and wash-basins to be provided was substantially reduced and so were the minimum requirements concerning circulating space.

The Ministry expanded its own Architects and Building Branch in order to develop and to suggest to LEAs cheaper and more economical designs. The Branch was to produce a series of Building Bulletins which advocated the most economical ways of designing and building new schools which would conform to the minimum standards required. That the purpose of expanding the activity of the Branch was to secure cheaper school building and that this was to be the only way of achieving the school building which the reforms enacted in 1944 would require was spelled out in the second bulletin.[19]

The growth of the Branch was not welcomed in all quarters. In the past the design of permanent school buildings had been left in the hands of the LEAs and their architects. The new development appeared to some of those in local government as a bureaucratic or political threat undermining its position. The Secretary of the Association of Education Committees wrote to the Ministry's Chief Architect seeking reassurances that Ministry architects were not 'virtually acting as architects for the building of schools'. He was, of course, sent a letter of reassurance, but the fears of local authorities for their independence or rights are never far beneath the surface.[20] In order to make cooperation closer and to ease relationships the Ministry held two educational building conferences for LEAs in September 1951. About 40 LEAs were invited to send the chairman of their education committee, their director of education and their architect. There were talks on different aspects of school planning and construction including the compilation and progress of the building programme, costs, and the special requirements of different types of schools and colleges.[21]

Thus under the pressure of adverse circumstances a close relationship developed between the Ministry and the LEAs. The authorities each put up their proposed building pro-gramme for the coming year. In drawing it up LEAs were mindful of the currently stated material priorities as seen by the Ministry as well as of local needs and pressures. The Ministry examined each programme and assessed the degree of priority to be accorded to the schemes it contained in accordance with current policies and perceived national needs. It approved as much of the local authority programmes as it could within the overall financial limits agreed between itself and the Treasury. The relationship between a large spending department like Education and the Treasury is, of course, fundamental and the rate of progress in providing schools depended on the extent to which the needs of the school building programme were accepted in the Treasury. Negotiations between the Treasury and the Ministry, as well as those between the Ministry and individual authorities, were much simplified and facilitated by the system of building regulations and national limits of cost per place. In view of the initial suspicions in local government when the system for administering school building was evolved, it may be of interest to note that 12 years later the chief education officers told the Select Committee on the Estimates that they acknowledged 'warmly the assistance and friendly help given throughout the period by the Ministry as a co-partner in this great enterprise and by the individual members of the staff of the Ministry of Education, particularly the Architects and Building Branch'.[22]

Aided by the new arrangements the volume of school building increased in 1950, although by the end of that year the physical shortages of materials which had diminished as the war receded began to worsen again with the outbreak of the Korean War. The tense international situation and the expansion of the defence programme led to a lengthening of the delivery period for such essential items as steel and components of every kind. These difficulties continued through 1951 and the building industry became so badly overloaded that the Government imposed a ban for three months from December on starting any new project except those needed for the defence, energy and housing programmes. To some extent the slow rate of completing school buildings also indicated the excessive pressure on the building industry for in 1951 £60,031,000 of new work was started, only £34,615,000 was completed and at the end of the year £111,498,000 was under construction.

The years from the end of the war to 1951 form a period when the Attlee Government had a strong political desire to push ahead with a large school building programme in order to bring nearer the fulfilment of the reforms held out by the Act of 1944.

Both of that government's Ministers of Education, Ellen Wilkinson and George Tomlinson, fought strongly and successfully for Education's interests within the administration. Given the enormous physical and financial problems which faced a greatly weakened national economy in a shattered post-war world, it was only the strongest political resolve that could prevent education from sliding back to the status of an also-ran from which it suffered in the pre-war era. The success which ministers achieved was recognized at the time. In one of the most difficult years, 1949, *The Economist* noted that 'In the struggle for men and materials which each year precedes the allocation of resources among the social service departments, Mr Tomlinson has battled successfully.' Following the major devaluation of the pound, *The Times Educational Supplement*, after reporting that the pace of school building was to be maintained and that total expenditure on public education was to be increased, commented that 'instead of public education being seen as a luxury to be lavishly lopped it is seen to be a bastion of national recovery and as such to be strengthened not debilitated'.[23]

The change of political control in 1951 did bring difficulties for education and especially for school building, not so much because the Conservative Party was not determined to push ahead with the Butler Act reforms, but partly because the new Minister, Florence Horsbrugh, and the Parliamentary Secretary, Kenneth Pickthorn, were to prove much less adept and successful than their predecessors in fighting for education's share of resources within the administration. The exclusion of the Minister of Education from the Cabinet from 1951 to 1953 – the last period in history when this was so – did not help.

The new Minister came into office in November and the more restrictive attitude to school building became apparent with the publication of a new circular in February 1952.[24] The need for financial economies and the overloading of the building industry meant that all efforts would have to be concentrated on the limited objective of providing places for children of statutory school age in areas of major new housing development. Building work designed to relieve overcrowding in existing schools, to enable all-age schools to be reorganized or to replace unsatisfactory premises would not be approved. Even if new building work were shown to be essential to meet the limited objectives stated, long-term considerations might need to be subordinated to the immediate need to cut investment. The circular suggested by way of example that in rural areas additional permanent building at a secondary school to accommodate rising numbers of secondary pupils would have to be postponed if the pupils could be accommodated more economically in temporary extensions to their existing all-age schools. The immediate post-war bulge in births would pass from the primary to secondary schools from 1956 and 1957 and the Minister expected the temporary postponement of the age of transfer to be 'widely adopted' as a way of overcoming this problem. On the day the circular was published, R. A. Butler, now Chancellor of the Exchequer, had spoken of the modern school which needed to be developed so as to provide a genuine, distinctive and full education for the great majority and added that here 'we have a long road to travel, and here again the road lies through the valley of retrenchment'. In a rather pious leading article next day, *The Times* commented that it was now up to Miss Horsbrugh to ensure that this development was 'not too greatly hindered by her building policy'.[25]

But the educational world was much alarmed. The AEC set up a special sub-committee to keep an eye on the effects of the new restrictive policy. The Ministry in fact removed projects amounting to £28,000,000 so that the value of the revised 1952-3 building programme amounted to £42,000,000.[26] LEAs struggled to cope as best they could, the fear was that there simply would not be enough places for the greatly increased number of pupils when needed. Through their organizations and publicity they sought not so much to attack the Ministry of Education as to strengthen that Ministry's hand within the Government. The Ministry believed that there could at least be a place for every child if 1,150,000 places could be built by the end of 1953 and in a letter in November 1952 to the AEC it claimed that only a general cataclysm could prevent that figure from being reached. The number of new school places actually completed by October 1952 since the end of the war amounted to 823,720.[27]

Under the restrictive programme now adopted it looked as though little progress could be made in bringing about genuine secondary education for all. A survey undertaken by the AEC showed that at the end of 1952 there remained 226,000 pupils over the age of 11 in all-age schools – about 150,000 in the counties and 76,000 in county boroughs. Perhaps the most remarkable instance of criticism of the Government's restrictive policy was to be found in the Report of the Commons Select Committee on the Estimates. The primary function of that body was, of course, to ensure the wise and economical use of public finds, but it felt driven to complain in 1953 that a Government target of 1,150,000 places was inadequate and that at least 100,000 more should have been provided by the end of that year. The main objects of the Government's building programme, like those of its predecessor, were to provide sufficient new school places to maintain the statutory period of attendance and to provide for those who stayed on at school voluntarily after 15 'and to extend the facilities available for technical education in order to increase productivity'. The Committee's conclusion was that the programme was quite inadequate to meet the needs so specified. The building of schools lagged seriously behind the building of houses in most places. This aggravated overcrowding, compelled local authorities to hire temporary school accommodation and committed them to exceptional and heavy expenditure on transport beyond that allowed for by statute. The condition into which numerous older schools had fallen was such that many should either be pulled down immediately or undergo drastic repair, even at considerable cost. The Committee did find that the actual procedure for planning and building new schools was satisfactory while the comparatively low cost of new school building represented 'a remarkable achievement on the part of local authorities and one to which the Ministry of Education, through their Architects and Building Branch, have contributed in full measure'.[28]

The political difficulties which the Minister began to encounter as a result of her failure to gain sufficient priority for her department's activities increased considerably in 1954. The Teachers Superannuation Bill which was introduced in that year and which would have imposed higher pension contributions on teachers and its subsequent abandonment served to weaken further the Minister's standing. Both Miss Horsbrugh's apparent failure to secure the resources needed for school building, and the strong opposition which the super-annuation proposals stirred among teachers served to weaken her standing with Conservative MPs. Edward Boyle has recounted in some detail the events within the Conservative parliamentary majority which led to an angry meeting of the full 1922 Committee and has analysed why it was that a majority of its members were so keen to avoid a running confrontation with the teacher's associations and the various education interests in the second half of a parliament with an election round the corner.

Following the débâcle over the Superannuation Bill, Florence Horsbrugh must have guessed that her days were numbered. I myself became a junior minister (at the Treasury) later that summer, and I remember her pressing for an increase in the school building programme within a week of her departure from office, but by now it was obvious that any additional resources were far more likely to be invested in her successors than in herself.[29]

On 18 October 1954 David Eccles was appointed Minister. He made full use of the opportunities open to him to inaugurate a remarkable decade or so of investment in educational facilities, not only in new schools but also in further and higher education. He began at once a series of consultations designed to move away from the restrictive policy embodied in Circular 245 and began by seeking to encourage the reorganization of rural all-age schools. Hopes for such a change began to spread rapidly. By the beginning of November a discussion which R.H. Turton, MP for York, North Riding, Thirsk and Malton, had had with the new Minister had been reported by the county education officer for the North Riding to Alexander at the AEC. The impression given was that a more expansionary policy would be introduced encouraging the building of new schools in the more rural areas so as to press ahead with reorganization.[30]

The new policy was embodied in Circular 283 issued at the beginning of December. It announced formally that the Government was making additional resources available for educational building. The bulk of new building would now have to be for secondary pupils whose numbers would increase by over 700,000 between the beginning of 1954 and the end of 1960. The minister wished to speed up the rate at which all-age schools were being eliminated. In many urban areas reorganization had made considerable progress as a by-product of building to keep pace with new housing and the increase in numbers. Eccles sought therefore now particularly to assist rural areas which had not benefited from policies previously in force. He proposed to add to the 1955–6 building programme as much work for the reorganization of secondary education in rural areas as could be started and county authorities were asked to inform the Ministry by 15 January 1955 of any projects which could be started on site by March 1956 and to indicate the all-age schools which would be reorganized as a result. County authorities were also asked to say what further work they proposed to start in 1956–7 for rural reorganization. The circular stated that it was 'confidently expected' that all the work needed to complete reorganization in the countryside would also have been begun before the end of 1959. The minister also took this opportunity to remove restrictions on the expansion of facilities for technical education.

It was quite clear that the situation had changed completely. *The Times* commented a little grudgingly that Sir David Eccles 'earns credit for being allowed to remove restrictions which Miss Horsbrugh was required to apply. The new and hopeful turn to educational policy is being bought by some millions of fresh money'. LEAs set about increasing their building programmes energetically and good progress was made. The building programme for 1955–6 was larger than any before. Not surprisingly difficulties were encountered in carrying out this programme. One major problem was the shortage of architectural and professional assistance in LEAs. Thus about 330 major school projects with a total value of about £30,000,000 had not been started by the end of the programme year and had to be carried forward to 1956–7, thus leading to the deferment of some projects due in the latter year in order to avoid congestion. During the later 1950s coping with the problems involved in actually handling large programmes and with the problems caused by closely drawn building cost limits at a time of steady inflation occupied much of the time and energy of LEAs. In its Report for 1958, the Ministry commented on the high rate of completions achieved. As may be seen from Table 1.2, the number of new secondary school places provided in that year reached a peak at 196,830.

Table 1.2   Number of schools built, 1945–70

Year	New schools completed		School places provided	
	Primary	*Secondary*	*Primary*	*Secondary*
1946			20,000	14,040
1947	7	3	22,320	62,165
1948	15	13	37,765	96,890
1949	97	21	68,720	50,610
1950	191	48	89,280	38,360
1951	288	65	120,230	38,565
1952	439	49	156,620	46,765
1953	384	116	177,740	84,495
1954	436	160	125,015	72,035
1955	284	147	115,650	96,470
1956	225	214	107,595	130,575
1957	278	300	117,855	162,570
1958	221	375	98,080	196,830
1959	217	273	86,810	159,265
1960	225	187	83,305	133,525
1961	258	152	91,035	112,580
1962	269	130	81,490	112,880
1963	308	174	102,340	127,015
1964	393	187	116,250	161,970
1965	375	176	113,985	132,325
1966	429	106	162,100	105,460
1967	614	115	216,565	116,100
1968	736	101	254,224	110,510
1969	664	83	233,506	134,130
1970	518	79	198,600	134,400

The new attitude to educational investment which David Eccles was able both to exploit and to foster was much appreciated by the other parties in the world of education. In 1956, at a time of another round of Treasury cuts, Eccles was able to protect the education building programme from any cuts. On behalf of the AEC, the Secretary sent a somewhat unusual personal letter to the Minister congratulating him.

This is the second time within a matter of months in which the education service, which up to then had borne perhaps more than its fair share of cuts and economies, has virtually escaped serious interference with its broad development. The Committee have asked me to express to you their very great appreciation of the efforts which must undoubtedly have been made to ensure that this result came about. They feel that it is in no small measure due to your personal efforts and, just as this Association has not been slow to criticise certain actions and policies which they thought not to be in the interests of the education service, so they hasten to express their thanks for the satisfactory decisions which have been made regarding the building programmes.[31]

The later 1950s and most of the 1960s have been described as golden years for educational investment. This was no doubt due in part to the current public mood of optimism and impatience and the widespread belief in the value to the national economy of better schools. But the significance of the success with which succeeding ministers of education exploited these sentiments so as to sustain their departmental programmes should not be overlooked. In this connection the efforts of Geoffrey Lloyd, Minister from 1957 to 1959, and of Edward Boyle, 1962 to 1964, as well as those of David Eccles, Minister from 1954 to 1957 and again from 1959 to 1962, served well the interests of education.

In evidence to the Select Committee on the Estimates in 1961, the Association of Chief Education Officers pointed out that the achievements in school building had been 'immense'. Continued high investment would still be needed through the 1960s not only to complete reorganization but also to replace the worst of the old schools and to re-model to modern standards the country's large stock of sound but out-of-date buildings which needed to be brought up to modern standards. The Report of the Select Committee contrasted strongly with that of eight years earlier and was broadly supportive of present arrangements and of the progress being made. The search for better value for money was described as thorough and continuing. There was some concern as to whether the cutting of capital costs was not pushing up the cost of maintenance and the committee welcomed the news that the Ministry intended to begin work on a building bulletin on maintenance. The cost of maintaining and of heating buildings erected cheaply has since often proved to be a serious burden.[32]

The Report urged that wide publicity should be given to the achievements of CLASP, a consortium of local authorities which sought to provide educational buildings more cheaply through a system of common design and production. The Ministry had been active in bringing about the establishment of the consortium which was formed following a meeting of interested LEAs under the chairmanship of the Minister, Lord Hailsham. The founder members were Derbyshire, Durham, Glamorgan, Nottinghamshire, the West Riding and the county boroughs of Coventry and Leicester; some other LEAs joined later. The use of standardized and prefabricated parts made it possible to erect new schools more rapidly, with a smaller site labour force and at figures well within the national cost limits.

The Ministry was already doing a good deal to publicize the activities of this consortium and to encourage other groups of local authorities to form similar consortia. Building Bulletin 19, *The Story of CLASP*, was published by the Ministry in June 1961. The attitude of those responsible for school building policy in the Ministry on the value of such consortia and on the relative contributions of local and central government may be clearly seen in this extract from a letter sent by Morrell of the Ministry to Alexander.

I think the point which I am keenest to have taken by the customers [the LEAs] is that here is evidence of partnership in development work between central and local government, and of the excellent results that can be obtained when both sides regard their contribution as complementary one to the other. At the centre we are perhaps better placed than authorities to undertake basic research and development – establishing principles and solving basic technical problems. But our work will not bear fruit unless it is built upon and continuously improved in the manner of CLASP by local authorities, who alone can integrate it with the whole process of design and production, and who can alone engage in continuous further

development within the essential context of a large building programme.[33]

There can be no doubt that Ministry and LEAs worked closely
together and got the maximum value from the money which
was available.

In 1962 a survey was undertaken of all existing school
buildings. The criteria adopted for judging whether school
buildings were satisfactory or suffered from shortcomings and
obsolescence were not entirely realistic. In the words of the
Report itself, the results shown were subject to important
qualifications 'inescapable in a comprehensive once-for-all
survey of this sort, which deprive them of immediate practical
significance'. Among other assumptions underlying the figures
produced were that the school pupulation would go on
increasing during the next decade, that the school leaving age
would be raised to 16, that the distribution of the population
would change and LEAs were asked to allow for the complete
elimination of all overcrowding. On this basis the estimated cost
of bringing all schools up to standard and raising the school
leaving age in 1962 was £1,368 million 'on the unreal hypothesis
that it could somehow be done overnight'. The survey did
confirm existing regional differences in that it showed that the
North-West needed most improvement while the Metropolitan
area was the best off. The Table 1.3 gave some idea of the age of
buildings currently in use, although many schools whose 'oldest
main building' dated from the nineteenth century might well
also have had some new buildings.[34]

Table 1.3   School buildings in use, 1962

Age of oldest main building	Pupils (thousands) on roll in 1962		
	Primary	*Secondary*	*All*
Pre–1875	775.0	145.3	920.3
1875–1902	1,056.0	367.7	1,423.7
1903–1918	612.6	403.1	1,015.7
1919–1944	702.6	827.8	1,530.4
1945–1962	993.2	1,087.3	2,080.5
All pupils	4,139.4	2,831.2	6,970.6

VOLUNTARY SCHOOLS

The mid-1960s is a significant landmark in the history of schooling in England and Wales because it was then, 20 years after the passing of the Education Act in 1944, that its main reform was eventually put into effect universally with the virtual elimination of the all-age school and the provision of a genuine secondary school place for all senior pupils.

As Eccles had stated, one of the main constraints on bringing this reform to pass had been the school building policies followed in the ten years following the end of the war. The effect of the drive which he launched to speed up rural reorganization from the end of 1954 may be judged from the details set out in Table 1.4.

Table 1.4   *Replacement of all-age schools*

| | All-age schools replaced | | | |
| | 1950–57 | | 1950–62 | |
	No.	*%*	*No.*	*%*
County	1,562	58.6	2,341	91.5
C. of E.	1,678	62.6	2,500	93.4
R.C.	255	27.5	568	61.2
Other	47	50.5	83	89.3

By 1962 there remained 228 county, 178 Church of England, 359 Roman Catholic and 10 other all-age schools.

The existence of a large number of denominational all-age schools, the inability of the churches to raise funds to build separate senior or post-primary accommodation and the failure to find any acceptable way in which public funds could be used to assist in this task went far to account for the failure of attempts to reorganize the schools between the two World Wars. R.A. Butler's principal personal contribution to the Education Act of 1944 was his untiring search for a compromise solution which would enable public funds to augment the resources of the voluntary bodies so that reorganization would become possible and a place in a secondary school might be the right of every senior pupil.[35] The terms of the compromise required that the churches themselves should make a considerable effort to provide their share of the capital costs if they were to maintain their full stake and ensure that their schools achieved aided status. Where a voluntary providing body could not shoulder the financial burden involved, the school became 'controlled', the LEA met all capital costs and the rights of the voluntary body were much reduced. This position was not at all acceptable to Roman Catholics and many Anglicans were also not prepared to accept it. The price of 'aided' status was to meet 50 per cent of the capital costs of improving and reorganizing the schools, the remainder of the capital being provided by way of government grant. Quite apart from certain logistic problems inherent in secondary reorganization where small numbers in separate systems were involved, the financial burden was certainly felt to be onerously obstructive by those who insisted on aided status for their schools. While the historic compromise patiently negotiated by Butler served as the *sine qua non* of secondary education for all, yet its delaying effects on aided school reorganization may be seen in Table 1.4.

It was not surprising that from time to time efforts were made to persuade governments to modify the terms of the compromise and to offer more generous terms. The Roman Catholic hierarchy claimed increased public assistance for the Church's schools before the election in 1950. After the election it was thought that the issue would be raised in the debate on the estimates so the matter was discussed in the Cabinet. The Cabinet accepted the Minister of Education's proposal that no change could be made in the percentage of cost to be met by the voluntary bodies. But a difficulty unforeseen in 1944 was the long delay inevitable between approval of aided status and actually carrying out and paying for the building work this would involve. Applicants had to satisfy the Minister before he decided that a school need not be taken over as a controlled school that they would be able, as well as willing, to meet the financial commitment involved in aided status. The church authorities complained that it was unreasonable to require them to prove at that stage that they would be able to meet all the expenditure which they might be required to undertake in the years to come. As an administrative matter the Minister was meeting this situation by allowing school managers to limit their assurances to a diminishing proportion of the total sums involved according to the time which would elapse before building work was undertaken. A paper prepared for the Cabinet showed that over 2,000 church schools had had their status settled. Not one existing Roman Catholic school had so far failed to achieve aided status while the proportion of Church of England schools achieving aided status was higher than had been expected in the Ministry. The Cabinet decided to make no change in the compromise of 1944, but possibly to legislate to permit 'provisional aided status' as a sort of waiting category until a final decision was taken if the Opposition indicated it wished to seek this.[36] In the event it did not. In the debate in the Commons Butler speaking for the Opposition pointed out the dilemma in which voluntary school managers found themselves if they opted for aided status – namely that those who succeeded them might find they faced unascertainable liabilities at some uncertain time. Even so he concluded by pressing on the government the desirability of reaching a settlement within the framework of the existing Act 'without, unless there is agreement among the Parties, any legislation on minor points'. The local authorities were also opposed to any change in the existing legislation. The Association of Education Committees' journal, *Education*, carried articles strongly opposing Roman Catholic claims in February and again in May.[37] Thus neither law nor practice were changed.

An Education Act in 1953 helped the application of the 1944 principles to voluntary schools. The legislators of wartime had not foreseen the extent to which the movement of population from the central area of cities to housing estates and new towns would complicate the application of criteria for the award of building grants for new aided schools for 'transferred' or 'displaced' pupils. Thus the 1953 Act,[38] while broadening the definition of 1944, took care to restrict any grant to school places that replaced existing denominational school places or were provided for identifiable 'displaced' pupils. This naturally involved a great deal of detailed investigation in each instance.

The case for raising the state's grant to 75 per cent for voluntary aided schools continued to be argued and it was pressed more vigorously in the later 1950s as the drive to provide secondary places for all senior pupils went forward. The Catholic hierarchy was particularly anxious not to see many of their own young people as a group deprived of improved educational facilities available to all other sections of the population. The Church of England as a matter of policy did not press its desire to retain aided status to the point where it would have interfered with progress on educational grounds. One of its representatives claimed that the rate of reorganization of Anglican all-age schools was slightly higher than that of the county schools and four times as rapid as Roman Catholic schools.[39] An example of the sort of situation which could retard Roman Catholic reorganization arose in East Sussex. By 1959 the county would complete its reorganization with the exception of one R.C. all-age school. Despite the opening of a new county secondary school in the same town the Church intended to keep its school open so as not to jeopardize its plan to erect a new aided secondary school even although this was unlikely to be accomplished for some years. The authority felt some concern for senior pupils in the all-age school being deprived of real secondary education which was now available. If the building grant were no longer tied to provision for pupils actually in existing aided schools, then it would no longer matter financially to the Church authorities if they were to allow such children to attend county schools pending the reorganization of their own schools.[40]

Early in 1959 consultations on the possibility of amending legislation to enable the churches to make more rapid progress with their share of the building programme were undertaken by the Ministry. The Roman Catholic hierarchy and the Church Assembly both sought an increase in grant to 75 per cent. The former wanted its extension to all new schools while the latter dissociated itself from this request. The Free Churches appeared to be persuadable over increasing the rate of grant but opposed to any extension to new schools. The Minister canvassed the suggestion that government be empowered to pay grant on building new aided denominational schools wherever they could be shown to be needed to provide proper secondary facilities to match existing voluntary primary facilities. The Minister believed that this would be especially useful in providing grammar and technical school facilities. By the summer sufficient common ground had emerged for the Minister to put two main proposals to Parliament. These were firstly to raise the rate of capital grant for aided schools from 50 to 75 per cent; secondly to offer similar grant for new aided secondary schools needed to match voluntary aided primary schools. The ministry considered that these proposals kept within the principles of the 1944 settlement while bringing the law up to date to meet changed circumstances. These changes were incorporated in the Education Act of 1959.[41]

The position of voluntary schools was to be further modified on two occasions after 1959. The Wilson Government of 1964 formally launched its drive to convert the maintained secondary schools to a comprehensive pattern the next year. Reconsideration of the terms for helping voluntary schools began in 1965 following a joint approach by the Anglican, Roman and Free Church representatives who sought more money to help with the new Labour policy. It is perhaps worth noticing how far the situation had changed from the difficulties faced by Butler 20 years earlier in getting the churches to accept any compromise. On this occasion such opposition as there was in the Commons came from humanists. Quite apart from the change which the Government sought in the pattern of secondary schooling, the intended raising of the school leaving age would add a further large number to the school population six years hence. The actual number of pupils in Roman Catholic primary schools had increased between 1955 and 1965 from 390,000 to 443,000 while the secondary school population had risen from 69,000 to 196,000. The ending of all-age schools had meant that there were far more children in Roman Catholic aided schools than could have been foreseen in 1944. Increasing numbers of pupils were staying on beyond the school leaving age in voluntary as much as in county schools. The birth rate had risen more rapidly than expected and there had certainly been a much greater movement of population than had seemed at all probable. The effect of this last factor was that denominational school supporters in growing areas were at a great disadvantage by comparison with those in old established areas. Some central areas had a surplus of grant entitlement for aided schools which would never be built or replaced. At the other extreme the point was made in the Commons 'the more urgently a school was needed by the Roman Catholic community, and the bigger the need for a school of viable size, the less promising were its prospects of grant'.[42]

The Education Act of 1967 accordingly increased the grant payable for new aided schools from 75 to 80 per cent. It also widened and simplified the possible circumstances in which grant could be paid by abandoning the need for conscientious officials to attempt to determine whether a new place was a 'transferred' or 'substituted' place or neither – a distinction which was said to have become metaphysical. In future the grant was to be payable in respect of all 'new places' provided in such schools.

Apart from aided schools, the Act made important changes in arrangements governing voluntary controlled schools, nearly all of which were Anglican. All capital costs of these schools fell upon the local authority and the circumstances in which the Secretary of State could direct an authority to pay for a new controlled school or its enlargement were in effect restricted to where it was needed to accommodate pupils for all of whom places in some other voluntary school had ceased to be available. Moreover no enlargement of an existing school could amount to the establishment of a school of a new character. In order to facilitate reorganization, the Government needed powers to agree to enlargements of existing controlled grammar or modern schools to make them comprehensive, that is, to enlarge and change their character. Moreover it also needed powers to agree to the establishment of new controlled middle schools where some but not all of the pupils might be from existing voluntary schools. As the Secretary of State put it 'in an area where nearly all the primary provision is in voluntary schools which would lose two or three of their age groups [to new middle schools] it may well be regarded by everyone as equitable that controlled schools should play a part in the middle school provision serving an area'. These changes were incorporated in the Act as was the power to direct a local authority to meet the cost of enlarging a controlled primary school. This was designed to meet those cases where new housing led to some increase in the number of pupils in an area with a controlled school but where the increase did not justify building a second, county, primary school – the only possibility as the law stood.[43] The political driving force behind most of the provisions of the 1967 Act were those associated with the Labour policy of comprehensivization. In the words of a Church of England spokesman 'it has not always been easy to find ways in which church secondary schools can cooperate in schemes of comprehensive reorganization'. Without the legal easement offered by this Bill it would have been very difficult to see how this could have been achieved in a number of situations'.[44]

The most recent legislation governing financial assistance to voluntary schools followed the return to office of a Labour administration in 1974. Government policy was again turned towards trying to achieve a comprehensive secondary system. The Education Act of 1975 had the effect of increasing the rate of building grant for aided schools from 80 to 85 per cent.

TOWARDS COMPREHENSIVE SCHOOLING

From the mid-1960s the issue of comprehensive reorganization tended to overshadow the school scene. The conflict between supporters of the grammar and comprehensive schools became a principal matter of contention between the political parties both nationally and in many local authorities. The future pattern of secondary schooling had been discussed at length by senior officials of the Board of Education when they were putting together the 'Green Book' on which the 1944 Act was based as early as 1940 and 1941. This group, which consisted mainly of the heads of branches presided over by Permanent Secretary, Maurice Holmes, were agreed that fees in secondary schools would have to be abolished and that every senior pupil would need to go to a post-primary school. There was less unanimity about the shape of school organization and the issues which were to become matters of public and political contention two decades later received an airing in this group during the second winter of the war. The common secondary school to which all children would go seemed to William Cleary, head of Elementary Branch, to be the only possible solution in the long term. The war was serving to emphasize the unity of the nation and to break down social and economic barriers and privileges. True equality of opportunity would be expected and this meant establishing equality of esteem between all post-primary schools. While grammar schools remained apart from other schools for senior pupils the greater social prestige of the careers for which they prepared their pupils would prevent any genuine equality of esteem from developing. 'The obvious and perhaps the only satisfactory answer is the multilateral post-primary school attended by all children over 11 alike.' There were many difficulties in trying to move to this arrangement. The existing comparatively small school buildings for instance would be quite unsuitable for large common secondary schools. Even so this system appeared to be 'the only full solution of the problem of a truly democratic education'.[45]

This argument was strongly opposed by the head of the Secondary Branch, G.G. Williams, on the grounds that 'parity of esteem is purchased at the expense of the grammar schools'. Continuing disagreement and conflicting memoranda from these protagonists of opposite viewpoints eventually led the Permanent Secretary to decide in favour of separate schools from the age of 11 largely on the practical grounds that the New Jerusalem would lose much of its value and political appeal if it was not going to be translatable into action for many years and given that they would have largely to make do with the existing buildings and staff, what became the tripartite system certainly seemed likely to be much more practicable in the immediate post-war years.[46] Thus while the 1944 Act itself did not seek to determine the form of secondary schooling which was to be established, the Ministry's policy and influence came to be thrown behind separate grammar, modern and technical schools and the great majority of LEAs put forward development plans on these lines in the years immediately following 1945 – even though Ellen Wilkinson herself had some doubts about the policy.

An early clash between the Ministry and a local authority on this question arose over the development plan submitted by Middlesex. The LEA proposed that its area should be served mainly by a system of comprehensive schools of 4, 5 or 6 form entry in size. The Minister – George Tomlinson – was not prepared to accept this arrangement. The Ministry's letter rejecting the proposals argued that the schools proposed would have difficulty in recruiting teachers normally suitable to grammar school work and that in such schools there would not be enough children staying on to ensure that Sixth-Form work would be established to any appreciable extent. 'The Minister does not understand why the authority believe that a standard and range of Sixth Form work comparable to that which could be produced by a multilateral school only of impossibly large size could be achieved in a comprehensive school very much smaller – so small indeed as 4, 5 or 6 form entry'. While a 'limited experiment' might be put in hand with three comprehensive schools, the Minister asked the authority to think again about their proposals for secondary schooling.[47]

The coming into office of the Conservatives in 1951 led to no immediate change in the Ministry's attitude. Multilateral or comprehensive schools remained unusual being seen as suiting special circumstances or as a matter for limited experiment. In some ways the increase in political pressure for those schools reflected an increasingly widespread feeling that the modern schools which were going up in considerable numbers were not fulfilling the hopes and expectations of parents. They were not winning equal esteem with the grammar schools. Cleary was in fact being proved right. Not least among the weaknesses of many modern schools as perceived by parents was the absence of the opportunity for pupils to take public examinations and therefore to obtain formal qualifications such as the General Certificate of Education (GCE). The elaborate efforts made by Her Majesty's Inspectors (HMI) and the Ministry in the late 1940s to 'protect' these schools from public examinations, which is discussed in the next chapter, helped to undermine their standing in the public mind.

Moreover as more secondary modern and secondary grammar schools were built and as the importance of secondary education for career purposes came to weigh much more heavily with more parents, so the debate about equality took a new form and became more widespread. It had become clear that for most of the country there was really no tripartite system but a bipartite one and this looked increasingly like a two-tier arrangement. Many parents were no longer prepared to accept that their children should be sent to what appeared to be – and too often was – an inferior secondary school while their neighbours' children might be sent to grammar schools on the basis of a difference of a few marks in a set of tests at the age of 11. Such blatant distinctions between neighbouring families of similar social and economic standing and aspirations seemed to be increasingly unbearable. Thus the pressure for a comprehensive system grew in that large middle band of society. One of the functions of politicians is no doubt to show an awareness of the electors' problems and to seek solutions. Thus as dissatisfaction mounted with the selective system so politicians came to take the abolition of selection more seriously both locally and nationally. It may be interesting to note that Conservative as much as Labour-controlled local authorities turned to non-selective patterns of secondary school organization as the social and political impossibility of continuing with the two-tier system became increasingly obvious – at first mainly in rural areas.

The Ministry's attitude began to change. As early as 1955 David Eccles had told the National Union of Teachers (NUT) Conference that he intended to apply five working rules to the pattern of secondary education.

(1) A range of 15 to 25 per cent for grammar plus technical school places would be expected.
(2) New technical schools would be approved where there was a very strong case.
(3) Modern schools would be encouraged to develop extended courses and to strengthen their links with grammar and technical schools, and with further education.
(4) Transfers should be made as early as possible to put right glaring mistakes in the examination. Otherwise the time for transfers – and more should be arranged – should be at 15 or 16.
(5) Comprehensive schools would be approved as an experiment when all the conditions were favourable and no damage was done to any existing schools.

The Conservative Government's 1958 White Paper, *Secondary Education for All: A New Drive,* marked a further step in this process. Geoffrey Lloyd, the Minister, committed £300 million for secondary school building over the next five years in the White Paper. It also admitted the case for comprehensive schools in country districts with sparse populations and on new housing estates where there were no well-established grammar schools. It opposed the closure of any good existing grammar school in order to give a comprehensive school a monopoly in an area. Since most LEAs would continue to operate their separate grammar and modern schools, it urged them to bring about an overlap of opportunities offered and of standards of work to be expected. Thus there ought to be the chance of taking GCE in modern as well as grammar schools. Edward Boyle, then Parliamentary Secretary at the Ministry, was later to comment that 'the 1958 policy came too late; the only possible means of preserving a bipartite system would have been the encouragement of GCE courses in all secondary modern schools *from the first*; and that is what some senior officials at the Ministry had wanted to do, but unfortunately they found themselves opposed (most unwisely) by Her Majesty's Inspectors'.[48] By the early 1960s there were indeed modern schools which were gaining more in terms of public examination results for their pupils than some grammar schools were achieving for their weaker streams. Yet even although it was possible to bring about overlap in the standards, opportunities and achievements of the secondary schools, there was still no overlap in parents' minds. Too many modern schools had become socially one-class schools, the bottom schools in their areas and even moderately ambitious parents were bound to react strongly to the news that their children, having 'failed' to pass their eleven-plus, would have to attend the modern schools.

There was also a sense in which the very success of the policy of overlap in some areas, where the growth of GCE courses in modern schools was widespread and successful, itself made it more difficult to explain why there needed to be separate school provision for children of varied abilities. Some of the large county authorities whose modern schools had been very successful, such as Hampshire, found the move towards comprehensive reorganization a natural next step. At the Ministry officials estimated in 1963 that 90 out of 163 LEAs in

England and Wales had completed or were working on comprehensive reorganization schemes for all or part of their areas. Politically it was, perhaps, paradoxical, that the bipartite system had come to make least sense in some of the Conservative-controlled county areas, while the LEA grammar school was most needed by the able pupil from a modest home in a poor district in a Labour-controlled mining area or city.[49]

The Labour administration that came to office in 1964 had promised to bring about a comprehensive secondary school system by ending selection at eleven-plus and by eliminating separation in secondary education. The House of Commons passed a resolution endorsing this aim in January 1965 and in the following July Anthony Crosland, the Secretary of State, issued Circular 10/65 which requested LEAs which had not so far prepared comprehensive plans to do so and to submit them and went on to give central guidance on ways in which comprehensive reorganization might be achieved. New schemes were to be built on the foundation of present achievements and to preserve what was best in existing schools. Six main forms of comprehensive organization were suggested.

(1) The orthodox comprehensive school with an age-range of 11 to 18.
(2) A two-tier system with all pupils going to a junior comprehensive at 11 and moving on to a senior one at 13 or 14.
(3) A two-tier system with all pupils going to a junior comprehensive but where only some move on to a senior school, the remainder staying put until school leaving age.
(4) A two-tier system where all the children go to a junior comprehensive and all move on at 13 or 14, some to a senior school offering courses to 18 and others to a school with courses terminating at the school leaving age.
(5) Comprehensive schools with an age range of 11 to 16 combined with sixth form colleges for pupils over 16.
(6) A system of middle schools which straddled the primary to secondary age range. Pupils would move to middle schools at 8 or 9 for four years, moving on later to a comprehensive school with an age range of 12 or 13 to 18.

Behind the different varieties of organization held out in the Circular lay the obvious fact that if the whole country were now to complete reorganization within a few years, the only way of achieving this would be to fit the new comprehensive system into the existing tri- or bipartite buildings. Hence some of the six commended forms of organization were only said to be acceptable as transitional schemes. This applied particularly to two-tier systems which involved schools taking pupils only up to school-leaving age (then 15) and providing no course terminating in an examination. As institutions which offered little more than the legalized passage of time until leaving age to boys and girls from 13, they were quite simply anti-educational and would presumably never have been commended by the Department of Education and Science (DES) had there not been party political pressure to achieve 'results' in an impractically brief span of time.

What was thought of as the 'orthodox' comprehensive school with a range from 11 to 18 was now said to need an entry of no more than 6 forms to achieve satisfactory and economical use of specialist facilities at the sixth-form level. Schools with smaller entry would be acceptable in rural areas and small towns. The 11–16 school followed by sixth form college was commended on an 'experimental' basis since experience with arrangements of this sort had been very limited.

The sixth possibility listed in the Circular, a system of middle schools, was said to be *prima facie* attractive, but the Secretary of State did not want to give approval to many such schemes in the near future while the age of transfer from primary to secondary schools was itself under consideration by the Plowden Committee. Middle schools owed their origins to the thought that was going on in the late 1950s concerning ways of breaking away from the two tier secondary school pattern for which the existing stock of buildings was mainly designed. Alec Clegg, Education Officer for the West Riding, worked at this idea and saw the possibilities in a school system organized around the age ranges 5 to 9, 9 to 13 and 13 to 18. This broke away from the division at the age of 11 required by the 1944 Act and would have been illegal and impossible unless the law itself were changed. In May 1963, Clegg wrote a personal note about this to L. R. Fletcher in Schools Branch at the Ministry 'not putting forward a properly thought-out case, but merely flying a kite'. A few days later he met Fletcher and Morrell to discuss the idea, but initially they were both cool about it.[50]

Clegg did not abandon the proposal. The possible alternative of junior and senior high schools with pupils of 11–14 and 14–18 seemed to him to be inferior for two reasons. Two years was too short a period of preparation for 'O' level, at the same time many of the post-war pedagogical advances made in the primary school could be carried through to 13 if 9–13 middle schools were set up. Clegg continued to press for support for middle schools in his own authority and saw that wide publicity was given to his proposals, copies being sent to chief officers of large LEAs and to the education correspondents of several national newspapers. He also continued to press Schools Branch. When the Minister, Edward Boyle, visited the Don Valley in 1964 he told C. T. Broughton, who was chairman of West Riding Education Committee, that he hoped an Act would be passed enabling LEAs to undertake arrangements of this kind. In fact one of his last actions as Minister before handing over to Quintin Hogg who succeeded him as the first Secretary of State at the newly-formed DES was to secure government approval for the introduction of a Bill which made middle schools legally possible. It seemed to him that this sort of secondary reorganization might well fit the needs and existing resources of a number of areas. When the Plowden Committee reported in 1967 it recommended a national system of 8–12 middle schools, but this was not adopted by the Government. Whatever the philosophical theory or pedagogical virtue behind the middle school, it was adopted on a pragmatic basis in many areas as the best means by which to adopt the comprehensive system within the strict limitations of the existing building provision. Circular 10/65 did indeed state that since during the next few years the increase in the school population, new house-building and the raising of the school leaving age from 15 to 16 would take up virtually all the resources available for new school building, LEAs should not plan on the basis that their programmes could be increased simply to take account of the need to adapt or remodel buildings on a scale which would not have been necessary but for reorganization.

POLITICAL POLARIZATION IN SECONDARY ORGANIZATION

The raising of the leaving age in 1970/71 was announced in 1964 and the DES and LEAs gave consideration as to how an additional 350,000 pupils could be accommodated on top of existing trends towards a larger school population. There was some consideration as to whether there should be a special national scheme after the pattern of the HORSA enterprise 20 years earlier. A meeting was held at the end of 1965 between officials of the DES and of the local authority associations at which reasons for the slow progress being made with the current building programme were discussed and the opportunity was taken to look at the needs of the additional age group from 1971. The Permanent Secretary, Herbert Andrew, felt that current difficulties in accelerating the existing building programme gave cause for concern over accommodation for September 1971 unless changes were made in current practice. It was explained that the building for the extra children would be included in the 1968–71 projects, the Department hoped to detach the investment allocation for raising the school leaving age from the rest of the school building programme and to make a block allocation to each authority, related to the extra children it would have to accommodate. The cost of the operation would be less than the full cost of providing new schools for the same number of children at current cost limits.[51]

It is impossible to consider school building or, indeed, other educational developments in the later 1960s without paying some regard to the increasing economic and financial difficulties facing the country. The sharp devaluation of sterling in 1968 was something of a landmark amidst these difficulties. The postponement of the date for raising the leaving age to 1972–3 was made known in 1968. The special building programme to accommodate the additional pupils was announced in 1969 and was spread over the three years 1970 to 1973. The total value of this programme was about £125 million.

After the close cooperation which local authorities had achieved with ministers and secretaries of state in the 1950s and

1960s, there was a distinct cooling of the atmosphere during Edward Short's period of office. An indication of how things stood became public in January 1969 at a press conference on the building programme given by the Secretary of State and which he was thought to have used to make a considerable attack on LEAs' 'extravagance' and 'lack of cost consciousness'. According to a report appearing in the *Guardian* next day Mr Short's anger was aroused by the size of the bids for the conversion of existing classrooms. 'Quite frankly some of the bids staggered me' he was reported as saying. A figure of £6,000 to re-equip an existing room was far too high. 'It is characteristic of local authorities that they do not look at their costs too carefully'.[52]

Irritation among some government supporters at what was felt to be the slowness and at times the downright refusal of a number of LEAs to cooperate in implementing Circular 10/65 was undoubtedly an important factor in the new situation. There was in any case bitter resentment and opposition to the drive towards comprehensivization. Supporters of the grammar schools could point to their fine record of academic achievement and of expansion. While such schools remained, the really able pupil from poor family or decayed area would have access to a publicly supported school which would enable him to fulfil his potential. Certainly there were some comprehensive schemes which seemed to be almost designed to take away this opportunity and which appeared to be ensuring that some districts would have such poor secondary schools that the promise held out by the 1944 Act would be denied. This was particularly true of some schemes that involved the housing of a single school on as many as three sites, each perhaps two or three miles apart. Moreover, where a well-established and respected grammar school was to lose its identity in one of these mish-mashed concoctions feelings naturally ran high. The greater the pressure for speedy reorganization, the more likely it was that such unsatisfactory proposals would come forward. If the widespread desire to avoid segregation and disqualification at the age of 11 were to be met without causing an impoverishment of the maintained school sector careful re-planning over an extended period was essential. Unfortunately such planning can seldom in the nature of things appeal to those who believe that well-publicized quick 'victories' are the surest way to gathering a good dividend in the form of votes at the next election.

Among those concerned with running the schools system there was a natural and proper reluctance to take sides in the party sense. From time to time chief education officers looked to the AEC for advice and guidance on their difficulties. The position which this and other local authority associations had traditionally supported was that an LEA had the right to determine the organization of schools in its own area. Writing to a chief officer in October 1969 the General Secretary made this point and went on to say 'but I do not think our people would continue to defend an organization which involved selection of 25 or 30 per cent going to grammar schools and the remainder to modern schools. I think our people have probably reached the point where they accept that this is socially divisive and is probably not the best organization of secondary education'.[53]

In 1965 Ministers had sought to avoid confrontation and to rely on pressure through granting or withholding building programme consents. There was difficulty with some LEAs such as Surrey and Cheshire but enough general progress was made to enable Anthony Crosland and Reg Prentice to resist back-bench pressure at that time. However, the introduction of a bill early in 1970 to compel LEAs which had not so far put forward comprehensive reorganization schemes to do so produced a strong reaction. The Association of Education Committees protested vigorously on the grounds that the measure would be an invasion of the prerogatives of local government and that it was unnecessary. In a letter commenting on the Association's views, Edward Short wrote that 'the Bill is mainly concerned with translating the request made to local education authorities in Circular 10/65 into a statutory requirement. The majority of authorities have cooperated excellently but a minority have not, and freedom for authorities in the education sector can scarcely include the possibility of frustrating national policy'. The Secretary of State's letter was considered by the General Purposes Committee of the AEC whose members agreed unanimously that their views remained unchanged. In replying they said they were most anxious that the education service should not be harmed in the current situation 'in which extreme is countered with extreme and educational policy tends to be determined by reference to a majority of votes at a time when it can quite easily happen that another Party is in power within a matter of months'. The Committee felt as dismayed at the prospect of the proposed measure being repealed by a Conservative government as they were at the possibility of the bill becoming law under a Labour government since both circumstances would harm the development of the service and be 'prejudicial to the sympathetic cooperation which exists in the majority of areas and is so infinitely to be preferred to enforced compliance with directives issued by central government'. In replying to this Mr Short made it quite clear that there was no question of the measure being withdrawn. He concluded 'my colleagues and I believe that comprehensive education has overwhelming support throughout the country and that we should be failing in our duty if we did not attempt to ensure, after this length of time, that all authorities begin to plan to achieve it'.[54]

However, the general election terminated this particular affair and at the end of the next month the new Secretary of State, Margaret Thatcher, issued Circular 10/70. Mr Short's bill was lost and Circular 10-65 was withdrawn. The period from June 1970 until the election of February 1974 was marked initially by giving LEAs a greater freedom to decide for themselves the future shape of secondary facilities in their areas. The circular itself spoke of recent rapid changes in secondary school organization imposing considerable strains within the education system. Where a particular set of arrangements was working well and commanded general support the Secretary of State did not wish to cause further change without good reason. It has been well argued that Margaret Thatcher from the first hoped that by this means grammar and comprehensive schools would co-exist in mixed systems. This would preserve some parental choice, if comprehensives were academically strong, parents would choose them; if they were weak then bright children would still be able to go to grammar schools where their ambitions, ability and hard work would be rewarded. The emphasis was to be on success. 'Little is heard of the secondary modern school. Rather the belief in individual effort and achievement that found its expression in the grammar school undermined the one nation concept with its harmonization of all interests based on social justice'.[55]

There were some grounds for expecting that quite a number of LEAs which had moved reluctantly towards comprehensive reorganization would withdraw their proposals. It was obvious that mainly Labour-controlled county boroughs would not do so, but it might have been expected that some of the larger counties would have taken advantage of the new situation. In fact, very few authorities seem to have done so. One of the most interesting cases was Surrey. By this time this large and overwhelmingly Conservative authority had only 7 comprehensives out of 90 secondary schools and 3 of those were Roman Catholic voluntary schools. The county's reaction to Crosland's circular in 1965 had been unenthusiastic. After much debate the authority decided on a course which would complete comprehensive reorganization by 1977 and rejected a proposal for a mixed system. Even where the mixed system approach was now adopted, it could lead in practice to movement towards a comprehensive system. The Conservative-controlled county borough of Walsall decided in 1971 to preserve two prestigious aided grammar schools but to comprehensify everything else. Thus selection would be reduced from 20 to 6 per cent. Since 94 per cent of children would go to the common secondary schools these would have to be suitably staffed and equipped to deal with the brightest children given the fallibility of the forecasting inherent in selection procedures. According to *The Times Educational Supplement*, this was 'much more than many more enthusiastic comprehenders can boast'.[56]

The desire which many Conservative-controlled authorities showed to continue with plans to reorganize their schools indicated among other things the strength of the value which many members of education authorities placed on continuity rather than attempting to change the system with changes of government. There was also the analysis of developments which Edward Boyle advanced: it was the achievements of the period 1951–64 – namely the growth of a middle-income society, the rise in educational standards, and the expansion of the universities – which made the continuation of a tripartite system with segregation at 11 less and less acceptable both in terms of educational and political common sense.[57] After a year in office, it was obvious that the administration could not rely on local option to check the coming of comprehensive systems. More positive action would be needed if mixed systems including grammar schools were to be introduced. Accordingly the Secretary of State fell back on Section 68 of the 1944 Act and used this against Surrey County Council over arrangements at Walton-on-Thames. Section 68 has been shown not to be a suitable means of pushing through a centrally favoured policy against an LEA since the 'reasonableness' of a decision under it by the Secretary of State may well be tested and found wanting in the courts. At this stage Mrs Thatcher then turned to Section 13 which dealt with government approval for establishing and closing individual schools and had been thought of in connection with possible local disputes over voluntary schools when originally put into the Act. Under the machinery here available the Secretary of State could receive parental and other representations directly, thereby by-passing local elected authorities and making them wait while she satisfied herself about any objections to their proposals as they might concern a particular school. Rejection of change in the case of a single school could quite easily make the reorganization scheme for a whole district impossible. Lengthy delays were virtually inevitable. The Association of Municipal Corporations as well as the NUT and certain local authorities apparently considered legal action to test the validity of this application of Section 13 powers, but the general election of February 1974 ended the matter. 'As it was so far as secondary reorganization was concerned, [Margaret Thatcher's] period as Secretary of State ended in confusion and recrimination'. Perhaps the position was most neatly summarized by *Education* which noted that 'under a Labour Government local authorities were firmly requested to go comprehensive but many were allowed to do as they wished, while under a Conservative Government authorities are told they may do as they wish but some are firmly prevented from going comprehensive'.[58]

Edward Short and Margaret Thatcher from their opposite viewpoints injected strong doses of party political warfare into the reorganization of secondary schools, thus assaulting the consensus of the 1960s created by educational administrators, leaders of teachers unions, sympathetic politicians and journalists. Events indicated the strength of this consensual movement and the figures in Table 1.5 which show among other things the continued growth of comprehensive schools between 1970 and

Table 1.5   Comprehensive schools and pupils in England and Wales 1965–76

Year	Comprehensive		Total secondary	
	Schools	*Pupils*	*Schools*	*Pupils*
1965	262	239,619	5,863	2,819,054
1966	387	312,281	5,798	2,816,793
1967	508	408,056	5,729	2,832,851
1968	748	606,362	5,576	2,895,387
1969	976	777,082	5,468	2,964,131
1970	1,250	973,701	5,385	3,045,974
1971	1,520	1,183,703	5,295	3,143,879
1972	1,777	1,412,174	5,212	3,251,426
1973	2,137	1,703,671	5,159	3,362,554
1974	2,677	2,310,103	5,079	3,723,743
1975	3,069	2,666,992	5,035	3,826,646
1976	3,387	2,976,408	4,982	3,935,500
1977	3,594	3,226,890	4,988	3,938,863
1978	3,901	3,436,637	4,962	4,093,032
1979	4,047	3,559,611	4,938	4,113,698

1974 are significant here. In 1970, 32 per cent of secondary school pupils were in comprehensive schools, by 1974 this figure had almost doubled to 62 per cent. Judged by the number of LEAs which had gained approval for schemes, the number with full or partial approval to reorganize was 30 at the end of 1966, 129 at the end of 1969 and 148 by March 1974 by which time only 15 had received no approval at all.

The change from Conservative to Labour administration in 1974 led to the re-establishment of comprehensive education as a central government aim and Circular 4/74 was issued reaffirming and updating the contents of Circular 10/65. LEAs were asked to inform the DES of the steps they were going to take to complete reorganization and to eliminate selection. Following the reorganization of local government itself in April 1974 the number of LEAs was reduced to 105 and many of the new bodies found themselves operating different forms of school organization in different parts of their newly acquired districts. It was left to each authority to decide whether to attempt to introduce some sort of homogeneity or to accept variety within its boundaries. In 1974, 67 of the new LEAs indicated that they expected to complete reorganization by the end of the decade; 31 committed themselves to reorganization in principle and subject to availability of resources while 7 made it clear that they would only reorganize if required to do so by new legislation. In the political atmosphere of the 1970s this led to the introduction of a new bill in December 1975 to enforce comprehensivization which received the Royal Assent on 22 November 1976.

Many local authorities continued to oppose new legislation as did some of their organizations, notably the Association of Education Committees and the Association of County Councils (ACC). Both organizations maintained the view that legislation turned 'an educational issue into a political issue'. In an exchange of correspondence with Fred Mulley, then Secretary of State, Alexander for the AEC again made the point that under the existing legislation a fully comprehensive system would in fact evolve as a natural process in the carrying into effect of consensus opinion which had been the basis of educational development for many years. Mr Mulley was hardly likely to heed this argument and replied that legislation was essential as public opinion only followed in the wake of reorganization. At the same time as wishing to complete reorganization speedily, he proposed to set no date for its completion nationally because of the danger of makeshift schemes through lack of resources.[59] The terms of the Act required authorities to follow the comprehensive principle in admitting pupils to secondary schools. The Secretary of State could call on LEAs or governors of voluntary schools to submit proposals for reorganization for his approval in such form as he might direct so as to complete the introduction of a fully comprehensive system.

Determined opposition to government policy on party lines continued in some areas and the extent of the Secretary of State's powers under Section 68 of the 1944 Act was held to be more limited by the Appeal Court and the House of Lords than the holder of that Office imagined when a writ of mandamus against the Conservative-controlled borough of Tameside was set aside.[60] Given the political context, it was inevitable that one of the first measures passed by Parliament after the general election of 1979 would be an act reversing the requirements of the 1976 Education Act. The Education Act 1979 removed all compulsion from the authorities and governors to reorganize on comprehensive lines and permitted those who had submitted proposals which had been agreed but were not yet carried out to apply to the Secretary of State to have these proposals revoked.

The steady progress towards a comprehensive form of organization for maintained secondary education has continued through these varied and 'exciting' episodes of political triumph and reversal. By 1979 about 85 per cent of secondary pupils were attending comprehensive schools. Of the six possibilities set out in Circular 10/65, three main patterns have been widely adopted:

(1)   schools with an age range of 11 to 18;
(2)   schools with an age range of 11 to 16 along with sixth form colleges for pupils of 16 to 18;
(3)   middle school systems with pupils moving on to comprehensive high schools at ages varying from 12 to 14.

The earlier belief was that comprehensives needed to have about 2,000 pupils in order to provide for an adequate variety of efficient and economically staffed 'A' level courses. In practice the average size of 11 to 18 comprehensives was rather below 1,000 pupils. There is undoubtedly a problem in trying to provide a sufficient range of 'A' level courses for traditional sixth-formers and developing courses suitable for 'new' sixth-formers within the limited staffing resources available to a smallish school. Attempted solutions can lead to a disproportionate amount of staff time being devoted to the sixth form. As the fall in the number of live births works its way through the secondary schools it has tended to make this problem even more difficult. Its effects can be particularly devastating in the central areas of nineteenth century cities and towns which are in any case losing population to suburban and rural areas. The closure and amalgamation of schools which may become necessary is nearly always a difficult undertaking for a locality. In some areas where middle schools were introduced because there simply was not enough room in existing buildings to accommodate the full secondary age range, the suggestion is now sometimes heard that there is space enough to abolish middle schools and concentrate the reduced number of pupils in the high schools. While this may fill high school buildings, it will not make any contribution to making sixth form numbers more viable.

The one group of secondary schools for which the central government had immediate responsibility were the direct grant grammar schools. In 1975 they numbered 174, about one third of these (54) were Roman Catholic and they often formed an essential element of an LEA's denominational provision. Among the remainder were a number of well known day schools such as the Manchester Grammar School. The largest single group were the 22 schools belonging to the Girls' Public Day School Trust. Direct grant status was the product of historical circumstances between the two world wars. They were left as a separate category in 1944 with the intention that they should form a sort of bridge between the maintained secondary schools in which fees were abolished and the entirely fee supported private or independent secondary schools which stood quite outside of the national system. Grant was paid directly to these schools by the DES, the principal condition being that a quarter of the places in a school must be made available to 11-year-old children from maintained primary schools without payment of fee. Other pupils paid fees with possible remission in accordance with parental income scales. An LEA had the right to take up a further 25 per cent of the total places if it wished. In the case of some Roman Catholic schools it sometimes took virtually all of the places.

Selection for direct grant schools was based on ability, thus from 1965 their future was in doubt. Their position was referred to the Donnison Commission on the Public Schools which reported on them abortively in 1970. The failure of the central government to deal successfully with its own group of secondary schools was probably due to its desire to do two things at once, firstly to end direct grant status and fees and to bring these schools within the maintained school orbit and secondly, to make their entry and organization comprehensive. After the Labour Party returned to office in 1974 the issue was taken up again and in March 1975 Reg Prentice made a statement in the Commons by which schools were urged to enter the maintained system and make a contribution to local provision. Where they were unwilling to do this, their grants would in any case be phased out, starting in September 1976. LEAs would not normally take up further places in the second group of schools. The Secretary of State expressed the hope that as many as possible would 'accept that they can best continue to serve the public by making the adjustments necessary to become an integral part of the local system of comprehensive education as maintained schools'.[61] The Roman Catholic schools accepted the invitation to enter the maintained system but most of the schools became independent.

The direct grant list had always been idiosyncratic, its composition had been the fortuitous outcome of administrative decisions taken by grant-aided secondary schools in the 1920s. Thus while many Conservatives regretted the withdrawal of direct grants, the list could hardly be revived in 1979. By way of substitute a completely new system of assistance for able pupils to attend independent schools was enacted as part of the Education Act 1980. The DES makes 'participatory agreements' with about 200 independent schools at which the assisted places may be held. Between 5,000 and 6,000 such awards were offered in the first year of operation. The case advanced in favour of this scheme was that many comprehensive schools were unable to meet adequately the needs of the brightest children who, therefore, needed public assistance to attend schools where their needs could be met. The scheme has been strongly opposed by supporters of the comprehensive principle who see in it a deliberate attempt to deprive the maintained schools of their ablest pupils. Others have objected to the scheme on the grounds that when the government is cutting heavily into the funds available for running the schools on the grounds that the state lacks the means to continue funding the maintained system at its existing level, it is not good enough for it to find also that the state does after all have the funds to set up a new scheme which channels public money into independent schools.

A FRAMEWORK FOR EXPANSION?

It is much easier for all sorts of reasons to cut planned capital investment rather than recurrent expenditure when the total resources available are reduced. During the early 1970s it appeared that the education service could look forward to further investment and further growth, but within a few years financial and economic circumstances began to take their toll. Provision for the necessary new building for raising the leaving age was achieved and the age raised by September 1973. A number of authorities planned the use of the RSLA (Raising of School Leaving Age) allocation to fit in with comprehensive reorganization. Somerset and Buckinghamshire planned certain of their RSLA projects in connection with youth service projects. The additional proportion of pupils who had to be catered for in different regions varied a good deal since the percentage of pupils staying on to a fifth year of secondary education on a voluntary basis had done so. In general more stayed on voluntarily in the South than in the North:

	1970	1971	1972
Northern Region	44.9	48.5	51.3
South East Region	63.8	65.1	66.2
Average (England and Wales)	52.8	53.8	55.0

With the return of the Heath government in 1970, Margaret Thatcher announced in December the 'first instalment of a large and systematic programme' starting in 1972 and intended to replace a considerable number of elderly primary school buildings. In October she had made the point in her address at her Party's Conference that her school building programme would concentrate on improving primary schools. She hoped after that to turn to the needs of nursery education. The programmes for 1972/3 and 1973/4 would improve or replace nearly 1,000 elderly primary schools. The resources for 1973/4 were distributed mainly according to the number of pupils still in pre-1903 primary schools. By 1970, 2.9 million of new primary school places had been provided since the War and there were then 4.9 million pupils; 2.6 million new secondary places had been provided and there were 3.0 million secondary pupils. There was a general feeling that primary schools had been kept short of capital investment while all resources had had to be concentrated on creating a secondary school system large enough to provide a place for everyone over 11 and to accommodate the additional age ranges brought in by raising the leaving age in 1947 and in 1973. This feeling was greatly reinforced by the Plowden report. It was as a result of its recommendations that Anthony Crosland was able to persuade Roy Jenkins then Chancellor, to add a special allocation to the school building programme of £16,000,000 to improve primary schools in deprived areas.

The publication of a White Paper, *Education: A Framework for Expansion,* in December 1972 seemed to promise a good deal of development in various directions. The White Paper was an attempt to consider the education service as a whole and to outline future policy. It was proposed and published in the heyday of the Heath government's dash for growth, when increasing public expenditure last played a prominent part in achieving an annual growth rate of 5 per cent in the gross national product. The White Paper placed special emphasis on launching a new policy for the under fives and was described as the first systematic attempt since 1870 to offer an earlier start in education. In support evidence was cited from the Plowden Committee pointing to the importance of the years before five in a child's education. It was thought that 700,000 full-time equivalent places might be needed by 1981/82. Given the progress expected for primary school building in the next few years, and the fall in primary school numbers from 1974, the White Paper also looked forward to taking some old school buildings out of use and in 1976/77 starting to replace or improve the worst of the secondary buildings. The addition of a secondary renewal programme to that for primary schools would pave the way for a more systematic long-term approach to the problem of renewal of school buildings. The White Paper was widely welcomed and the Secretary of State was congratulated on securing for the schools 'a pleasing prospect for the next decade, with a greater share of the available resources than they have enjoyed in the last 10 years'.[62] The following summer the Secretary of State announced the nursery building allocations to LEAs in England for building starts in 1974/75 and 1975/76. The total cost was £34 million and this would enable LEAs to provide nursery education for up to 130,0000 with 70,000 new places.

Before the end of the year the financial crisis struck which has really persisted ever since with varying degrees of intensity. The cuts in public expenditure meant that school building was cut back to the basic need for providing additional places where essential. There would be no money for improvements in schools and the £95 million programme for this was axed. A 10 per cent cut was also imposed on local authorities' revenue expenditure other than salaries and wages. The Secretary to the AEC commented that 'this is the most terribly serious setback in the development of the education service in my lifetime'. The Chancellor's December statement in the Commons in fact included cuts of 20 per cent in all public building programmes and 10 per cent of all spending on supplies, goods and services.[63]

At much the same time as the national economic difficulties intensified, it became increasingly clear that there was going to be a very considerable drop in the number of children for whom school places would be needed. There is always great difficulty in forecasting the likely course of the number of live births and during the present century these figures have, in fact, proved to be unpredictable – with difficult consequences for the planning of school provision. At the time of the White Paper in 1972 it was thought that although the number of live births had been declining it was about to rise again. The figures used by the government at that time are shown in column A of Table 1.6. Within two years those estimates were shown to be false. The actual number of live births was still declining so the future projections were also moved down (column B). As may be seen from column C, they were not moved down far enough.

These figures would in any case have made it difficult to sustain a strong claim on national resources for an ambitious programme of school building even if the economic situation had not become so depressed. As it was, they seem to have been seized upon by government agencies anxious to find economies

Table 1.6   Live births, actual and projected, in England and Wales (thousands)

Year	Actual numbers and projections		
	White Paper 1972 (Column A)	1974 (Column B)	(Column C)
1964	876	876	
1965	863	863	
1966	849	849	
1967	832	832	
1968	819	819	
1969	798	798	
1970	784	784	
1971	783	783	
1972	806	725	
1973	825	676	(Actual)
1974	833	640	640
1975	837	635	603
1976	840	637	584
1977	843	644	569
1978	847	657	596
1979	851	679	638
1980	856	710	
1981	862	741	
1982	869	767	

Sources: DES, Reports on Education, no. 80, Dec. 1974; Office of Population Censuses
and Surveys, England and Wale, Live Births.

as a reason why financial cuts in educational investment should
be very large indeed. The ambitious programme for the
building of nursery accommodation launched in the 1972
White Paper could hardly be expected to survive. It has been
possible to carry out some of the work of providing more
accommodation for nursery education by adapting existing
buildings. The DES was anxious to encourage LEAs to follow
this path. In 1977 the Department pointed out that opportunities for providing new buildings would be very restricted but
that advantage might be taken of the fall in primary school
numbers. These would fall from a current figure of 4.7 million
to a projected 3.9 million by 1982. The primary school space
thus released could be converted to accommodate nursery

classes at considerably less cost than that involved in new building. The Department's Architects and Building Branch undertook a pilot scheme in Nottinghamshire remodelling surplus space in four of their primary schools and gave some publicity to this.

CHAPTER 2

Curriculum and Examinations

Detailed prescription of the curriculum by the central government had long since been abandoned in England and Wales. The final ending of payment by results in 1898 enabled teachers in the public elementary schools to exercise a greater freedom of judgement. The Elementary Code only set out very broad requirements. A *Handbook of Suggestions for Teachers* was first published by the Board of Education in 1905. The preface to the 1918 edition stated that

The only uniformity of practice that the Board of Education desire to see in the teaching of public elementary schools is that each teacher shall think for himself and work out for himself such methods of teaching as may use his powers to the best advantage and be best suited to the particular needs and conditions of the School. Uniformity in detail of practice is not desirable, even if it were attainable.

From 1944 the Code itself finally disappeared and the statutory requirement was simply that pupils should be educated according to their age, ability and aptitude.

One of the most important consequences of the abandonment of the concept of 'elementary' schooling and its replacement by 'primary' and 'secondary' education was the impact which the change in concept had on the curriculum. The Consultative Committee's *Report on the Education of the Adolescent* in 1926 and its *Report on the Primary School* in 1931 had both helped to advance the need for a distinctive approach to the curriculum for the older and younger children within the public elementary schools. The pre-war reorganization of all-age schools into senior and junior elementary schools in many cases had helped teachers to focus the curriculum and teaching

52

arrangements to match more closely the needs of boys and girls above and below the age of 11. But it was only the legislative separation that eventually enabled the primary curriculum and teaching methods to develop their distinctive qualities in the way that they have during the last 30 years.

One of the principal external influences on the curriculum of many primary schools in the years following the Second World War was the 'eleven-plus' examination. As a higher proportion of parents became increasingly anxious that their children should not lose at the age of 11 the opportunity of eventually entering the more sought-after occupations, so the pressure on many primary schools to achieve a high rate of passes in the 'eleven-plus' intensified. In view of the nature of the tests this produced a strong emphasis on English and Arithmetic in the form in which they were tested. In som schools it also led to classes being instructed in and practising intelligence tests. In an effort to reduce the effects of this standardized testing on the primary schools, efforts were made in a few areas to devise alternative ways of selecting children for grammar school places. This was attempted in some districts of the West Riding of Yorkshire where pupils were allocated to secondary schools on the basis of recommendations by junior school staff.

Of its very nature the principal business of the school is learning while teaching is the main supporting activity designed to ensure that learning takes place. The Plowden Report commented on the extent to which ideas associated with Jean Piaget had come to influence the approach to learning in primary schools. One of the most important conclusions for practical purposes was that the great majority of primary school children could only learn efficiently from concrete situations, either as lived or as described. All learning called for the organization of material or of behaviour on the part of the learner, and the learner needed to adapt himself and underwent change in the process. Learning took place through a continuous process of interaction between the learner and his environment. Thus each new experience reorganized to some slight degree the structure of the mind and contributed to the child's world picture. It followed from this that teachers needed to observe their pupils closely so as to adjust their requirements to their pupils' stage of development. From this developed the concept of 'readiness' in reading and in mathematics. Thus for the youngest children the curriculum has tended to be more undifferentiated. As pupils moved up the primary schools so the conventional organization of subjects became more relevant. But even as pupils reached the stage where they could profit from a more structured subject approach, the subjects themselves still merged and overlapped and if one teacher was in charge of a class most of the time, it was easy for this to happen and for the maximum advantage to be drawn from it.

These ideas have had more influence on the way in which and on the stage at which different topics are taught rather than on the curriculum itself. The primary curriculum has continued throughout the post-war period to give priority to the acquisition of the basic skills in language and mathematics – to reading, writing, speech and arithmetic. In 1977 the Senior Chief Inspector reported that outside these key areas the pattern of the curriculum also remained fairly common. She ranged these elements in descending order of time given and successful practice:

(1)   work related to learning about self and society – religious education, history and geography;
(2)   aesthetic subjects – art, craft and music;
(3)   physical education – 'more in the form of gymnastics and games than of movement, dance and drama';
(4)   finally 'in a very insecure position at the bottom of the list', science and French.

The Plowden Committee commented that the force of tradition and of the inherent conservatism of all teaching professions makes for a slow rate of change. It might also be fair to add that the basic need which the young have for literacy, numeracy, some idea of the world in which they have to live and so on is not likely to change very much and the primary schools rightly seek to meet the needs of their clients.[1]

FROM SCHOOL AND HIGHER SCHOOL CERTIFICATE TO THE GENERAL CERTIFICATE OF EDUCATION

The position in the secondary schools since 1945 has proved to be much more controversial and, at times, more highly charged

in a political sense. Given that the central government's policy
was to move towards a tripartite form of secondary school
organization, presumably this would require not only different
approaches and teaching methods but also different curricula
at least for the older pupils. But since the curriculum in schools
was not prescribed by regulation, the usual process of influencing developments through publications, courses for teachers
and HMI advice would need to be employed. In the secondary
schools the powerful medium of the external public examination was obviously bound to play a considerable part in
influencing what went on. This was most obviously so in such
detailed matters as syllabus content or standard of attainment
required, but examinations were also influential in a wider
sense by their mere presence or absence. If the 'new' secondary
schools were to be free of public examinations, this would
surely limit the career opportunities of their scholars and
therefore the regard in which these schools were held by the
public. Thus examinations were bound to play their part in
limiting and casting doubt on the long-term acceptability of the
new secondary modern schools.

In the traditional secondary schools the curriculum had been
largely guided and maintained in its particular mould by the
School Certificate and Higher School Certificate examinations.
Preparations for the legislative reconstruction of the education
system in 1940 and 1941 made it desirable that the curriculum
and examinations in secondary schools should be reconsidered
as part of the wider problems of recasting educational arrangements. Hence a committee was appointed in 1941 under the
chairmanship of Cyril Norwood – then President of St John's
College, chairman of the Secondary Schools Examination
Council and previously a public school headmaster – 'to
consider suggested changes in the secondary school curriculum
and the question of school examinations in relation thereto'.
The Board of Education had some difficulty in restraining the
Chairman from leading his committee into undertaking a
report on most aspects of secondary schools. On the curriculum
itself the committee put forward four main points in its report.
It pointed out the need for a common curriculum for children
aged 11 to 13 so as to facilitate the movement of pupils between
different types of secondary education at this early stage. At all

ages it urged that emphasis should be placed on the importance of physical education, on the development of 'character' and of facility in the use of the English language. The committee perceived and condemned the 'narrow specialism' of many secondary schools and called for the reinstatement of the form master in the traditional public school sense – this would be of 'incalculable benefit to real education'. Finally schools ought to have greater freedom to devise curricula suited to individual needs.

The most time-consuming and controversial aspect of the committee's business proved to be examinations.[2] The members had great difficulty in coming to a set of recommendations on these and the longer-term proposals never won enough support in the teaching profession, among parents or in the public at large to prove acceptable. The importance of these proposals lay in the framework they set for the controversies out of which the GCE at 'O' and 'A' level and the subsequent Certificate of Secondary Education (CSE) all emerged. The Norwood Committee recommended that the School Certificate examination should eventually give way to internal examination and assessment by individual schools. For a transitional period of seven years the examination should continue to be carried out by the university examining boards and should become a subject examination. Pupils would therefore be able to take any subject or combination of subjects as they wished and the requirements of passes in a number of subjects chosen from certain groups before a certificate was awarded should be dropped. Thus there would in the longer term be no external school leaving examination at the age of 16. To meet the requirements of entry to the universities and to the professions a school leaving examination should continue for pupils of 18+. Pupils would specialize and take in this examination subjects required for their particular purpose; it was not to be used to provide evidence of a 'general or 'all-round' education. In order to increase public confidence in the assessment which schools made of their own pupils at 16+, the Inspectorate should be increased in numbers and greater emphasis was to be placed on the keeping of school records from the primary stage to the end of the school course.[3]

The publication of the Report in 1943 marked the opening of

a long period of campaigning and manoeuvring by the various interest groups. Much of this was concerned with the advisability or otherwise of permitting pupils of about 16+ to take an external, public examination. Both Norwood and the secretary to the committee, R.H. Barrow – staff inspector for classics – pressed the Board of Education to accept and implement the recommendations. Since the Secondary Schools Examinations Council (SSEC), consisting of representatives of the university examining boards, teachers' associations and LEAs, was largely critical, Barrow urged the head of the Secondary Branch, G.G. Williams, to set it aside. 'It is composed of vested interests, looking at educational problems with more than a trace of myopia' he wrote, and added that 'many of the people whose views we are compelled to consider are not of the quality which entitles their views to consideration.' Williams could only resist this pressure to act however much he might have sympathized with the recommendations in the Report. As he pointed out to Barrow, he could not advise the President to authorize major changes in the examination system without being quite certain that he would not have to withdraw them later on account of a clear expression of public opinion against them. Opposition in the grammar schools and in the examining boards hardened. The attitude of most members of the SSEC was only too clear. This was fully recognized by Cyril Norwood who continued to attack the SSEC even as he remained chairman of it. In writing to Williams he claimed that of its members 'the teachers are likely to prove inconvenient and the Examining Bodies intractable'.[4]

Something like stalemate continued for two years and it was only in 1946 that the Ministry was ready to try to move on this issue. In the early summer of 1946 the general attitude of the Ministry under Ellen Wilkinson was set out in a circular. This rehearsed briefly the original purpose of the School and Higher School Certificates and went on to indicate that the current view of senior members of the inspectorate had been accepted by the Minister. Accordingly it was 'impossible to ignore the view of [the Norwood] committee that the secondary schools will be better able to study the real and varied need of individual pupils and to develop their potentialities to the fullest and widest possible extent, if they are free from any form of external examination for pupils under the age of 17 or 18'. There was therefore no longer a place for an external examination at the age of 16 and 'it should be discontinued as soon as circumstances permit'. At the same time 'certain responsible quarters' believed there might be a place for the examination to continue as an internal school examination. Before reaching a final conclusion the minister proposed to seek the advice of the Secondary School Examinations Council.[5] But before seeking its advice, the Council itself was to be drastically reformed.

In February the Ministry had circulated a draft circular on the future shape of the SSEC. This had run into considerable opposition from the local authorities with whom discussions ensued so that the circular was not issued until the end of June. There were two central criticisms of the draft. The Minister proposed to state that she was no longer justified in limiting her functions to those of a coordinating authority as in the past, 'she will accordingly assume in the future full responsibility for the direction of policy and general arrangements with regard to school examinations'. This raised in acute form the fears of other parties in the government of education since it looked very much like a bid by the central government to take control of the curriculum. In its comments on the draft, the executive committee of the AEC pointed out that the 'substantial influence which is exercised over the school curricula through the medium of the SSEC renders it undesirable that the Minister should assume responsibility for the direction of policy in regard to school examinations'.

The second criticism was of the proposed composition of the SSEC. The proposal was to replace the existing arrangement of ten representatives from each of the local authority associations, the teachers and the examining bodies by six from the universities, five from the LEAs, ten from the teachers and three from the Ministry. The authorities stated that they were unable to accept this and suggested that the previous composition be retained. The Ministry was determined to get rid of the representatives of the university examining bodies and to replace them with a smaller number of university representatives, but it conceded three more places to the local authority associations so that the CCA, the AMC and the AEC were each to nominate two members, not one. At the same time the Ministry increased the number of its own nominees from three to five. The Chairman of the reformed Council was to be the former permanent secretary, Maurice Holmes. By way of response to the first criticism, the circular was modified to read that the Minister would assume 'full responsibility *with the assistance of a reconstituted SSEC* for the direction of policy and general arrangements in regard to school examinations'.[6]

Since the secretary to the Norwood Committee, HMI R.H. Barrow was to be secretary to the SSEC and since M.P. Roseveare, then Senior Chief Inspector, was to be an assessor, there was little doubt but that the full Norwood recommendations would be kept in mind. The Council decided to work in two panels, one to deal with examinations at 18+ and the other to consider the position two years earlier. The Higher School Certificate Panel submitted its report to the full Council in January 1947. There had been much difficulty within the Panel in agreeing, but the recommendation was not for two separate examinations, one for leavers at 18+ and the other for aspirants to university entrance, but rather one examination at 'A' and 'S' level. The School Certificate panel was divided in its report. The majority recommended no external examinations for pupils until they were old enough to take the new replacement for Higher School Certificate. For purposes of employment, school reports and the results of 'Eleven-plus' type tests of intelligence would suffice. The minority recommended that the School Certificate should be retained although as a subject examination.[7]

By the fourth meeting of the SSEC it was clear that the Council was not going to reach agreement on the main issues before it. On some major questions there was serious division with the university and grammar school representatives on one side and the local authority, ministry and some teacher representatives on the other. Finally Roseveare prepared a paper in consultation with Philip Morris (acting chairman) which formed the basis for a unanimous report. This paper necessarily contained a number of significant concessions to the minority – largely, it seems, to prevent the universities from setting up their own examination arrangements for admissions, thus bypassing and possibly even undermining a reformed state system. The Report has proved to be a significant document for it contained the basic recommendations for the GCE examination system which has played a central part directly or indirectly in guiding the curriculum and teaching in secondary schools for the last 30 years.[8]

The Report opened with uncontentious general principles about ages, abilities and aptitudes, on the need to avoid premature specialization and to encourage children to stay at school beyond 16. It urged that fuller school records should be kept and that leavers should be given a comprehensive school report about their abilities and potentialities. Periodic objective tests were commended as were experiments in the external assessment of internal examinations. On external examinations the Council recommended that there should be a GCE with papers set at three levels, 'Ordinary', 'Advanced' and 'Scholarship'. The ordinary examination was to provide a reasonable test in a subject for pupils who had studied it up to about the age of 16 or who had studied it in a non-specialist way in the sixth form. Advanced papers were to test two years of specialist study in the sixth form. Scholarship papers were to be designed to give specially gifted pupils an opportunity for showing distinctive merit and promise. No 'group' or minimum number of subjects was to be required. The standard of the ordinary level was to approximate to that of a 'credit' in the School Certificate Examination while the pass at Advanced level was to approximate to the existing pass standard in the Higher School Certificate Examination. No pupils should be permitted to take the GCE before the age of 16.

The main proposals concerning examinations proved to be generally acceptable. It appeared that universities and professional bodies would find it possible to relate their entrance requirements to the GCE. The Minister made it known in April 1948 that he accepted those recommendations and intended to bring them into effect. The proposal minimum age of entry to the GCE became a matter of acute controversy when a circular was issued detailing the steps by which the new arrangements were to come into force. Circular 168 stated that the GCE would be introduced in 1951 on the lines proposed in the SSEC

Report including the minimum age of 16 for entry – possibly rising to 17 in due course. The majority of the SSEC had certainly wished to ensure that modern and technical schools remained free of external examinations and of the constraints these would impose on their curricula. The minimum age restriction was therefore in accordance with that view. Criticism of the age limit grew among grammer school teachers in spite of efforts to answer it by the Minister and by officials. Tomlinson told the annual meeting of the Incorporated Association of Head Masters at the end of 1948 that the age limit was not 'a political device of my own' but a necessary part of a new system of examinations which was not designed to review the general work of the lower forms of a school but to test children in subjects they had studied to an age of relative maturity. He also stated that he wished to dispose of the suggestion that he had imposed the age limit 'solely in order to protect the modern school'. This might not have been the *sole* reason, but it does seem to have been an important reason for doing so in the minds of those HMIs and others who took the Norwood Committee's attitude to school curricula and external examinations.[9]

Although the Association of Education Committees (AEC) accepted and supported the minimum age arrangement, a number of LEAs were moved to add their weight to complaints to the Ministry. In replying to a letter from Essex the Ministry explained that the object in 1950, as in future years, 'would be to reserve the younger children for later examination at a time more nearly relevant to their needs'. A few months later Cleary explained in a letter to the AEC that the age requirement was 'conceived in terms of a full secondary course from 11 to 17 or 18 and of the individual requirements of each pupil. A pupil who leaves at an early age and wants credentials can always take examinations for the General Certificate as a student at a Further Education Institution'.[10]

Some authorities, including Kent, were anxious to extend the GCE to their modern schools and took the matter up with the Ministry. By 1950 Tomlinson apparently considered that all secondary schools should be encouraged to develop facilities for pupils of 15 to 18, including modern schools. Since the new examination could properly be taken by pupils who had studied beyond the minimum age, this provision was needed for some modern school pupils would require GCE passes to enter teaching and nursing. This was clearly a departure from the earlier view. In a discussion paper following this correspondence, the AEC noted that hitherto applications from modern schools in Kent to enter pupils had been turned down by HMIs but it now appeared to be the Ministry's view that the taking of these examinations in modern schools should be actively encouraged. The paper went on to consider the effect of this on well established aspects of education policy. For instance, if the Minister considered there would be enough pupils in the average modern school capable of taking several subjects (as his reference to future teachers and nurses implied) 'are not local education authorities going to be obliged to ask themselves (a) whether their selection system is working properly or (b) whether it really matters'.[11] This particular issue was only resolved eventually by moving away from the tripartite arrangements which – at least logically – became increasingly untenable even as many more secondary school places were being built on the tripartite pattern.

The GCE examinations were held for the first time in 1951. Although the standard for the 'O' level pass was to rise to that of the former School Certificate 'credit'. On the assumption that the standard of entry remained substantially unchanged, the pass figures for 'O' level reflected the policy accurately. There was a good deal of criticism of the standard of the new examination because of the high proportion of falures, but the main weight of criticism continued to be directed against the age limit.[12] Heads of grammer schools were perhaps the most consistent and energetic group of opponents of the minimum age requirement. There was a good deal of sympathy for their views in the press and eventually from the Conservative Party. By the time the Conservatives were returned to office in 1951 opinion generally had moved against the age limit and it became clear that it was likely to be modified. Thus it was not surprising that when the SSEC published its review of examinations in secondary schools in 1952 it suggested that head teachers should be given the discretion to enter pupils for the examination under the minimum age if they were able to confirm that this was educationally desirable.

Although the SSEC's Report appeared early in 1952, it was not until the following October that the Ministry ammended its grant regulations to give effect to the proposed change. The LEAs apparently feared that there would be an appreciable increase in the examination fees which they would have to pay under the regulations if more pupils could be entered for the GCE and they attempted therefore to win for themselves the right to decide whether or not to pay for any pupil under 16. Beloe, Chief Education Officer for Surrey, complained that pupils were already being entered for more subjects than they were likely to pass. 'Financial wastage' would increase if children under 16 in grammer schools were entered and this would be even more wasteful if modern schools began to enter their pupils under 16 in one or two subjects. Alexander took the matter up with the Ministry and wrote to Beloe 'I have now had a chat with the Ministry boys and they are, I think, quite clear that there must be a means which will enable a local education authority to limit its responsibility for paying examination fees. I have suggested a form of words [for the grant regulations] and at the moment the Ministry are checking with the legal branch.'

In fact by the end of July the Ministry had decided that it could not leave the payment of fees to the discretion of LEAs. The fees would have to be paid by LEAs for any pupil above or below the age of 16 who was entered in accordance with the conditions laid down by the SSEC. All the LEAs got was the promise of exhortation through a circular 'in which we should say: "The wholesale entry of young pupils would be a misuse of the examination; but provided the revised conditions of entry are strictly and faithfully fulfilled, the Minister would expect that the fees of pupils entering below the prescribed age should automatically be paid from the public funds." '[13]

THE ASSOCIATED EXAMINING BOARD

The majority of members of the SSEC certainly wished modern and technical schools to remain free from any external examinations because of the constraints which these placed on the curricula of schools. Most members probably agreed with the Norwood Committee's contention that pupils in all forms of secondary education should be free from external examinations until the latest possible age. So far as the LEAs were concerned, this feeling was reinforced by the apparent jealousy which some of them had shown between the wars towards the influence of university examining bodies on the curricula of 'their' secondary schools. Thus in 1952 the AEC urged the Minister of Education to publish and circulate widely a pamphlet on the GCE 'so that present misunderstandings may be removed'. The much more limited scope of the new GCE by comparison with the former School and Higher School Certificate had been completely overlooked. Comments on the BBC and in the press showed that the whole scheme of the GCE was widely misunderstood. In the minds of most people the new examination was merely the old one under another name and 'it is principally an employment ticket which is issued to successful pupils attending grammer schools.'[14] This LEAs took a somewhat equivocal attitude towards the initiatives of various bodies to establish examinations for children who would not be candidates for the new and more difficult GCE. An organization called the Combined Schools Examinations was set up and wrote to chief education officers and others offering to conduct external examinations at a level somewhat lower than the GCE. There was to be no age limit and the standard required would approximate to that of the old School Certificate. There was some discussion of this body's intentions in the Ministry in the summer of 1952 but those involved were apparently unwilling to accept that such bodies only brought forward proposals because there was a demand for them among the general public. The Ministry's attitude at this time was reasserted a few months later in a circular which again suggested that a school report would provide much better evidence of a general education than any examination. 'It may be idle to suppose that the examination certificates will not continue to be used in this way. Even so, it appears to be quite unnecessary for nationally attested certificates to be made available on the same scale as in the past.'[15]

It would have been difficult for those who wrote this circular – or, indeed, for most of those who read it – to believe that they were on the eve of a great expansion of public examinations which would within two decades come to be used to assess more than half of thepupils passing through the seconadry schools. Even when the circular appeared, much progress had been made towards the creation of an additional examining body for the GCE itself. When it became clear that the new GCE would not be simply an examination to be taken by the senior classes in grammer schools but rather a subject examination, available to senior pupils still at school or after they had left, the position of those regional bodies whose examinations had been widely taken in technical colleges and schools appeared to be affected. For instance at a meeting of the Northern Counties Technical Examinations Council in 1949 it was thought probable that many students on leaving technical schools would take part-time courses of study in order to add subjects to their GCE and that there would be a diversion from the examinations of regional examining bodies. It was precisely to meet this problem that the SSEC appointed a group to confer with representatives of the City and Guilds of London Institute, the Royal Society of Arts, the Northern Counties TEC, the Union of Lancashire and Cheshire Institutes and like bodies. At a meeting held on 1 March 1949 it was agreed that it was desirable for those other examining bodies to be associated with the new examining system in some way so as to avoid a serious danger of duplication. It was thought that the experience of these bodies would be well worth utilizing in dealing with candidates for GCE from technical institutions and secondary technical schools.

It seemed to be impractical to modify the existing university examining bodies and a new GCE examining body appeared to be a possibility although there was some doubt as to whether such a body would have the same standing with students, universities, employers and professions as a university examining body. It had been suggested that a new body might cater specially for a limited range of 'technical' subjects, but the chairman, Sir Philip Morris, thought the SSEC would want to be satisfied that the new body would also provide more comprehensive fare for its clients and cover a broad stretch of the curriculum at a reasonable standard. A great deal of further discussion was necessary before the various bodies could be brought to agree on the creation of a new, ninth, examining body. Much of the negotiation fell on Cyril Lloyd of the City and Guilds Institute. The creation of the proposed body was in accordance with the desire of the AEC that there should be no extension of the influence of the university examining boards, consequently the local authority bodies supported this development. The Minister finally gave his formal approval to the 'Ninth Examining Body' in September 1953. It took the name of the 'Associated Examining Board for the General Certificate of Education'. In the summer of 1954 it submitted its draft regulations to the SSEC for approval together with 47 syllabuses at 'O' level and 35 at 'A' level with the intention of conducting its first examinations in 1955.[16]

THE CERTIFICATE OF SECONDARY EDUCATION (CSE)

Dissatisfaction with various aspects of the 'O' level examination was widespread in the 1950s. After the age limit had, in effect, been dropped, there was pressure for change in three main directions, for the re-introduction of some system of grading to show merit (in place of the pass/fail arrangement), for the abolition of the single subject certificate and a requirement for at least three subjects and for the creation of a lower level of pass. This last was sought since work in many fifth forms was said to be 'gravely handicapped through the sense of frustration engendered in the less able pupils by the knowledge that they have little chance of sucess in an examination which must determine their course of study'.[17] A further frequent complaint was that the new subject system resulted in ever earlier specialization. The Ministry resisted any change and on the advise of senior members of the Inspectorate continued to work towards the goal of a system of secondary education which would be free from examinations until the end of the sixth form. Initially the AEC also continued to argue that the GCE was not appropriate for use as a leaving examination, that it was to be regarded as a qualification for admission to universities and to certain professions and that the modifications urged were therefore inappropriate.

However, dissatisfaction with the new arrangements came to be expressed by a number of education committees and

Alexander certainly changed his attitude in the face of demands for an externally-based leaving certificate. It has been pointed out that confronted by Ministry opposition to any extention at all of secondary school examinations, Alexander was able to channel the AEC's expression of this pressure away from any modification of the GCE into a campaign for a completely new examination, appropriate to the needs of a considerable proportion of pupils in the secondary modern schools and – an important point – not under the control of the university examining bodies.[18] It may well have been this last point which made him continue to oppose demands for a lower pass in the 'O' level itself even although many saw this as the best way of meeting the situation. Nottingham County Borough, for instance, put a strong case to the Ministry for reinstating a pass in the GCE at the pass level of the old School Certificate. The authority told the Minister that it was confident that such a change would enable 'a substantial number of secondary modern school pupils to take the GCE examination with reasonable prospects of success in several subjects'. Had reforms been carried through on these lines it would certainly have avoided the problems that have arisen and persisted for so long over trying now to bring GCE and CSE into one 16+ examination. [19]

Certainly from 1953 the evidence indicates that the Secretary to the AEC was convinced of the need for a leaving examination designed for the good average pupil, 'by that I mean the average of the whole age group and not of grammar schools'. By the end of 1954 a number of bodies were pressing the need for suitable examinations for secondary modern and techncal schools and some such as the Royal Society of Arts (RSA) and the College of Preceptors were coming forward with examinations which they had devised or were offering to set up and manage in order to meet an increasingly pressing demand from many parents and schools. The AEC and NUT Joint Working Party considered the problem and urged the Minister in 1954 to set up a committee of inquiry. By the beginning of 1955 the Minister had not replied. The AEC therefore pressed again for an 'urgent inquiry' into the whole question of leaving examinations and continued to maintain its pressure through correspondence.[20]

The immediate results of the representations made to the Minister were embodied in Circular 289 which was issued in July 1955 and which indicated an unwillingness on the part of the Ministry to move very far. The Minister welcomed the small but increasing number of modern school pupils taking 'O' level but warned that the interests of an able minority in these schools must not be allowed to take precedence over the needs of the majority. He stated that he did not favour either the establishment of any new examination of national standing for secondary schools or the widespread use of examinations run by outside bodies. Finally in the Circular once again the more general use of school records and references from head teachers for employers was commended. A new examination

on a national basis for modern schools would induce uniformity of syllabuses, curricula and methods at stages and ages where uniformity would be most undesirable. Schools would feel unable to resist pressure to enter pupils for it and the Minister fears that it would prejudice the more widespread development of the varied and lively courses already to be found in the best modern schools. There is also the risk that it would be regarded as an index to the efficiency of schools, a conception which would be unrealistic or even oppressive in view of the wide differences in their circumstances and in the ranges of ability of their pupils.

The Circular invited comments from the various educational interests and these showed to what extent pressure was building up in favour of a fuller system of external examinations in the modern schools. The AEC urged the Government to set up a departmental or other committee specially to examine this whole question. As for the apparent handicaps which the Minister found external examinations imposed on the freedom of teachers and on pupils, schools which took external examinations 'seem to derive substantial public esteem as a result and, indeed, the teaching staff in such schools tend to argue that the examinations are desirable rather than undesirable'.[21]

Two years later a further circular indicated very little movement by the Ministry in spite of pressure. While an examination could prove to have value as an incentive, there was no reason for it to be external, thus internal examinations were to be encouraged. Moreover, since the Central Advisory Council (the 'Crowther Committee') was looking at the education of children over 15, these items could not properly be considered apart from the wider question of the general provision for older children. The local authority associations all expressed strong disappointment and similar sentiments were widespread in the press and among the public. The Crowther Committee was not a suitably representative body and there was doubt as to its adequacy or competence to deal with examination matters. An increasing number of LEAs were adopting plans for regional leaving certificates. Such independent bodies as the College of Preceptors and the Royal Society of Arts found a growing demand for their examinations from candidates from modern schools. It was clear that official policy was coming under greater pressure and it was equally clear that on this issue the local authorities, organized by Alexander, were doing all they could to bring about change. Because of the influence of the local authorities and advocates of change in the SSEC the Ministry had decided, probably for tactical reasons, to try to still the campaign by referring the whole issue to the Crowther Committee. Here, it hoped, its views would be given full weight by one of the few educational committees on which the AEC did not nominate any representative as of right. It has been suggested that this step was taken in part to remove the matter from the persuasive personal pressure of Alexander who had been pushing the need for a new examination so vigorously both inside the AEC and inside the SSEC.[22]

During the winter of 1957/8 two new names came to occupy offices which were intimately involved in this question. Geoffrey Lloyd succeeded Lord Hailsham as Minister and Dr J. F. Lockwood succeeded Sir John Wolfenden as chairman of the SSEC. The Ministry became slightly less resistant on the matter of an inquiry and the new chairman of the SSEC sent an uncharacteristically forthright letter to the Minister following a meeting of that body on 25 March 1958. Dr Lockwood's letter amounted to a threat to go it alone if the Ministry advised by its Inspectorate continued to obstruct. He wrote

I was asked to put to you once again a strong plea that you should yourself appoint an *ad hoc* committee at an early date. . . . Indeed, some members of the Council feel so strongly on this issue that it seems likely that at their next meeting they will, in default of an alternative, propose the appointment of a sub-committee from amongst their own members, with such additions as they may think it necessary to make by cooption, to undertake an immediate investigation of the problem.

Geoffrey Lloyd's reply began by denying that his predecessors had ever been opposed to the use of 'examinations as such' in secondary schools and much of the letter was devoted to defending and explaining the negative attitude the Ministry had taken. But the essential point in the letter came with the opening of the last paragraph. 'If, however, as I understand from your letter, the Council now wish themselves to conduct a . . . study of the problem of examinations below GCE 'O' level, I would not wish to stand in their way.'[23]

The SSEC therefore established a sub-committee 'to review the current arrangements for the examination of secondary school pupils rather than by the GCE examination, to consider what developments are desirable, and to advise the Council whether, and if so, what, examinations should be encouraged or introduced, and at what stages and levels'. The sub-committee consisted of six members of the SSEC (R. Beloe as chairman, W. P. Alexander, E. L. Britton, A. Hay, H. Wyn Jones and Miss O. M. Hastings). It was agreed that a further two members, preferably from non-grammar schools should be added in view of the nature of the investigation. Later it was also agreed to invite the Central Advisory Council (the Crowther Committee) to send an observer. The setting up of this subcommittee marked a crucial stage in the development of examinations policy. It was largely the result of pressure by Alexander and the AEC. If the matter had been left to the Central Advisory Council alone under Crowther as the Minister had wished, the outcome would have been very different for that body did eventually recommend that no new national examination should be established but that developments be watched for five years.

At its first meeting the Beloe Committee decided that the first step would be to obtain all the information it could as to the examinations other than GCE currently being taken. These fell into four categories – national (such as those of the RSA); regional (such as those of the Union of Lancashire and Cheshire Institutes); local (like Harrow district scheme) and internal. The Committee decided to seek evidence from the bodies conducting the examinations, from LEAs on what was actually happening in their schools and directly from a sample of schools since one member of the committee had suggested that many schools had branched out in contravention of official policy and would therefore be loth to confide in the LEA. The attitude of the Chairman was certainly not predetermined before the Committee began its task. He had appeared to be rather inclined to the view that no new examination was necessary but that schools should be allowed to choose for themselves and letting the existing bodies seek to find the right form of examination for pupils of 16. As it progressed the Committee found itself attaching importance to the proportion of pupils who could manage GCE 'O' level with a reason- able group of subjects for this clearly left a considerable number of children with an interest in extended courses to the age of 16 sometimes with a distinctly vocational bias or interest.[24]

The evidence presented to the Committee ranged from complete opposition to any extension of the examination system to strong support for a new secondary school examina- tion. Head teachers, education officers and others were divided in their views. A. B. Clegg from the West Riding and S.T. Broad from Hertfordshire were two of the best known members of the education establishment who opposed the proposal, largely on the same grounds that had persuaded the Norwood Committee. According to Broad, the question was fundament- ally and essentially a professional matter. 'The teacher should not have to be looking over his shoulder at the "employer" or the "public", wondering what such uninformed people are going to commit him to.' Witnesses from commerce and industry felt that examinations could provide a stimulus to pupils but appreciated that examinations might have undesir- able effects on educational grounds on which they were not well qualified to speak. According to a letter representing the view of the heads of secondary modern schools in Ealing, it was not the generally accepted view that a leaving examination was 'not only a useful incentive but also a necessity vocationally'.[25]

The Beloe Committee accepted the idea of a new examination and recommended certain criteria that it should meet. The examination was to be suited to pupils at the end of the fifth year of the secondary school course when they would be 16+. On the assumption that about 20 per cent of the age group might attempt GCE 'O' level in at least four subjects, the new examination ought to meet the needs of the next 20 per cent below these in four or more subjects with a substantial majority obtaining passes. Up to a further 20 per cent might attempt individual subjects. The examination should be on a subject and not a group basis It should be specifically designed to meet the needs and interest of pupils in the ability range concerned and should not merely replicate GCE examinations at a lower level. The examinations should be largely in the hands of teachers serving the schools which would use them. The examining bodies were to act under the general guidance of the central consultative body. On the publication of the Beloe Report comments and reactions were sought. These were considered by the sub-committee and submitted to the SSEC to form the basis of its Fourth Report.[26]

The major organizations primarily concerned, the teachers' and local authorities' associations – with the exception of the County Councils Association (CCA) – were found to have endorsed the Beloe Committee's proposals. GCE examining bodies raised no major objections and a number of existing non-GCE examining bodies expressed a readiness to come into any scheme which might emerge. The CCA and the West Riding LEA objected in principle: opinions amongst teachers and others were divided on whether examinations at this level did more harm than good, they therefore favoured 'the view of the Crowther Committee that the time has not yet come to make a decision concerning the creation of a national system of examinations'. The sub-committee discounted this objection and suggested that the CCA had not realized the extent to which external examinations by independent examining bodies had, despite official discouragement, grown so rapidly that there was serious danger of the curriculum and teaching in the schools coming under external control and that after another five years the Minister would probably find himself faced with a situation much more difficult to remedy. The other objections were on specific points such as the age at which the examination should be taken and the number of regional examining bodies that should be set up. The SSEC was recommended to advise the Minister to accept the general principle that there should be a new subject examination as already outlined. Details of arrangements for bringing the examinations into being should then, it was suggested, be remitted by the SSEC to a small working party.[27]

The SSEC met to consider these reactions on 1 March 1961. It was clear that the great majority of pupils remaining for a fifth year in a secondary school were being entered for external examinations already. The Council accordingly recommended the Minister to accept the Beloe proposals. On 17 July the Minister told the House of Commons that while he accepted the proposals, he did so 'reluctantly'. He realized that he had to choose between either prohibiting all examinations other than the GCE for this group of pupils or trying to improve examination arrangements on the lines recommended by the SSEC. In taking the latter course he asked the SSEC to work out a more detailed scheme, urged that attention should be paid to the view of those teachers who feared that new examinations would cramp their freedom and stressed the need for further experiments with internal school examinations externally assessed. In order to strengthen the SSEC to take on its new responsibilities it was reconstituted in October so as to bring in members with knowledge and experience of non-selective schools. The total membership of the Council was increased from 32 to 39 and a smaller standing committee was set up to work out detailed plans for introducing the Certificate of Secondary Education.[28]

The process of reporting by committee, awaiting comment and reactions, then making recommendations definitive was repeated again and during 1962 and 1963 the actual details of the new Certificate of Secondary Education became firm. A regional examining body was to be set up in each region and could not undertake examinations in the area of another body. Subject panels were to have a majority of serving teachers and the regional examining bodies were to have a majority of their members drawn from serving teachers on the subject panels. The CSE itself was to be offered in three ways:

(1)   an external examination on syllabuses provided by the regional subject panels;
(2)   an external examination on syllabuses provided by a school or group of schools and approved by the regional subject panels;
(3)   examinations set and marked internally in a school or group of schools but moderated by the region.

The standard was to be suitable for pupils in the 20 per cent of the age group below the 20 per cent who attempted GCE 'O' level in four or more subjects. Perhaps the most novel of these recommendations was the third mode of examining – the papers being set and marked internally but with regional moderation. The strongly critical attitude of the West Riding referred to above where the Education Officer, Alec Clegg, particularly feared the cramping effect of examinations on the curriculum, led to the setting up of the West Riding and Lindsey Regional Examining Board which largely reflected his views in that it placed great emphasis upon and has provided valuable experience of Mode 3.[29]

The standing committee of the SSEC was enjoined to consult with the Ministry's Curriculum Study Group in the course of its work and the report on the Scope and Standards of the Certificate of Secondary Education was produced after such consultation. The main conclusions were that there should be a five point scale with two reference grades, 1 and 4, to which examiners would allocate candidates on the basis of available evidence. A sixteen year-old pupil whose ability showed that he might have secured a pass at GCE 'O' level if he had an appropriate course of study was to be placed in grade 1. A pupil of average ability who had applied himself to a course of study of the subject regarded as appropriate to his age, ability and aptitude, might be expected to achieve grade 4. All candidates between 1 and 4 were to be allocated to grades 2 and 3 in equal numbers. Grade 5 was to be used to describe performances below grade 4 but which had enough merit to show the candidate had been properly entered for the examination.

Lower performances would be ungraded. Certificates of Secondary Education were to be issued to candidates who secured at least one grade in the range 1 to 4; where issued they would also include grade 5 results.[30] Arrangements went ahead smoothly and 14 regional examining boards were set up. Nine of these offered examinations in 1965, the remainder started the next year.

It is of interest to notice that the creation of a system of public examinations for secondary schools in the middle years of the century went forward in response to pressures from 'outside' sources – parents, some schools, some teachers, employers – and in the face of strong opposition from the Ministry and the Inspectorate. Far from school leaving examinations ceasing as foretold by the Norwood Committee and the SSEC working party of 1947, they have grown to embrace in some way the majority of school leavers. Secondary education for all apparently included in the popular mind the right to take a secondary

Table 2.1   Candidates for public examinations, 1947 and 1977

(a)	1947		
	Candidates entered for:	School Certificate	107,356
		Higher School Certificate	26,322
		TOTAL	133,678
(b)	1977		
	Candidates entered for:	CSE alone	258,500
		CSE and 'O' level	360,700
		'O' level only	614,400
		'O' level and 'A' level	49,300
		'A' level only	252,700
		TOTAL	1,535,600
(c)	1977		
	Subject entries:	'A' level	554,500
		'O' level	2,852,000
		CSE	2,782,300
		TOTAL	6,188,800

Sources: (a) *Education in 1947,* table 32 (p. 134).
         (b) *Statistics of Education, 1977,* vol. 2, table ix (p. xiv).
         (c) Ibid., table xi (p. xv).

school leaving examination. The previous table gives some idea of the growth of public examinations over the three decades following 1947. The number of candidates from all sources taking CSE and GCE almost doubled in the decade from 1967 to 1977 when it exceeded 1.5 million (see Table 2.1). The main increase occurred in the group taking CSE following the raising of the school leaving age.

THE CURRICULUM STUDY GROUP

The very fact that outside pressures led to a system of examinations far removed from that envisaged over the years by the Ministry further encouraged some reconsideration of the Ministry's own organization for dealing with the curriculum and examinations. In retrospect it could be argued that successive ministers were offered advice that was not very sound and there seemed to be a gap within the Department which needed to be plugged. There was a feeling within the Ministry that Schools Branch needed to add a new dimension to its work. Growing interest in the curriculum internationally – through UNESCO and OEEC meetings – also brought home to senior officials the fact that they could not make any effective contribution to the discussion of educational questions if they could do little more than incant the doctrine that in Britain the teacher was a law unto himself. This gave the impression that the Minister and the Ministry neither knew nor cared who learned what. It would be very helpful to be able to show that the Minister stood for a course of action recommended as advantageous or expedient. Since the relationship of inspectors to officials was that of adviser to actor, both the Inspectorate and Schools Branch needed to add a new dimension to their work in that a joint group should be set up to investigate and develop policies on defined questions. Such a group might be headed jointly by a staff inspector and an assistant secretary.[31]

Against this background the recommendations of the Beloe Committee that the SSEC needed the assistance of a small but highly qualified professional team to study in depth the problems posed by the introduction of a new system of national examinations-offered the occasion for the Ministry to come forward with its Curriculum Study Group which, it said, could fulfil just this sort of task. On 9 March 1962 Mary Smieton, the Permanent Secretary, sent a letter to teachers' and local authorities' associations to let them know what was afoot. The Ministry was in the process of setting up a Curriculum Study Group which would concern itself with the curriculum and examinations and their administrative implications. The main job of the unit would be to improve the value of the service that the Inspectorate and the Department were able to offer in this area. She went on to explain that a team was going to be formed to deal with CSE examination matters and would be concerned with advising the SSEC and its committees. This would not change the functions or responsibilities of the SSEC itself; the new unit would merely be offering a service function.[32] In this letter and in the subsequent speech by the Minister, care was taken to reassure teachers and local authorities that the existing pattern of powers would not be disturbed in any way.

Initially the response of the other partners was cautious rather than hostile. In its reply to the Permanent Secretary, the AEC accepted that the Ministry had a major contribution to make in the area of the curriculum and examinations but also added that the fundamental distribution of power between the three partners – central government, local authorities and the teachers – should be sustained. This point was made more specifically in *Education*. LEAs and teachers must be fully consulted on what researches were to be undertaken. It was unfortunate that the Minister had not consulted the other partners before setting up the Group, but assurances had now been given and it was to be hoped that these would be fully carried out. The press was more favourably disposed. *The Times Educational Supplement* welcomed the Curriculum Study Group and called it 'Eccles' most imaginative and far-reaching legacy to education.'[33]

As has been described above, the development activities in the Ministry's Architects' and Building Branch had been successful in terms of school building and also in the political sense in that it had not provoked jealous hostility among the LEAs but rather had worked well in collaboration with them.

D. H. Morrell had been responsible for this work within the Ministry and he had been removed to Schools Branch as an assistant secretary in February 1962 assuming responsibilities in connection with the SSEC. When the Curriculum Study Group was formed it was announced that it was to have joint heads, one from the office, Morrell, and the other a senior HMI, R. W. Morris. Quite apart from his other qualities, no doubt Morrell's successful experience in guiding from the Ministry a new development in what had been traditionally more of a local authority area, school building, indicated that he was well suited to handling the new Group and any difficulties that it might encounter.

The creation of the Group served however to reawaken the whole issue of who should control the curriculum. Morrell's address to the annual meeting of the National Foundation for Educational Research in which he said that the work of curriculum development required the active participation of other agencies such as the central government and local authorities as well as the teachers, served to intensify feelings. From the education committees the view was put that since the Group had been established without consultation, its activities should be placed under the guidance of a representative body on which there would be representatives of the Ministry, LEAs, teachers' associations, universities and other appropriate agencies. If this was not done, the Minister must expect the activities of the Group to be regarded with considerable suspicion by his partners in the education service. In October 1962 a deputation from the AEC went to the Minister to press for a much more representative body to supervise the Curriculum Study Group. The Minister, Edward Boyle, agreed that there did appear to be some danger of control of the curriculum by an unrepresentative body, but thought that there were constitutional difficulties in the AEC's suggestion. It was left that he would give further consideration to ways of meeting the case put forward by the LEAs and the teachers.[34]

THE SCHOOLS COUNCIL

During the winter of 1962/3 thought was given to various ways of dealing with this matter. The possibility of reconstituting the SSEC and concerning it in the affairs of the Curriculum Study Group was canvassed. In February, Morrell sent Alexander a copy of a paper he had prepared entitled 'Proposed Schools Council for the Curriculum and Examinations' and in a covering letter explained that he would welcome any comments on it and that he was sending it, in confidence, a few days later to a small number of people, 'Gould, Lockwood, Keith Murray', for their views. Although there were to be major changes in these proposals, this initial paper is important in two ways; it set out the problem of control over the curriculum very clearly and it proposed a discussion model for what did in fact grow into the Schools Council after further modification. The memorandum argued that the only two bodies which could claim to be the corporate voice of the schools on the curriculum were the SSEC and the Ministry with the Inspectorate. Neither of these bodies could provide an authoritative national forum for the discussion of curriculum matters yet there was a need for such a body which should also have the means of coordinating and stimulating developments and of formulating and expressing the voice of the schools in curriculum and examination issues. At the earliest opportunity, therefore, the SSEC should be expanded and reconstituted to form a new Schools Council for the Curriculum and Examinations. 'The long tradition of *laissez faire* in curriculum matters had created a vacuum within the schools.' This had been acceptable in a relatively stable society in which a teacher who had trained a quarter of a century earlier might not be seriously out of date. But the pace of change – social, economic, technical – and of the expansion of knowledge were combining to force the pace of necessary educational change to an unprecedented extent. The vacuum was being filled by such outside pressures as the entry requirements of professional bodies and institutions of higher education and 'by the desire of parents and employers to have more and more children ticketed by means of public examinations'.[35]

The proposed Council would have 60 members drawn from the various teachers' associations, local authority organizations, the universities, commerce and industry. The Council would operate through a series of committees and sub-committees including a Curriculum Committee, an Examinations Committee, a Research and Development Committee, a Liaison Committee and a Welsh Committee. There would also be subject committees and sub-committees. The Minister would appoint assessors from the office and the inspectorate and a secretariat from the Curriculum Study Group.

At the end of May the Minister made public the knowledge that consultations were going on through the device of a Parliamentary answer. It was hoped to hold a meeting at the Ministry over which the Minister himself would preside on 19 July for a preliminary discussion of the proposal with representatives of the various bodies likely to feel concerned.[36] Most organizations welcomed the proposed meeting, but fear of centralized control of the curriculum and of possible Ministry domination was quite widespread. In order possibly to lessen this antipathy the Minister changed the venue for the meeting from the Ministry to the NUT headquarters at Hamilton House. The politics of control over the curriculum served to dominate the discussions and deliberations over setting up the Schools Council. One of the London County Council (LCC) representatives before the meeting on 19 July circulated a critical note which elaborated the view that 'tradition and experience alike require that it is the local authorities not the Curriculum Study Group which should provide arrangements such that the ideas of teachers can be tried out, developed, assessed and made available to other teachers'. At the meeting Edward Boyle in his introductory statement explained that no one was being asked to enter into any commitment beyond joining a working party which it was proposed should consider in detail the ideas put forward in Morrell's memorandum. If a Schools Council were eventually set up it would have an advisory function of the traditional kind only in relation to those matters which fell within the Minister's statutory powers and responsibilities. In respect of all other matters the Council would be quite autonomous in relation to the Minister. Representatives of the teachers were more welcoming and supportive of the Ministry's initiative than were local authority spokesmen. The CCA, the AMC and the LCC all expressed reservations. The AEC suggested the Schools Council might need an independent secretariat. The meeting agreed to appoint a working party under the chairmanship of Sir John Lockwood with one representative from each of the bodies present 'to consider how effort could best be given to the matters discussed and to make recommendations'.[37]

On the initiative of the County Councils Association (CCA) local authority representatives met before the first meeting of the working party to air their reservations and political fears. This meeting rather reluctantly agreed that the working party would probably accept that there must be change and that some means would have to be found for ensuring effective cooperation between Minister, LEAs and teachers. 'It was difficult to see how this could be done without the establishment of a strong national body on which both teachers and authorities would be represented.'[38]

To lessen some people's fears of Ministry domination, the working party met at Birkbeck College, London, of which its chairman was Master. A number of papers had been prepared by the Secretariat, which included Morrell, at the request of the chairman. The original memorandum was put aside and these were concerned with an outline of the problem, a possible solution, the Curriculum Study Group and research and development.[39] In effect the working party at its early meetings traversed the ground which brought its more reluctant members to accept the need for moving towards a Schools Council. Morrell prepared detailed proposals on finance and staffing and at the chairman's suggestion the original constitutional proposals were recirculated. Morrell, however, revised these in close consultation with Alexander in November 1963. In order to reconcile the need for wide representation with detailed professional handling of difficult problems, Morrell suggested a dual organization. This would have a policy organization with a fully representative Council plus three representative steering committees, a Welsh committee and a general purposes committee. These bodies would be in charge of the executive organization so that no study or project could be initiated without the agreement of the representative bodies. The studies themselves would be organized by a professional coordinating committee which would control the executive organization. This somewhat complex plan was intended to ensure both representative control of policy and professional units of manageable size and simplicity for carrying out the Council's functions. It is interesting to note that since any further Ministry proposals might have been viewed by some members of the working party with suspicion, Alexander put in the revised proposals in his own name. As he had been working closely with Morrell this was not inappropriate. He was able to argue the case for these proposals in the working party with much greater freedom than a member of the secretariat could possibly have done and Alexander in fact got these proposals through the working party at its third meeting at the end of November.[40]

This meeting made a great deal of progress. It not only agreed the constitutional proposals, but also the arrangements for financing and staffing the Council. The Curriculum Studies Group was to come to an end and its members were to work directly under the Council which would control their work. In view of this progress the chairman proposed that a small drafting committee be appointed to oversee the preparation of a draft report. This consisted of the chairman, Alexander, Elvin and Miss Stewart of the NUT. It was not inappropriate that after this meeting there was an exchange of letters between Morrell and Alexander in which the former congratulated the latter on his masterly handling in the meeting of the paper on the constitution while Alexander in his reply wrote of his admiration for Morrell's ability to sit silent while another argued the brief which he had prepared.[41] Only minor changes were made in the draft at the full working party's final meeting. The Minister wrote a preface welcoming the proposals and the *Report of the Working Party on the Schools Curricula and Examinations* was published in March 1964. A full meeting of representatives of the various bodies which set up the working party took place at Hamilton House on 12 June 1964 and accepted the Report.

The Schools Council held its first meeting on 27 October 1964 at the offices of the County Councils Association. Sir John Maud, Master of University College, Oxford, and a former Permanent Secretary of the Ministry of Education was the first chairman. A majority of the 55 members were teachers. There were three joint secretaries, one DES administrator

(D. H. Morrell), one HMI (R. W. Morris) and one local authority administrator (J. G. Owen). To begin with the Secretary of State met the Council's overhead costs (staffing, accommodation etc.) and also agreed to an annual g: ꞏ ꞏt of up to £100,000 for the support of research and development work commissioned by the Council. This figure was clearly inadequate and the Council was heavily dependent on the Trustees of the Nuffield Foundation. At its first meeting the Council had before it requests for additional representation from the NUT – which had initially 11 places – and from numerous organizations which were unrepresented such as the Association of University Teachers, the Confederation for the Advancement of State Education, the Association of Heads of Secondary Technical Schools and the National Union of Students. The only additional representation agreed was one place for the Free Church Federal Council and one extra place for the NUT,[42] but pressure for places continued from other quarters and the Council – or later Governing Council – grew so that by 1970 there were 75 members. The Constitution was first revised at the end of 1968. From 1 April 1970 the Council became an independent body financed equally by the DES and by the LEAs. The constitution required that the majority of members on all the committees except finance should be teachers.

One striking feature of the first year of the Council was the amount of work already going on for which it became responsible. The SSEC passed on a great deal of work in preparation for the new CSE examinations as well as a good deal of work on the development of the GCE. The staff from the former Curriculum Study Group brought with them experience of working with the contemporary 'Nuffield' development teams in such areas as science and primary-school French. Thus of its two-sided task, the Schools Council became responsible for examinations just when the full flood of GCE 'O' and 'A' level and CSE which have since become a familiar feature was building up. On the development side three major new programmes were initiated. In English 'a far-reaching and necessarily long-term programme of research and development' was begun. Priority was given to this because difficulties in communication were thought to lie at the heart of educational and social wastage. A programme of inquiry, research and development was launched to help schools prepare for the then forthcoming raising of the school leaving age to 16. Thirdly, a programme of inquiry and research was initiated with the intention of providing the basis for new patterns of sixth-form work.

These three programmes were all concerned in their different ways with helping the schools to meet problems of the curriculum which arose out of this changing clientele. The raising of the minimum leaving age in the early 1970s would obviously require teaching programmes which would meet the needs of those who would never have stayed on at school for a fifth year on a voluntary basis. The proportion of the age groups staying at school beyond the statutory leaving age increased steadily throughout this period. In 1955 about 1/6 of the 16+ age group remained in the maintained schools whereas by 1968 this proportion had increased to 1/3. Many of those who stayed on were, in fact, attracted to courses for external examinations and sought to acquire qualifications. For those pupils the examinations to some extent shaped the curriculum. In preparation for raising the leaving age, the Schools Council proposed a programme centre around some 17 inquiries ranging from studying the way in which other countries sought to meet the curricular needs of this age group to establishing the possibilities of programmed learning and other new teaching aids which might be developed.[43] By the time the leaving age was raised the Council had issued a very considerable number of relevant publications. Some of these were the findings of national development projects in mathematics, science, humanities, English, history, geography and religious education. Others were concerned with a survey of early leavers, their attitudes and expectations and the attitudes of parents and teachers. Teachers had themselves played a leading role in the preparation of teaching guides and materials.

The Schools Council was itself the product of the reaction to fears that one party was going to seek to control the curriculum. Thus in its approach to curricular research and investigation it could hardly be expected to formulate a strong directive model of the curriculum and initiate projects in support of that model. On the contrary it has operated by responding to the expression of needs from outside and most of its projects have been designed to meet apparent and immediate problems. In the contemporary jargon, the Council's approach was non-directive. Proposals were usually put to it and those that achieved acceptance were developed and funded. Most of the projects were based in universities and colleges of higher education. By 1978 the Council had financed nearly 200 projects. Rather more than half of these were related to the teaching of school subjects while others concerned school organization and resources, the relationship between school, home and community and examinations. Quite the most expensive project was that on teaching modern languages while other large projects have been those on careers education and guidence and the communication skills project. Table 2.2 gives the number of projects and cost in each of the main fields of investigation.

Table 2.2   Schools Council research and development projects, 1963–78

Field of investigation	Number of projects	Cost
English	22	1,278,376
Humanities	19	1,738,983
Languages	6	1,067,621
Creative Studies	10	628,322
Mathematics	15	1,096,909
Science	24	1,008,098
Interrelated studies	24	1,857,937
Special Education	5	270,901
Wales	10	600,535
School, home and community	5	55,440
School organization and resources	16	698,628
Examinations	25	767,803

Source: *Schools Council Projects,*1978.

THE CERTIFICATE OF EXTENDED EDUCATION

The much larger number of pupils staying on at school to attend sixth forms meant that the traditional curriculum and examinations were not suited to a growing number of pupils.

The purpose of the Council's sixth-form programme was to provide the basis for new patterns of work. The programme was in two parts. Firstly a series of largely factual inquiries were undertaken relating to the changing character of the sixth form and to the expectations and needs of various groups – pupils, parents, teachers, professional bodies and employers – concerning it so as to inform the Council about possible ways in which new courses and examinations might be developed. Secondly, the Council began to consider possible new patterns of courses which might enable schools to build up curricula from a range of major and minor examined courses along with an allocation of time for non-examined general studies. Any programme of work for young people from 16+ to 18+ is bound to be closely concerned with qualifying for various forms of further study or employment and hence with public examinations. Thus the continuing concern of the Schools Council with this age group over the years has tended to take the form of discussing the various possible ways of reforming or changing in some way 'A' level of GCE. In retrospect there really does seem to have been a great deal of time and effort spent on considering the possibility of moving from 'A' to 'Q' and 'F' or to 'N' and 'F' although none of these possiblities has eventually gained general acceptance.

The increasing number of pupils staying on at school for further study beyond the age of 16 after having obtained a number of pass grades in the CSE led to a considerable investment of energy in the development of a possible Certificate of Extended Education (CEE). During the later 1960s a certain amount of impetus grew among CSE boards for an examination at a later stage suited to the needs of those who had met with some success in CSE. For some time the Schools Council as such did not become involved in this matter for two reasons. The Council had prompted the two sixth-form working parties which it had set up earlier to make a fresh attack on the problems with which they had been trying to deal for two years and any attempt to design a CEE in detail would have been premature. Secondly, the replacement of 'O' level GCE and CSE by a common system of examining at 16+ would remove at least some part of the basis for an extended form of CSE itself. The regional examining boards were not deterred by these circumstances and at a meeting of the Governing Council on 13 January 1972 this resolution by the CSE Boards was noted:

Whilst recognizing the need to see the proposed Certificate of Extended Education as part of the general pattern of examining at the post-16+ level, the Regional Examining Boards remain firmly of the opinion that it is urgently necessary to meet by way of the CEE the needs of increasing numbers of pupils at this stage in their development, for whom the present provision is unsatisfactory. As envisaged by the Regional Boards, the CEE needs to be established in its own right, being neither an intermediate or subsidiary level of an existing examination nor merely an extension of the CSE based on so-called mature syllabuses.

The Council in noting this added that the boards should be encouraged to formulate proposals for CEE examinations on an experimental basis which would allow investigation into the feasibility and development of such examinations in their regions.

Constitutionally the boards could only introduce a new examination with grades going beyond those used in the CSE with the authority of the Secretary of State. Accordingly they asked the Schools Council to seek that authority for them for an initial period of five years from 1973. This proposal was debated but defeated and the boards proceeded on the more restricted, experimental, basis. Four boards decided to conduct pilot examinations in 1973. Some of them decided to indicate to candidates what their CEE grades would have been by means of a letter of credit but this would not be endorsed by the Schools Council or bear the counter-signature of the Secretary of State's representative.[44]

The issue of whether there should be a CEE was one which served to exacerbate relations between teachers and LEA representatives within the Schools Council and, in some areas, regional examining boards. One region where there was difficulty was the South West where the Chief Education Officer for Somerset, R. Parker, supported by his authority, was one of those who strongly opposed the new examination. Somerset's opposition produced correspondence to the AEC, the CCA and to the DES in the early 1970s criticizing the CEE

on a variety of grounds – educational, financial and constitutional. Parker feared that the teacher-controlled examining
boards would be able to establish a new examination without
the consent of the LEAs 'who will have to provide the funds'.
According to E. Warren, Chief Education Officer for Bath,
most of his colleagues in the South West shared this concern
about LEAs possibly having to finance CEE through pupils'
entry fees. Parker reported that he had had a meeting with
secondary school heads with the purpose of establishing exactly
which group of children needed to stay on and for whom neither
further education nor CSE itself was appropriate. 'In the end
we discovered one clear case only. This was a dwarf who was
kept on at school as being too immature physically to enter into
employment.' At a time when resources were beginning to
become more strained, LEAs were likely to be much more
anxious about any possible financial implications. Parker may
have put the views of a number of LEA members and officers
when he added 'External examinations, teacher participation
and mode 3 assessment may be splendid concepts but do
they really merit such priority in the allocation of our
resources?'[45]

The Schools Council continued to find itself divided on the
issue of the CEE. The LEA representatives generally felt very
doubtful about this additional examination. Because they saw
no way of preventing them, they accepted that there might be
experiments but they feared that before very long they would be
faced with a *fait accompli* and the CEE would have arrived.[46]
During the second half of the 1970s the Schools Council found
itself caught up in the wider troubles which have beset the
education system. In 1976 it formally recommended to the
Secretary of State that the CEE be established. The Government was not prepared to accept this recommendation as it
stood. To some it suggested that the Schools Council was
simply acting under the influence of the teachers' unions. The
question of the CEE was therefore referred to the Keohane
Committee to consider in relation to other examinations for
those for whom CEE was intended – both in the schools and in
further education. This Committee reported in November
1979[47] by which time the Government currently in office was

Conservative. While in opposition the Party had rejected the CEE proposals as being likely to confuse pupils, teachers and employers. The Keohane Committee did, in fact, recommend that the Secretary of State should introduce the CEE officially as an examination suited to meet the needs of 17-year-old pupils staying on for one year beyond the school leaving age. It would be designed for those who had reached CSE grades 2 to 4 at 16. The Committee did also propose changes in the content of the CEE. To make it more acceptable to employers it should also include proficiency tests in reading and writing, in spoken English and in numeracy. *Education* suggested that the Committee had thereby 'gift-wrapped' the examination to make it acceptable to the Conservative Government.[48]

Reactions to the Report were very mixed. The education committee of the Association of County Councils overrode the advice of its own officers and advisers and rejected the proposed new CEE for political reasons, claiming that there was not enough demand from employers. The teachers' associations supported the official introduction of the examination. The Schools Council also backed the CEE. The new sixth-formers who stayed on at school for a year wanted something to show for it on entering employment. For a large and growing group of pupils this would be more appropriate than 'A' levels 'which leave many students dispirited and disillusioned at present'. The government's policies by this time were entirely directed by a quest for economies and by a determination to enter into no new commitments which might have the consequence of increasing expenditure. In April 1980 a written Parliamentary answer indicated the likely ministerial response. A little over half of the comments received at the DES had supported the Keohane proposals but the objections were said to 'question the wisdom of inaugurating a separate new examination alongside existing examinations for a similar target group who follow pre-employment courses in further education'. Thus when the DES issued a green paper later it was not surprising to find that it was suggesting that a new vocational examination on the further education pattern would best suit the needs of the 17+ group by preparing them more aptly to meet their possible future employers' needs.[49]

THE GROWTH AND CULTIVATION OF 'CONSUMERISM'

The difficulties encountered by the proposal to establish the Certificate of Extended Education as an official examination may well be seen in retrospect to have arisen from the changed political and social context in which the education system found itself from the 1970s. *Black Paper One: The Fight for Education* was published in March 1969. The emergence of the views expressed in this and subsequent Black Papers was hardly surprising in that the enormous expansion and recasting of the maintained school system in the quarter of a century following the 1944 Act was so far reaching that it was probably bound to provoke a certain measure of reaction. The increasing economic difficulties of the 1970s followed by the failure of a considerable part of manufacturing industry especially since 1979 have served to nourish these criticisms as part of a general loss of confidence in the nation's political, financial and social institutions.

The Black Papers were perhaps more concerned originally with attacking comprehensive schools and organizational manifestations of equality than with the curriculum although 'modern maths' and 'discovery methods' and other manifestations of contemporary curricular developments and teaching methods were censured by various Black Paper authors. The growth of public support for the critics might perhaps be gauged by the interest which James Callaghan began to take in this matter in 1976 when a request went to the DES for a memorandum on what was happening in the nation's schools. The request followed a meeting with Fred Mulley, Secretary of State. This was one of a series of meetings which the new holder of the office of Prime Minister held with senior ministers about the work of their Departments.

The request fitted in well with the apparent desire in the DES to take a much more active part in curricular matters in the schools. It has been remarked that both William Pile and his successor as Permanent Secretary, James Hamilton, had made it clear that they believed the Department should be more actively involved in governing the curriculum. The obvious instrument for this purpose was the Inspectorate whose head apparently agreed with her administrative colleagues. Thus the Inspectorate compiled the so-called Yellow Book dealing with the teaching of the three Rs in the primary school, curricula for secondary schools, examinations and the education of those of the 16 – 19 group who would not be going on to higher education.

The political circumstances which led to the compilation of this document made it inevitable that it would be critical rather than judicial. Thus while informal methods and free expression in the primary school could produce admirable results in the right hands the memorandum concluded with the suggestion that the time was almost certainly ripe for a corrective shift of emphasis away from the newer and freer methods. In the secondary schools the Yellow Book admitted that the initial confusion caused in many cases by comprehensivization had led to difficulties so that middle-class parents feared that their children would receive a less rigorous education than would have been the case in a grammar school. Yet teachers were, on average, below what was to be expected in good grammar schools. Some teachers were putting too much emphasis on preparing pupils for their roles in society and too little emphasis on preparing them for the labour market. A further source of worry was said to be the variation in the curriculum followed by pupils in different schools. Modern languages and physical sciences received too little attention. The time had probably come to try to establish generally accepted principles for the composition of the secondary curriculum for all pupils, that is a 'core curriculum'. The Department and the Inspectorate were both described as having 'misgivings' about the CEE since the educational programmes followed by some of the pupils concerned were of doubtful relevance to their needs. The replacement of CSE and GCE 'O' level by a common 16+ examination was a development of greater merit but the Schools Council had not succeeded in producing a workable scheme for achieving this.

The Schools Council was said to have performed moderately in commissioning development work in particular curricular areas but to have had little success in tackling examination problems despite having far more resources than its predecessor, the SSEC. It had barely begun to tackle the problems of the curriculum as a whole. The general performance of the Schools Council on both curriculum and examinations was, in fact, mediocre. Because of this and because the influence of the teachers' unions had led to an increasingly political flavour – in the worst sense of the word – in its deliberations, the general reputation of the Council had suffered a considerable decline over the last few years. Since the performance of the Council had been disappointing, there would have to be a review of its constitution and functions. Whatever proposals might come from the Schools Council, the Department ought to develop its own thinking on the different functions of examinations and their interactions. The work of the Assessment of Performance Unit – directly under the control of the Department – should be increased.

Finally the Yellow Book showed the desire of officials to exploit fully the apparent opportunity to increase their own power and influence.

It would be good to get on record from ministers, and in particular the Prime Minister, an authoritative pronouncement on the division of responsibility for what goes on in school suggesting that the Department should give a firmer lead. Such a pronouncement would have to respect legitimate claims made by the teachers as to the exercise of their professional judgement, but should firmly refute any argument – and this is what they have sought to establish – that no one except teachers has any right to say what goes on in schools. The climate for a declaration on these lines may in fact now be relatively favourable. Nor need there be any inhibition for fear that the Department could not make use of enhanced opportunity to exercise influence over curriculum and teaching methods: the Inspectorate would have a leading role to play in bringing forward ideas in these areas and is ready to fulfil that responsibility.[50]

The contrast with the atmosphere of cooperation which had earlier brought central and local government and the teachers together in the partnership of the Schools Council could not be more striking. One of those who were reported as welcoming this was Rhodes Boyson who commented that 'There will be a great sigh of relief among parents and Black Paper writers everywhere.' On the other hand the teachers' organizations were, not surprisingly, hostile in their comments. In words which have proved more prophetic than he might have expected, the General Secretary of the NUT claimed that the DES only seemed to be concerned with fitting children for the labour market 'and heaven knows how uncertain that is nowadays'.[51] The speech at Ruskin College, Oxford, which the Prime Minister subsequently gave in which he expressed his attitude to the Yellow Book and its proposals was moderate. He showed that he cared about primary and secondary schooling and to some extent he echoed some of the criticisms made, but he did not endorse the bid made by the Department and the school inspectors for giving them a larger role in deciding education objectives.

Attempts to develop and sell to the schools the ideas of a 'core' curriculum seem to have had reasonably little practical effect in the last six years. The DES has, however, seen a return on its efforts to modify and downgrade the Schools Council. A reform of the constitution and working arrangements of the Council seemed inevitable. The outcome of a revision was to ensure that of the three senior committees proposed the Finance and Priorities Committee would be the central, coordinating body. Here teachers' organizations had twelve places, LEAs eight and the Secretaries of State eight also. The aim of this committee was to 'draw together with three main partners . . . and determine the broad direction of the Council's work and the priorities for implementation'. Apart from controlling finance, this committee was to convey recommendations from the other two senior committees to the Secretaries of State with its own advice being added. The other two senior bodies which were set up were Convocation with 56 members, a discussion forum where the various interests could make their views known, and the Professional Committee with 37 members, 23 of them teachers of whom the NUT was to nominate 11. This committee was to give professional advice to the other bodies and to have responsibility for the 'main work' of the Council. In the interests of efficiency the Council was to have a chief officer or secretary on a permanent basis to take over from the existing joint secretaries who had simply been seconded to the Council's service. This revised constitution was formally adopted early in 1978. The new constitutional arrangements were obviously a compromise, but probably the best that could gain general acceptance among the wide variety of interests

involved. Peter Sloman, education officer of the AMA, summarized the position succinctly. 'The first point is that the
Schools Council has survived. It has had strident and various
critics, but at the moment of truth no one wished to abolish
it.'[52] Even if LEAs might agree with the DES's criticism that
teachers' unions had been too influential in the Schools
Council, they certainly had no desire to see the central
government take charge of the curriculum.

After the election of 1979 and the change of political control,
the Secretary of State re-opened the question of the future of the
Schools Council. Nancy Trenaman, Principal of St. Anne's
College, Oxford, was asked to review the functions, constitution and methods of work of the Council. A great deal of
evidence was submitted to the inquiry; there were 150 written
submissions. The DES submission was very critical but Mrs
Trenaman was apparently struck both by the amount of
support for the continued existence of the Council and by the
degree of criticism of aspects of its performance and organization. She commented on the degree to which the various
interests – teachers, parents, governors, councillors – were in-
stitutionalized and politicized. She also found the anti-intellec-
tual atmosphere of discussions and meetings of the Council's
committees' tiresome and unnecessary: certainly I never heard
the word academic used save in a pejorative sense'. The Report
accepted the need for curriculum development on a national
basis and that this was not a function which DES officials or
HMIs could perform. The overwhelming weight of evidence
was in favour of maintaining the Schools Council as a body
financed by central and local government, somewhat distanced
from both but with both represented on it. A number of changes
in committees and membership were recommended as was the
proposal that the Council should act as a clearing house for
curricular development being carried out by other agencies.
Finally, the Schools Council should continue with its present
functions and it should not be made the subject of further
external review for at least five years. In fact the Secretary of
State has decided to close down the Schools Council and to
replace it by two advisory bodies – one for the curriculum and
one for examinations.

It is not possible at this stage to set in perspective some of the most recent developments. One factor which is making itself felt and which must have a considerable impact is the decline in the number of pupils of secondary school age. This could mean smaller schools, limitations of the curriculum as staff numbers diminish and the consequent total loss of some subjects in certain schools. This is a large issue and it has received attention elsewhere.[53] But one cardinal principle in the government of education is the need to carry the support of the various education interests involved if a policy is to be successfully applied. This truth is perhaps most self-evident in dealing with the curriculum and examinations.

CHAPTER 3

The Supply and Training of Teachers

The extent of the growth in the numbers of pupils in the schools of England and Wales has been discussed above. The success with which teachers were recruited and professionally trained in order to meet the growing demands for their services may be judged from Table 3.1. The total number of teachers in the schools more than doubled in these years and, while the proportion with degrees did not quite double, the actual number of graduate teachers increased steadily and by 1977 had more than quadrupled from 28,253 to 123,647.

Table 3.1   Number of full-time teachers in service, 1947–77

Year	Primary	Secondary	Total	Graduates	Graduates as a % of total
1947	118,363	58,772	177,135	28,353	16.0
1950	130,412	77,256	207,668	32,998	15.9
1953	139,982	85,481	225,463	36,957	16.4
1956	149,087	95,081	244,168	42,380	17.4
1959	145,594	115,945	261,539	49,344	18.9
1962	141,878	136,585	278,463	55,630	20.0
1965	138,171	145,779	283,950	58,782	20.7
1968	144,396	152,389	296,785	62,202	21.0
1971	172,281	170,541	342,822	71,309	20.8
1974	194,081	209,870	403,951	97,030	24.0
1977	202,887	233,409	436,296	123,687	28.3

Sources: *Annual Reports*, 1947–60; *Statistics of Education* 1961–77.

In the later 1930s the Board of Education believed that too many persons were training to teach and in 1936 brought about the closure of three training colleges. The impact of the war, however, led the Board to fear a shortage of teachers and there was talk of an emergency training scheme. An office committee was set up in 1943 under the deputy secretary, R. S. Wood, which found that the drop in the number of teachers between 1938 and 1942 was matched by a fall in the number of pupils. More significantly, however, the number of teachers employed had come to include 37,000 'stop-gap' staff, mainly those beyond retirement age who would wish to leave once the war ended. The office committee forecast an immediate shortage of 40,000 teachers once hostilities ceased after allowing for the return of teachers from the armed services on demobilization. This figure allowed for the school-leaving age to be raised to 15 but it was assumed that there would be no reduction in the size of classes. The committee proposed that about 50 emergency training colleges should be set up offering intensive courses lasting for a year. The Treasury would finance these colleges, but they would be operated by LEAs acting as agents for the Board. It was recognized that there would be fears of dilution of their profession among teachers and that LEAs might be reluctant to appoint emergency trained teachers. Within the Board there was, however, a belief that the experienced ex-service candidates for whom the scheme was intended 'may be better staff than the normal entrant to the profession, whose background and experience are too often deplorably narrow'.[1]

The Board set up an advisory committee under the chairmanship of G. N. Flemming which included representatives of LEAs and the teachers' associations to work out the implications of the emergency training schemes. Teachers' associations were persuaded to go along with the proposals in spite of their misgivings at the prospect of presenting persons of any qualification or none with a short-cut to the status of certificated teacher. In order partly to meet these misgivings emergency trained entrants were to serve as probationary teachers for two years instead of one.[2] The scheme attracted large numbers of applicants and by the time it was terminated in 1951 more than 23,000 men and 12,000 women teachers had qualified. By the early 1950s about 15 per cent of the teachers serving in primary and secondary schools were emergency trained. The story of the emergency scheme has been fully told elsewhere.[3] It succeeded in its immediate objective of avoiding a breakdown in the staffing of the schools just after the war and it enabled the school leaving age to be raised from 14 to 15 in 1947.

One important change in government policy was won by the teachers' associations when they were being asked to support emergency training and that was the abolition of the grade of 'uncertificated teacher'. A deputation from the NUT to the Board in 1943 had raised the position of uncertificated teachers and the position which would be created for them by the arrival of the proposed emergency trained. The Board was receptive and set up a special committee, which included NUT members, to review their position. The outcome was that the grade was to be abolished by granting the status of qualified teacher to those who had been teaching for 20 years and by offering special one year courses to those who had been uncertificated teachers for at least five years. Those with less service were expected to take an initial training course. The special courses were launched in 1946 and all the costs involved were met entirely by the Treasury. By 1950 some 2,000 applications had been received from eligible teachers and about 500 were offered courses each year. Employing LEAs appeared to the Ministry to have had no great difficulty in releasing such teachers for a year to take courses. As no uncertificated teachers had been appointed since 1945 no more courses were needed after the early 1950s.[4]

The reorganization and reformation of the permanent training college system followed the lines proposed by the Report of the Committee on the Training of Teachers and Youth Leaders with Arnold McNair as chairman. The Board of Education believed that the post-war reforms could only serve their purpose if the teachers serving in the schools were able to translate the new legislation into practice. Thus while more teachers were needed, it was not just a question of numbers. In the view of S. H. Wood, head of teachers' branch, it would have been utterly deplorable if the necessary teachers could only be obtained at the expense of lower standards. Thus the need to widen the basis of recruitment for the profession, to improve the quality of training and to enhance the status both of the profession and of the training institutions were among the aims of the government policy.

Wood's proposal to the Committee was that it should recommend that each university should set up a school of education which would include the existing department of education and the joint examining board for the colleges of the area; it would also be the centre for educational research and for in-service courses for teachers. While the colleges would retain their separate existence, the school would influence the appointment of teaching staff who would need to be of a standard which would justify their being regarded as recognized teachers of the school of education. Such reforms as the length and nature of the course, the standard of both staff and students could all be dealt with inside the new framework. In a letter written about this time, Wood set out his aim as being to ferret the universities 'out of their hiding places and give them a chance to do for teaching and the teaching profession' what they ought to be doing. In the long run 'it would be disastrous if one passed the universities by in this matter. Whether they could be shaken up sufficiently to see the job in its right perspective I do not know.'[5] Wood's ideas dominated the committee's thinking. About half of the members went along with them and about half feared that the accretion of such large responsibilities in teacher training would unbalance the universities and proposed instead a much looser arrangement, a regional training council on which the university, LEAs and the teaching profession would be represented. Thus the final report of the McNair Committee set out two schemes, A and B. The first was in effect Wood's proposals for university schools of education, the second the Joint Board Scheme, as it came to be called.

Scheme A for university schools of education attracted widespread support among teachers, local authorities and the press. There was a disunity within the Committee of Vice-Chancellors which reflected the contrasting reaction of different universities. At a meeting in July 1944 the Committee of Vice-Chancellors set up a sub-committee to frame a third scheme whose main feature was the avoidance of any constitutional change in the existing arrangements but would have permitted the establishment of Institutes of Education to encourage cooperation between colleges and universities. It was assumed that these institutes would be paid for by the

Ministry of Education. The position taken up by the universities – or perhaps their failure to take up a single position
– prevented the Ministry from adopting the central recommendation of the McNair Report for Scheme A during Butler's
period of office and led eventually to the adoption of varying
schemes in different places under the general term of area
training organizations during the succeeding Labour Ministers
in 1947 and 1948.

The position was accurately appraised by the Deputy
Secretary in a minute to Butler when he wrote that it was
impossible to say that if the universities would not adopt
Scheme A they must go out of teacher training completely since
it would be difficult to refuse to recognize their training of their
own graduates. It was also undesirable to have some teachers
trained under a School of Education scheme and some under a
Joint Board Scheme since this would lead to all sorts of alleged
inequalities of standing and prestige. He went on to sketch out
an alternative which he believed would be much simpler to
introduce and to run because the Ministry would handle the
whole matter more directly itself. Precisely for this reason it
came to appeal later to Ellen Wilkinson. The Ministry would
take responsibility for the supervision and organization of
teacher training, colleges and universities were to be grouped
regionally under regional training boards composed of a
representative from each institution and LEA nominees under
a chairman to be nominated by the Minister. This body would
be responsible for training arrangements and examinations in
both universities and training colleges.[6]

In August 1944 Butler met a deputation from the Vice-
Chancellors' Committee to see if any progress could be made,
but the meeting illustrated yet again that each university tends
to go its own way and that they can only come together to
defend themselves in a negative sense: it is not possible to agree
positive initiatives. At this meeting Hele of Cambridge explained that universities had no interest in the professional
education of teachers since although they took the products of
the schools, teaching students of 18+ was totally different from
teaching anyone under that age. Butler pointed out that an
improvement in the status of teachers and of their training was
vital to the success of the educational reforms; Vice-Chancel-

lors would have noticed that the educational world favoured the proposal to set up schools of education 'so it is important that if this were to be turned down it should be on social grounds and not be open to the accusation of prejudice'. In the Ministry it was felt that the 'somewhat irresponsible' expression of opinion by the three Vice-Chancellors who came to the meeting (Horton (London) and Loveday (Bristol) in addition to Hele) should not be accepted as typical of the attitude of the universities. In spite of this episode, the Parliamentary Secretary, Chuter Ede, a former schoolteacher, believed that universities could supply a much richer culture than training colleges and urged that a strong appeal should be made to the universities to consider the possibility of making Scheme A workable.[7] There ensued discussions with the chairman of the CVCP, Hector Hetherington, and then letters were sent to individual universities.

By the time the universities had given formal consideration to the letters and had replied there had been a general election and Ellen Wilkinson had become Minister of Education. An analysis of the replies showed that London, Manchester, Birmingham, Nottingham, Exeter and Southampton were ready to set up schools of education more or less on the pattern of Scheme A; Bristol, Durham, Leeds, Liverpool, Reading and Sheffield put forward schemes for education centres on the lines of a suggestion originating with a group of vice-chancellors. Oxford declined to express a view and Cambridge proposed a joint board scheme. The Deputy Secretary, Sir Robert Wood, advised the Minister that it would be impossible either to refuse to approve of schools of education in universities which proposed them or to force them on universities that did not want them. It looked as though the Minister would have to accept that there could not be a uniform system. Miss Wilkinson, however, wanted a uniform plan of the Scheme A type and proposed to press for this with such local variations as could not be avoided. On this desire to press for a uniform plan, the Deputy Secretary felt obliged to point out to the Minister the difficulty. 'You are aware that the Ministry has no statutory control over universities?' he wrote. Further meetings both among officials on their own and with the Minister led him to propose going ahead with Scheme A wherever possible and letting other universities wait. On this minute Ellen Wilkinson wrote 'This is just what I *don't* want.'[8] She was anxious to secure a much more direct role for the Minister to play than any of the schemes seemed to permit. She objected to the Central Training Council proposed by the McNair Committee on the grounds that the Ministry 'must do its own work under the new Act and not follow the modest habit of the Board of Education of farming out responsibilities'.

By the beginning of 1946 the new Minister had settled into office and the limitations of her position had to be accepted. In a statement that went to interested parties early in 1946, the Minister agreed that she would in principle accept a measure of diversity between schemes in different areas because of the stage negotiations had reached before she had assumed office, the independence of universities and her desire to work with them. But whatever local proposals were put forward, all schemes would have to meet the following conditions:

(1)   The area training councils responsible for the training and assessment of the those seeking qualified teacher status must be constituted in a way acceptable to the Minister.

(2)   She reserved the right to appoint members to each council and to appoint HMIs to serve as assessors.

(3)   The geographical area to be covered was to be approved.

(4)   All training arrangements in both universities and colleges were to be open to inspection by HMIs.

(5)   A single body in each area was to be responsible for submitting to the Minister the names of students recommended for qualified teacher status.

Thus in May 1946, arrangements for negotiations with individual universities were put in hand, those institutions which had put forward proposals in line with Scheme A being taken first. In June Circular 112 was issued outlining the future pattern for the organization of the training of teachers.[9]

In the event most universities chose to follow some version of Scheme A – usually after internal struggles. In only three cases did universities decline to accept full financial and constitutional responsibility so that at Reading, Liverpool and Cambridge the new institutes of education were funded directly by the Ministry of Education. The area training organization system was to last for a quarter of a century and it proved to be the agency by which the training colleges moved from being little more than institutions achieving not much more than sixth-form level work to becoming genuinely part of the higher education sector. This closer association with the universities did much to raise the status of teacher training and to broaden it into teacher education.

THE SUPPLY OF TEACHERS AND THE NACTST

While these professional and academic arrangements proved to be well founded and effective, questions associated with the supply of teachers produced a number of intractable problems. Issues concerning the number of teachers to be trained were of obvious concern to the three parties in the education sub-government and the McNair Report's suggestion that there should be a Central Training Council was one way of enabling the partners to come together to find solutions. After her initial period of hostility to such a council, Miss Wilkinson came to accept that there were good grounds for some permanent machinery to handle the receuitment, supply and training of teachers. Late in 1946 the Ministry suggested to the local authority and teachers' associations that a council be set up for this purpose composed of representatives of the new university area training organizations (ATOs), LEAs and teachers' associations. Because of the urgency of some of the matters to be considered, the Ministry suggested that an interim committee, 'broadly representative of the main interests to be represented on the proposed Council should be assembled as soon as possible and should be available for consultation with officers of the Ministry'.[10]

The first meeting of the interim committee was held in February 1947, when it considered a balance sheet of forecast gains and losses in the teaching body up to March 1950. The meeting was much concerned with the likely shortage of women teachers and it proposed to try to meet this in the short term by making every effort to reduce the 'abnormal wastage' of women by persuading suitable married women teachers to remain in employment and by skewing recruitment into the emergency training scheme away from men towards women. While the number of male applicants showed that emergency colleges for men would be needed for another three years or so, it appeared likely that some of those for women would no longer be required beyond 1948. It was, therefore, decided to begin discussions with LEAs so that in suitable cases emergency colleges could be taken over to provide training facilities for candidates of the normal type.

The shortage of women teachers, the need to encourage married women teachers to continue in post or to return to the classroom and the possibility of a surplus of men teachers were to be recurrent themes of the policy-makers. The rapid rise in the number of births was a significant factor underlying this issue. During the period 1946 to 1951 the children leaving school were drawn from those 2,382,000 born from 1932 to 1936, but the number born between 1942 and 1946 and therefore entering school at the infant level amounted to 3,595,000. Given that the youngest groups of children were usually taught by women, this made the shortage of women teachers more acute. Within the Ministry there were fears that the large influx of men, many of them trained to teach at the secondary level, might even result in some unemployment. This fear was increased by the slow progress of the building programme since the estimates for the number of teachers required had been based on the assumption that the building needed to make some progress in reducing the size of classes would be done. An internal minute in 1947 said that it was 'pretty certain that this assumption will not be realised. That being so, which is the better course, to reduce the size of classes by forming extra classes in halls and such other free spaces as are available or to hang on to the free spaces?' The position was summarized fairly at a meeting of the Interim Committee early in 1948 when forecasts of the position to 1953 showed that unless there was a rapid fall in the birth rate it would be extremely difficult to deal with the situation in the primary schools. There needed to be the maximum possible increase in the supply of women teachers as well as the employment of the greatest possible proportion of men teachers within the total.[11]

Ministry policy in the late 1940s was conditioned by the fear of imbalance between men and women entrants to the teaching profession. While the emergency training programme was to be phased out, every effort was to be made to open as many new permanent colleges as possible for women while no encouragement at all was to be offered to the expansion of permanent training colleges for men. When the claims of men and women were apparently in competition, those for women were to take precedence. While there was little doubt of the desirability of extending the normal length of the training for teachers from two to three years, no attempt could be made in the existing circumstances to fix a date for this change but every effort was to be made to increase the number of supplementary or third year courses available to teachers.

The shortage of suitable teachers was noticeably more acute in some area than in others and the Interim Committee appointed a working party in 1948 to assess the position and to consider as a matter of urgency what steps should be taken. Figures produced for the working party showed the extent of the problem (Table 3.2). Against these averages the position in certain county boroughs was a great deal worse (Table 3.3).

Table 3.2   Pupil/full-time teacher ratios, 1947–48

Type of LEA	Primary	Secondary
Counties – urban	32.1	21.0
Counties – rural	24.3	21.0
County boroughs	33.5	21.3

Table 3.3   Pupil/full-time teacher ratio in certain county boroughs, 1947–48

LEA	Ratio (Primary schools)
West Bromwich	38.7
Dudley	38.0
Walsall	37.7
Darlington	37.5
Birmingham	37.4
Coventry	36.8
Grimsby	36.6
Hull	36.1
Liverpool	36.0

A ratio of 36.0 implied actual average class sizes of over 40 and the existence of many classes with more than 50 pupils. There was therefore need for special action in authorities with ratios above 36.0. Within the working party itself Alexander for the authorities thought it essential to place an embargo on the appointment of mobile teachers by LEAs with favourable ratios so as to help areas in difficulty, the alternative to control being complete breakdown. There was some opposition from representatives of the teachers to anything which appeared to imply direction of the individual. At a subsequent meeting it was agreed that the Ministry should write to LEAs giving them provisional maximum establishment figures for women teachers. Those authorities with more teachers than their establishment would permit were to hold back from recruiting while those below the proposed limit might recruit up to the specified figure.[12] A measure of central control was not an entirely new departure. Before the war LEA staffing establishments had been reviewed annually by the Board of Education. This was abandoned on the outbreak of war but from 1941 each LEA was assigned a quota of newly trained teachers. This scheme had been ended in 1946 since it was hardly appropriate for teachers returning from the services. Quota arrangements in some form were only to be abandoned again in the very different circumstances of 1976.

By 1948 the experience of the Interim Committee led it to 'recognize the necessity for the formation of a Central Council for Teachers, among whose functions would be the consideration of questions connected with recruitment, training, qualifications and distribution of teachers' and it resolved that the time had come for its establishment to be considered in detail by the Ministry. The new Minister, George Tomlinson, hoped to inaugurate the new permanent council early in 1949.[13] This body, known as the National Advisory Council on the Training and Supply of Teachers (NACTST) included representatives of the various local authority and teachers' organizations on the Interim Committee along with representatives of the area training organizations which had by now been established.

The first meeting of the NACTST was held on 20 July 1949 with Sir Philip Morris, Vice-Chancellor of Bristol University, as chairman. Two standing committees were set up reflecting the two principal aspects of activity: one to handle training and conditions of qualification, the other the recruitment and distribution of teachers. The teachers' associations and ATOs were much more heavily represented on the first while the LEAs had twelve members on the second committee against only two on the first, this reflecting what was thought to be the main thrust of their interests and expertise. Thus general questions concerning the balance between training college places for primary and secondary teachers and between men and women along with such issues as quotas for LEAs became a staple part of the business of the Council. More specialist issues such as the supply and training of technical teachers or of graduate teachers were usually considered by ad hoc working parties. It is not possible here to follow in detail the issues with which the Council had to deal, but many appear in retrospect to have been perennial. In February 1950, for instance, when it was reported that university education departments could fill up with history graduates but had great difficulty in finding applicants with good degrees in science, Standing Committee A 'agreed that this was a very serious question of the use of the nation's manpower' and that the Council should consider what should be done about it. At the same meeting one significant decision for future policy was that it would be worth trying to build up facilities for training graduates in the colleges to about 500, even at the cost of losing some two-year training places.[14] At the same time there were 3,250 places in universities; by 1980 there were to be as many Postgraduate Certificate in Education places in public sector colleges as in the universities.

STRENGTHENING TEACHER EDUCATION

During the 1950s the ATOs brought training college staff into a much closer relationship with universities than had existed hitherto. There was a general strengthening and broadening of both the academic and professional aspects of college work. That it was feasible to extend the minimum period of training from two years to three and a few years later to introduce degree schemes were both indicative of the fundamental change wrought in training colleges since the Second World War. Indeed, it was becoming difficult to recall that the typical college in 1939 had 120 students spread over the two years and had only six or seven academic staff.

By the mid-1950s there were signs of an easing in the overall teacher supply situation, partly because there was some improvement in recruitment, but, more important, there was a reduction in the wastage among serving teachers – more married women continued teaching than had been expected and rather more returned to teaching. This apparent improvement in the prospective staffing position led to two policy modifications. The first of these was the dropping from 1 January 1956 in the teacher training regulations of the much criticized 'pledge' – that students training for teaching should sign an undertaking to teach in a state aided school before becoming eligible for grant while at training college. The pledge had been particularly disliked by teachers since it was seen as demeaning recruits to teaching by comparison with trainees in other professions who were not bound in this way and for many years the NUT had made its abolition one of its aims.

The second development that an apparent easing in the supply situation made possible was the extension of the minimum period of training from two years to three. In 1956 the NACTST suggested that 1959 or 1960 would be the best years in which to introduce the three year course since by the early 1960s the supply situation would have improved while the immediate post-war swollen birth rate cohorts would be being replaced in the schools by the smaller age groups born in the 1950s. The Council expected the number of pupils in the schools to reach a peak betwen 1958 and 1961, thereafter it was expected to fall so that by 1967 there would be about half a million fewer pupils. Thus these years of fairly rapid fall were seen as offering a 'peculiarly favourable, possibly unique, opportunity to introduce the three year course'.[15] Lord Hailsham announced the Government's acceptance of this advice in a statement in the Lords on 6 June 1957. Students entering teacher training courses from September 1960 were to be required to spend three years qualifying. The effect of this would be to make 1962 a year of 'intermission' in teacher supply since there would then be no entrants to the profession from the main source – the general training colleges. In order to accommodate the third year, the numbers admitted were to be reduced to two-thirds of those accepted hitherto, thus permanently cutting the supply by about one-third. The decrease expected in the number of pupils was such that further reduction in the size of classes was still thought to be possible even though at a reduced rate. The Minister invited the NACTST to advise on the content and scope of the new three year courses. It must be said that the advice it gave was singularly unambitious.[16] In the event many colleges achieved a good deal more than the Council appeared to suggest.

For over a century the standard course in the training colleges had been of two years' duration. This was, therefore, a profound change. Unfortunately it soon became clear that the projected over-supply of teachers which had persuaded the government that the time had come to make the change proved to be too optimistic. Wastage among teachers began to increase significantly in 1957. In the period from 1950 to 1956 there had been an annual average net increase of 6,500 in the number of teachers. In 1957 this dropped to 5,000. Doubts were raised in the Commons as to the wisdom of lengthening the course at this time but Sir Edward Boyle on behalf of the Ministry stated that the Government regarded itself as being absolutely committed and that it would not change its mind. Even so there was some public controversy about the decision. *The Times* suggested it was more important to reduce the size of classes than to lengthen the training of teachers. *The Economist* claimed that the three year course would worsen the supply of teachers without doing much to improve the quality. It said that some people regarded the whole affair 'as the manifestation of the non-graduate teachers' chip on the shoulder itch for "parity of esteem" with graduates'.[17]

The extension of the normal length of training college course to three years, the usual period of study required for a degree, was bound to stimulate further the hopes of those who wished to integrate the training colleges more closely in the world of higher education. The setting up of the Committee to report on

the future provision for higher education under the chairmanship of Lord Robbins in the winter of 1960 led to a close
examination of the issues involved. The Association of
Teachers in Colleges and Departments of Education (ATCDE)
believed that the time had come for establishing the government of training colleges on a national rather than a local basis.
Evidence on these lines was submitted to the Committee. Some
local authority associations submitted evidence seeking to
show that the training colleges should remain with them rather
than be transferred elsewhere. The AEC looked forward to a
structure which would to some extent have integrated the
monotechnic training colleges with other institutions on a
regional basis. Alexander himself believed that concurrent and
consecutive forms of training should be available side by side
and that in some way the isolation of future teachers from those
students entering other walks of life should be ended. He also
believed that an increase in the annual supply of newly-trained
teachers to about 35,000 could only be achieved after considerable re-shaping of the training arrangements.[18]

The main recommendations of the Robbins Committee on
the future of teacher training colleges were that they should
come entirely within the university pattern through university
schools of education and that they would be financed through
UGC earmarked grants to the universities. This would complete their evolution towards the higher education sector and
the new degree of BEd should be established for suitable
students who would stay to take a four-year course. The
proposals were welcomed by the ATCDE and by ATOs. They
were opposed by many LEAs. The UGC consulted the
universities and found that most of them accepted the proposals and were willing to cooperate in their implementation.
Some universities were only willing to accept the academic
proposals if the administrative and financial proposals were
also accepted. The chairman of the UGC felt that academic
should be separated from administrative and financial questions and that the academic proposals for the degree of BEd
should be accepted. The reasons he gave for not wishing to
accept the administrative and financial arrangements really
amounted to two. Firstly he feared that such arrangements
might lead to prolonged local argument. Secondly he feared

that the principle of non-accountability in respect of university expenditure might be jeopardized because of the degree of public and government interest in this field. In retrospect it may be noted that the principle of non-accountability for university expenditure vanished very soon after this even though the UGC declined to accept the financing of the colleges of education.[19]

Soon after the Robbins Report was published, Alexander had written to Dacey, Secretary to the County Councils Association, suggesting that they could have avoided the pressure from the colleges if they had found ways of giving them more status 'several years ago'. He suggested that the Ministry now felt it had to do something for the colleges but that if approached on these lines it would 'not be unsympathetic to the importance of keeping LEAs in the picture in the interests of expansion'. Dacey concurred and there were informal exchanges with the Ministry on these lines. At a meeting some time later the Secretary of State (as he was now styled) commented that while it was plain that illiberal government of the colleges by the LEAs was not a problem everywhere, yet there were serious deficiencies in some places. 'Moreover in all areas there would be need to reassure the colleges that the decision was not being taken against their best interests.' In reply to Prentice, Alexander said that early action to make degrees available and to reorganize governing bodies should rapidly assuage any feelings of disappointment. He also suggested that the question of the composition and powers of college governing bodies should be referred to the DES for review. Thus the Government issued a statement in which it concluded that the academic and the administrative and financial aspects were separable and that fundamental changes should not be made in the administrative and financial structure of the teacher training system. The statement went on to promise a review of college governing bodies and to accept that the colleges might be appropriately renamed 'Colleges of Education'. Political and bureaucratic hopes and fears were much less concerned with academic issues and here the Government contented itself with saying it was 'glad to know that most universities have expressed their readiness to consider making degrees available to suitable students'.[20]

One reason advanced by local authority spokesmen for wanting to keep their colleges of education was that just at this time the colleges were undergoing very rapid expansion and that any administrative or financial rearrangement would disrupt this. By 1958 it had become apparent that there would have to be a considerable expansion of the training college system. The extension of the course from two to three years could not be overcome by a decline in the demand for teachers as had been expected. When this extension had been authorized in 1957 it had been reckoned that the school population would stabilize in size in the early 1960s and remain steady throughout the decade. Moreover the teaching body was increasing each year by more than 6,000. This forecast was falsified by a number of developments. In the late 1950s a considerable surge began in the birthrate and demographers began to suggest that there would be eight million children of school age in 1970 and nine million by 1980. Secondly the rising birthrate from 1957 was accompanied by a more rapid withdrawal of young married women teachers from the teaching service. In 1962, 19,000 women teachers were recruited but 17,000 left, many after only a few years' service in the schools. Indeed calculations showed that at one stage the average period of teaching service after three years of training was only 2½ years before departure – although many returned later. By 1963 the Ministry calculated that 100,000 extra children would be entering the schools for the next 20 years. To produce a teacher for every 20 of these meant producing an annual increase in the teaching force of 5,000. The current recruitment of 30,000 was only producing a net increase of 4,000. Moreover a further 100,000 would be needed to get rid of oversize classes by 1970. To achieve this, because of wastage, about 400,000 would need to be recruited during the decade.[21]

Against this background, the National Advisory Council in 1958 had recommended that 16,000 additional places be provided in the colleges by 1962. The Minister at that time accepted a programme to provide an additional 12,000 places. The next year he announced his intention of adding a further 4,000 by 1964. During the 1960s the targets had to be raised further. The aim of 80,000 places in the colleges by 1970 was superseded by a target of 111,000 places by 1974.

Further plans for expansion were initiated in 1965. In 1967 five departments of education were established in technical colleges and in that year the number of new entrants to the colleges exceeded 37,000. The total number of students in the colleges reached 100,000 in 1968.[22] The very remarkable increase in the number of students recruited is shown in Table 3.4.

Table 3.4   Students admitted to initial teacher training courses (excluding university departments), 1959–68

Year of admission	Students admitted
1959	15,700
1962	17,700
1965	30,000
1968	39,000

During the 1960s considerable progress was made in setting up the degree of BEd. It was awarded after four years of study, usually on the basis of the normal three years for the certificate plus an additional year for about 10 per cent of students who would then be eligible for the award of the degree. A few universities first awarded BEd degrees to college students in 1968 but in most cases the earliest awards were not made until 1969. Following the discussions with LEAs noticed above, a study group was set up with T. R. Weaver, a DES official, as chairman. The aim of the group's report was to broaden the membership of all college governing bodies and to ensure that LEA colleges actually had effective governing bodies. It also proposed procedures for considering internal academic matters. The recommendations of the study group were adopted and instruments and articles of government incorporating the new arrangements should have been made for all LEA colleges by 1 July 1969. The changing position of the students was shown from the inclusion in the great majority of the governing bodies of student members. At the same time the governing bodies of voluntary colleges amended their constitutions to include student members.[23]

THE JAMES COMMITTEE REPORT

The very rapid expansion of the colleges of education during the 1960s produced some signs of strain and tension within the teacher education system. A great deal of the expansion was undertaken by local authorities. At the time of the Second World War they had provided about one-third of the colleges, the other two-thirds being provided by the voluntary bodies – mainly the Anglican and Roman Catholic Churches. By 1968 these proportions had been reversed, the local authority colleges had increased in number from 23 to 113 while the voluntary bodies provided just over 50. The replacement of the Churches by LEAs as the major providers of teacher training facilities made the McNair area training organization arrangements less expedient – especially since the DES had rejected the advice of the Robbins Committee on the structure of higher education and had developed a binary system which pushed the local authorities into creating a series of higher education institutions which some of the more thrusting officials and councillors saw as constituting an autarkic sector of higher education, unconnected with universities and to which their colleges of education should belong.

Moreover the speed and extent of the expansion had led to serious doubt in some quarters about the quality and suitability of some of the courses leading to qualified teacher status. This produced a number of separate inquiries. In 1970 the Secretary of State invited area training organizations to undertake inquiries into the curriculum and methods of their colleges. In July 1969 the Commons Select Committee on Education and Science took teacher training as a topic for inquiry. Various teachers' associations and some local authority organizations also favoured an inquiry about this time. The body which had kept both supply and training under review and on which they had been represented, the NACTST, had gone out of existence in 1965. The DES had come to regard it as of little value and, on the resignation of its chairman Sir Alan Bullock, took no steps to appoint a successor and to keep the Council in existence. Hence the only meeting place for the discussion of teacher training issues by the parties most involved had vanished at a critical time. The DES was opposed to a national committee of inquiry such as other bodies sought believing that any weaknesses in the training arrangements were due to the rapid expansion and that a period of quiet consolidation would best serve to strengthen any weakness which had been produced by the rapid expansion. However, in the course of the general election the Conservative Party gave an undertaking to set up an inquiry if victorious, hence a committee came to be appointed with Lord James as chairman.

The terms of reference were very wide, 'to inquire into the present arrangements for the education, training and probation of teachers' and among the particular issues to inquire whether a larger proportion of intending teachers 'should be educated with students who have not chosen their careers or have chosen other careers'. The small – and strangely unrepresentative – committee of only seven members produced a set of proposals which would have completely recast teacher education and training. There was to be a separation of personal education and training. The first cycle was to be two years of more or less academic study for a diploma in higher education or three years for a degree. The second cycle was to consist of one year of training in a college or department with emphasis on practical work followed by a year of induction to a school. The year of induction was to replace the existing year of probation. The third cycle of education and training was a fully-organized system of in-service training with one term in every seven years of refresher courses for every serving teacher. New developments and constant changes in the schools were believed to make this essential. The existing organization through university based area training organizations was to be replaced by a National Council for Teacher Education and Training with 15 Regional Councils for Colleges and Departments of Education below it. The National Council was to be empowered to award the diploma in higher education and the BA(Ed). This degree was to be awarded at the end of the second cycle in place of any form of teaching certificate – it was, in fact, a renaming of the various certificates. The Council might also confer the degree of MA(Ed) as an in-service award.[24] The Report met with a hostile reception from the various education interests. The new BA(Ed) for instance, appeared to some to be a mockery of the long held desire for an all-graduate teaching profession. The main recommendations were still-born. The leading members of the James Committee were known to be strongly critical of the existing, McNair type of teacher education arrangements, but they failed to convince the education service generally that their views were sound or that the reforms they proposed would be beneficial. The whole exercise also had a lesson for the DES. The committee of inquiry which is broadly representative is likely to be of much more value in formulating and advancing policy than an earnest, unrepresentative group, however distinguished its membership might be.

There is some evidence that the looming issue of cutting back the number of students proposing to teach was one which the James Committee considered but which – for reasons best known to members of the Committee and to senior officials in the DES – it did not deal with in its Report.[25] The fall in the birth rate from 1964 ensured that the large increases in the size of the college system in the second half of the 1960s would quickly become an embarrassment. Within the DES from an early stage the policy followed was to bring to an end teacher education as a distinct sector of higher education and to merge it into further education. In this way the buildings and capital provided to produce teachers could be used to expand public sector advanced further education which the Department had sought to build up since the effective departure from the Robbins proposals and the movement towards the 'binary' arrangement.

THE SHRIVELLING OF THE SYSTEM

By the middle of the 1970s three factors combined to worsen what would in any case have been a difficult problem of over-supply of teachers. Against all predictions the number of live births continued to decline as may be seen from Table 1.6. The size of the salary award to teachers by the Houghton Committee in 1974 was such as to reduce appreciably the wastage from teaching and thus to limit further than had been expected the number of openings for newly trained teachers. Finally the OPEC inspired world-wide increase in the price of oil led to financial and economic problems which made the continued availability of large new capital funds for public sector higher education and further education extremely unlikely. Thus the pressure to reduce the number of teacher training places, to fuse teacher education with further education and to redeploy its capital assets became much greater. Some of the consequences of the new policy were enunciated in a parliamentary answer by Reg Prentice in March 1975. The teacher training capacity outside the universities was to be reduced to 60,000. Thirty colleges would have to give up teacher training and in as many cases as possible their buildings were to be used for other educational purposes.[26]

Any attempt to fuse the colleges of education with the further education sector required the ending of the McNair area training organization system for the regulation of courses and the recognition of qualified teachers. In a White Paper the Government noted the 'widespread misgivings' caused by the James Committee's proposals for new administrative machinery and said it shared them. Thus it ended the ATO system and offered colleges the choice of validation of their courses either by universities or by the Council for National Academic Awards. It accepted the need for the careful organization of in-service training, the one important recommendation of the James Committee which had attracted widespread support, but it put on one side the creation of new regional committees for this function and 'shadow' ATOs were to continue their work here for the time being. In place of the NACTST there was now established an Advisory Committee on the Training and Supply of Teachers on which much the same bodies were represented as on the former National Advisory Council. Although the Advisory Committee on the Training and Supply of Teachers has itself now been replaced by the Advisory Committee on the Supply and Education of Teachers, there has so far been no permanent settlement of machinery at the regional level.

Towards the end of 1976 the Secretary of State, Shirley Williams, told the Commons that a further contraction of the system to about 45,000 places outside the universities had become necessary and that the reduction would need to be achieved by 1981. This would probably require about another 30 institutions to cease from initial training. Earlier Mr Mulley had announced that in view of the prospective over-supply of teachers, he had decided to limit the entry in September 1977 to 12,000 non-graduate students for three and four year courses and 10,000 graduates, including the number entering the university education departments.[27] The limits remained at this level until the 1980s.

It is not possible to relate within the limits of this chapter the actual story of cuts and closures which the Department enforced. There was much criticism of the methods employed and of the apparent veil of secrecy surrounding its policy. Little or no convincing effort was made by those responsible to explain the criteria they used to select which institutions should be closed or amalgamated with polytechnics or other colleges. In response to criticism and after most of the decisions had been taken a paper was circulated to members of the ACTST entitled 'Criteria for Restructuring the Teacher Training System'. Policy for teacher education was said to have three aims:

(1)   Teacher education should be fully integrated with other higher education and where practical should take place in major institutions such as universities, polytechnics and major colleges of higher education.

(2)   Initial and in-service teacher education should be closely related.

(3)   The teaching profession should become all-graduate and existing certificate courses were to be phased out.

Apart from these aims, an objective of reorganization was to preserve special facilities of which the schools had need such as successful experience of training teachers for slow learners or for shortage subjects. A further point was that advice from the Inspectorate and validating bodies was that the average size of a teacher training unit should not be below 600 places including those allocated to in-service training.[28] As criteria these were fairly vague. In practice it seems that there were occasions when the officials concerned ended by achieving reductions where they could without encountering too much political or administrative difficulty. A number of threatened institutions survived by mounting polical pressure, thus diverting the cuts on to those which showed less aptitude in this direction.

It is too early to attempt to put the events of the last few years in perspective, but it is possible to see very considerable achievements in teacher training in the period since the Butler Act of 1944. In spite of the enormous increase in the demand for teachers with the number of pupils in the schools doubling, classes being reduced in size and a much greater degree of specialization becoming necessary since a secondary school place became the right of every pupil over 11 instead of only 15 per cent, it was possible to meet this and still to raise the standards of entry to the profession. Teacher training came to be accepted as part of higher education. The minimum period of training was increased from two to three years and by the end of this period a degree came to be required of all those entering the profession. Even before the final abolition of the certificate and its replacement by the BEd much progress had been made towards bringing more graduates into teaching. Table 3.5 shows both the growth in the absolute number of graduate teachers and the steady increase in the proportion of the rapidly growing teaching body which graduates came to represent.

The issue of admitting untrained graduates to teaching has

Table 3.5   Graduate teachers in service, 1947–77

Year	Graduate teachers			% of the total teaching body
	Primary	*Secondary*	*Total*	
1947	4,033	24,320	28,353	16.0
1950	4,265	28,733	32,998	15.9
1953	4,892	32,065	36,957	16.4
1956	5,888	36,492	42,380	17.4
1959	5,701	43,643	49,344	18.9
1962	5,263	50,367	55,630	20.0
1965	5,700	53,082	58,782	20.7
1968	6.704	55,498	62,202	21.0
1971	8,320	62,574	71,309	20.8
1974	13,616	84,414	97,030	24.0
1977	20,696	102,951	123,647	28.3

Source: Annual Reports of the Ministry 1947–50; Statistics of Education, 1962–77.

almost been dealt with. In September 1969 Edward Short announced the introduction of a training requirement for graduates. There was a high rate of turnover of untrained graduates and, as the shortage of teachers became less severe, the Secretary of State believed the time had come to enforce training and remove the difficulties for their pupils that arose from its absence. The requirement came into effect in the primary schools first for here the educational case for training was at its strongest and those who graduated after 31 December 1969 would not be permitted to teach in maintained primary schools without taking a course of professional training. In secondary schools those who graduated after the end of 1973 would not be able to teach without professional training.[29]

Another significant development which should not be overlooked has been the growth from a very low base in the amount of in-service work among serving teachers. This has become increasingly important as a means of enabling those already in service both to keep abreast of new developments and to adapt themselves to meet the changing needs of the schools. In the last few years the sharp reduction in the number of newly trained teachers entering the profession has made in-service work more important than ever before. It is unfortunate that provision for it by some LEAs remains quite inadequate by any yardstick.

CHAPTER 4

Social and Welfare Provisions

SCHOOL MEALS AND MILK

Although the years following the Second World War are frequently regarded as the time when much of the welfare state was created, the main welfare factors associated with the education service have their origins and their most rapid period of expansion before 1945. School milk had been widely provided in the 1930s at a rate of 2½d (1p) a week for ⅓ of a pint daily. The driving force behind the institution of the subsidized distribution was the dairy industry which sought to enlarge sales during the years of agricultural depression between the wars. The National Milk Publicity Council had sponsored a scheme in the 1920s and this grew when the Government as part of its proposals for the utilization of surplus milk gave the Milk Marketing Board a subsidy which permitted ⅓ of a pint to be sold to each pupil for as little as ½d (0.2p) a day.

Public funds were first made available to assist in the provision of a meal at school for necessitous children in 1906.[1] By 1939 about half of the 315 LEAs which then existed were making some provision for needy children; rather more than 100,000 or 2.4 per cent of the elementary school population were receiving free meals and these were mainly in the towns and cities. Other LEAs resisted Board of Education attempts to persuade them to make provision and maintained that no need existed in their areas. Alongside this arrangement for poor children, in many secondary schools dinners were provided in return for payment. Secondary schools often gathered their pupils in from a wide area and the provision of a dinner in the midday break was a useful service which could virtually pay its way. The emergence of the school meals service in modern form was due to the circumstances of the war. Initially the Board's efforts to persuade more LEAs to provide meals – especially to help with the problems of evacuation – met with little success. By March 1940, 95 LEAs had replied to the Board that they saw no need to take any steps at all, 12 did not respond. The real drive to wider provision came from Clement Attlee who became Lord Privy Seal in the Coalition administration in 1940. In the context of feeding the population adequately under war conditions Attlee wanted school meals available for all children with no discrimination between those who paid and those who did not. He brought the matter to the Food Policy Committee of the War Cabinet and got strong support from the Minister of Food, Lord Woolton.[2] The Board of Education believed it administratively impossible to provide a meal daily for every pupil as decided by the Food Policy Committee. But with the aid of increased grant the number of meals served daily rose to 425,000 by September 1941 while nearly 3,000,000 children now had milk daily.

By 1943 the food supply situation had become critical and Lord Woolton saw school dinners as the only way of ensuring supplementation of the general ration which was regarded by his advisers as inadequate for children. By now the Board of Education had itself become convinced of the need for more vigorous action and Butler and Woolton made a joint approach to the Ministry of Works for the necessary priority for new prefabricated buildings. This was agreed. The target was to provide 2,000,000 school dinners a day by April 1944 and 3,000,000 by April 1945 for England and Wales. But by October 1945 a total of only 1,782,000 had been achieved.[3] Even if the ambitious targets had not been met, a great deal had been achieved. The nature of the service itself had been transformed. The shadow of the poor law had given way to the approach of the welfare state and the standard practice was now to provide for the majority of normal children and not merely a rescue operation for those in need.

The wartime Coalition Government had inclined towards free meals and milk for all pupils as part of a system of family allowances. The Treasury certainly favoured the idea of benefits in kind rather than cash payments which might not be used for the benefit of the children. The Chancellor told the

Commons in 1943 that the Government was perfectly ready to consider a free meals service for all school children.[4] In due course the Government announced its intention of introducing a 5 shilling (25p) children's allowance plus free school meals and milk and reaffirmed this in debate in the Commons in November 1944. On the question of date the Minister of Reconstruction was more hazy. 'What do a few years matter', he asked rhetorically, 'considering that we are inaugurating a system which is going to last the whole life-time of everyone in this chamber?'[5] The Education Act of 1944 laid on LEAs the duty of providing meals and milk for pupils in schools and left it to subsequent regulations to determine whether these would be free. In fact as early as January 1945 the Government's policy of waiting for a while was set out in a circular which explained that a wholly free service could not be introduced until the existing dinners service was further enlarged to cope with the number of pupils who might be expected to use it if it were free of charge. This was envisaged as 75 per cent of the school population.[6] This intention was never to be fulfilled. The regulations provided for a charge which for some years was not to exceed the cost of the food provided. Where parents could not afford this charge the meal was to be free. The Government fixed the price of the meal which increased rather more rapidly than the general rate of inflation. From 1951 the regulations simply required payment 'according to an approved rate'; the additional limitation that this 'shall not exceed the cost of the food supplied therein' was then dropped.[7]

From the end of the war notionally the central government bore the entire cost of the school meals service. The Ministry exercised control through a careful system of unit costing. Under this LEAs were required to submit estimates of unit costs incurred in providing the service and, in agreed form, these became the basis for governmental reimbursement. Local authorities expressed their opposition to having to commit themselves to final fixed unit costings so far in advance when unforeseen changes could so easily occur. In spite of local authority complaints, the system survived for, as Alexander admitted in 1959, the AEC had been watching the working of the system for ten years and found that the Ministry's argument that it was the most satisfactory available was a difficult one to counter.[8] The introduction of a general grant system for local authority expenditure in 1958 made little difference since the specific grants for meals and milk continued. However, the system was ended by the Local Government Act of 1966 which had the effect of terminating the special grant arrangements since the expenditure was in future to be taken into account in deciding the rate support grant.[9]

The milk scheme had been paid for from the end of the war until 1952 by the Ministry of Food, the milk being supplied without charge to pupils. The decision to transfer this expenditure to the Ministry of Education from 1 April 1952 was reached after protracted inter-departmental discussions on the grounds that financial and administrative responsibility ought to be in the same hands.[10] Two years later formal responsibility for providing milk in schools passed to the LEAs supported by a 100 per cent grant as for meals and with similar unit costing arrangements. Since this expenditure was now borne by the Education Vote the Ministry was particularly anxious to obtain the lowest possible prices from suppliers. The dairy trade tried to enforce the maximum price for milk and in the autumn of 1954 the Ministry wrote to chief education officers pointing to evidence of an organized attempt within the dairy trade to maintain prices. Some local authorities such as Monmouthshire and Derbyshire managed to crack 'the milk ring'. After a year or so of struggle authorities more generally began to secure some discount, although early in 1956 Ministry officials noted that while the 'full price' ring was broken a new 2.5 per cent discount ring seemed to have formed.[11]

The end of specific grants for meals and milk following the introduction of the rate support grant system in 1966 was soon followed by the growth of pressure to limit the extent of the services and therefore to reduce the costs now apparently falling on local authorities. The financial crisis of the late 1960s led the Labour administration to introduce legislation to remove the requirement that LEAs should supply milk to pupils at maintained secondary schools. It was estimated that this would save annually £4.5 million in England and Wales.[12] Questions also began to arise over the provision of school meals. Here too financial pressures were growing more acute and some began to argue that most families were sufficiently well off to provide adequately for their children's nutrition at home. LEAs saw themselves in competition at the local level for resources under the block grant arrangements and began to complain of the government's exploitation of the new arrangements to shift responsibility for the finance of the service on to local authorities. The actual charge for the meal was itself subject to various pressures arising from wider considerations associated with incomes policy and pay bargaining. The effect of this on the proportion of the cost borne by an authority may be illustrated by some figures prepared by the Somerset authority in Table 4.1.

Table 4.1   School meal costs in Somerset, 1971–5

Year	Total cost per meal	Permitted charge	Deficit borne by LEA	
1971/2	18.75p	12p	6.75p	36%
1972/3	20.06p	12p	8.06p	40%
1973/4	22.32p	12p	10.32p	46%
1974/5	30.30p	12p	18.30p	60%

Source: AEC, E73, Taylor (Somerset) to Alexander, 21 July 1975.

The extent to which the deficit borne by the LEA really fell on Somerset – or any other authority – depended on the degree to which the effect of freezing the price per meal was allowed for in the course of the annual discussions in fixing the overall rate support grants. The situation was to become even further aggravated early in 1976 when an increase in the permitted national charge from 15p to 20p had been announced only to be set aside as part of the agreement reached between the Government and the TUC on pay limits. The frustrated increase had itself been proposed as part of a new policy of annual adjustments to keep constant the proportion of the total cost to be met by subsidy.[13]

As the financial situation worsened, local authorities found themselves forced to choose between meeting financial limits imposed by the Government and meeting the needs of the school meals service. The situation was resolved by the Conservative administration which took office in May 1979 with reduction in expenditure on education as a guiding principle. The reduction was to fall largely on meals, milk and transport for pupils. The charge for school dinner was raised from 25p to 30p in the June 1979 budget and a further increase to 35p was announced from February 1980. These increases were essentially interim measures for the Education Act of 1980 converted the previous *duty* on LEAs to provide meals and milk to a *power*. The only duties remaining were to provide somewhere for children who brought their sandwiches to school to eat them and to provide a free midday meal – not necessarily a cooked meal – for the children of needy parents. Thus the question of what charge should be made is now a local matter as is the issue of whether to have any meals service at all.[14] The effect of these recent steps on the number of dinners served may be seen from Table 4.2. The proportion of pupils taking meals fell in 1981 to a figure not seen since the 1950s. Owing to its chronic surplus of dairy products, the EEC has recently offered to subsidize milk in schools. Responsibility for administering these subsidy arrangements was transferred from the DES to the Ministry of Agriculture in 1981.[15]

Table 4.2   School meals in maintained and assisted primary and secondary Schools, 1948–81

Year	No. meals served (000s)	% of pupils present taking meals
1948	2,743	52.6
1951	2,824	50.2
1954	2,850	46.1
1957	2,847	45.9
1960	3,408	52.4
1963	3,849	59.2
1966	4,655	68.4
1969	5,169	70.1
1972	4,802	64.4
1975	5,552	70.3
1978	4,856	61.7
1981	3,515	49.0

Sources: Ministry of Education, *Annual Reports;* DES, *Annual Reports;* DES, *Catering in Schools* 1975.

THE SCHOOL HEALTH SERVICE

The 1944 Act imposed on LEAs the statutory duty of providing medical and dental inspection in all types of maintained primary and secondary schools and the duty to provide or to secure the provision for children attending maintained schools of all forms of medical and dental treatment – other than domiciliary treatment – without cost to the parent. Medical inspection had been a statutory duty since 1907 and from 1918 LEAs had been obliged to offer treatment for defective vision, dental disease, enlarged tonsils and adenoids and certain other ailments. Some authorities had gone a great deal further than this might suggest and the extension of the school health service by the Butler Act was entirely in line with previous development. By this time the Ministry of Health was itself attempting to devise a form of universal health service for the post-war years and the extent to which this might make separate LEA provision unnecessary was not clear in 1944.

Accordingly the Ministry took steps to deal with the immediate situation by asking authorities early in 1945 to concentrate on improving existing services which dealt with ear, nose and throat diseases, eye diseases and defective vision, child guidance, speech therapy and the treatment of rheumatism. Authorities which had done little to develop these services were urged to make greater efforts. In the interim period LEAs were asked to extend their range of free provision for treatment by making arrangements with existing voluntary and other hospitals for the treatment of school children suffering from other forms of disease. The actual terms for these arrangements were to be agreed locally between the authority and the hospital which contracted to provide treatment. In the case of dental treatment this was to be maintained on the existing basis and was to be expanded as soon as more dentists became available.[16]

After the general election in 1945 the new Minister of Health, Aneurin Bevan, was determined to introduce a full state health service as soon as possible and set about preparing what became the National Health Service Act of 1946 that came into force in 1948. In September 1945 Bevan wrote to the new Minister of Education suggesting that since the Government's aim was a free service for everyone, LEAs should seek to provide inspection but to refer school children to the national health service for treatment – all treatment being taken over by the new service when it was in a position to do so. This letter really only repeated the view set out by the Ministry of Health in a white paper in 1944 which stated that in due course 'the child will look for its treatment to the organization which the (new health) service provides – and the education authority, as such, will give up responsibility for medical treatment'. The Ministry of Education accepted that Bevan's letter stated the understanding that already existed between the two departments except that it had never agreed that *all* treatment would be given by the new service and none by LEAs.[17] Education succeeded in maintaining its position when the new health service began to operate in 1948.

Detailed arrangements for the school health service were set out by the Ministry in 1948 and these were to continue for a quarter of a century. The circular stressed that LEAs should do their utmost to ensure that the effectiveness of the school health service should not be impaired. 'For many decades the building up of the school health service has been a work of the highest national importance and it is vital that there should be no relaxation.' Medical inspection and the ascertainment of the various forms of handicap were not affected by the new service. All consultative and specialist work being carried out under agreements with hospitals became free of charge to LEAs and the future organization of such work became the responsibility of regional hospital boards. Even here LEAs might provide any specialist service for school children if they believed this desirable 'notwithstanding the facilities otherwise available'. The school dental service was not affected, speech therapy also remained an LEA provision. Child guidance centres were to continue to be the financial and administrative responsibility of local authorities but children found to be needing psychiatric treatment were in future to be referred to national health service clinics. Local authorities were concerned about various aspects of the new arrangements and there was a series of meetings covering local authority associations and with the Ministry in an effort to determine new guidelines and working practices.[18]

Thus the school health service really developed as a preventive health service for children at school and the prevention or limitation of disability was to be achieved through close cooperation with the national health service. Improved social conditions were largely responsible for the change in the nature of the school health service from its preoccupation in the early days with infectious diseases and malnutrition. In the late 1940s and early 1950s most authorities arranged medical inspections shortly after children first entered school, at about the age of transfer to secondary schooling and again just before the time came to leave school. Pressure on time when the number of school doctors did not keep pace with the increase in the school population led to a greater flexibility in the arrangements and to the concept of selective medical inspections. The case for the initial entry examination was a strong one since it enabled defects to be detected an an early stage, introduced mothers to the service and ensured their understanding that the school doctor worked with the family doctor. After this stage the selective approach has really relied upon teachers reporting any pupil showing emotional or behavioural traits out of the ordinary or any evidence of ill-health. The chief medical officer believed that this approach brought parents, teachers and school health service closer together and focused attention on the children most in need of medical service and help. It avoided the situation where school doctors spent much of their time examining a large number of healthy children while many others with serious handicaps and emotional or educational difficulties needed more attention.[19]

The 1944 Act set the age at which LEAs are required to assume responsibility for handicapped children at two which is late for those with hearing difficulties. Most of the authorities made special provision in one way or another for those suffering from serious hearing defects. In 1967 just over 3,000 were receiving special educational treatment as partially hearing and about the same number as deaf. About half of the former were in 191 special classes in ordinary schools. In the same year 23,000 new entrants to schools in England and Wales were found to need treatment for defective vision. The number of pupils in schools for the physically handicapped was nearly

17,000 and included those suffering from cerebral palsy, poliomyelitis, heart disease, congenital deformities, spina bifida and those seriously injured in road or other accidents.

The number of children in special schools for the educationally subnormal was 49,000, 40,000 in day schools and 9,000 in residential. As late as 1968 the DES commented that there were problems in some areas where authorities were still without a school psychological service. For many years the Department has followed the policy that no child should attend a special school if his needs could be met satisfactorily in an ordinary school. Two recent developments have given added impetus to this policy. In 1976 one provision of the Education Act passed in that year required handicapped pupils to be educated in county or voluntary schools in preference to special schools unless doing so would be impractical, against the educational interest of the pupils (whether handicapped or non-handicapped) or involve unreasonable expenditure. The Report of the Warnock Committee in May 1978 also made recommendations with the effect of taking this policy further. An Education Act broadly derived from some of the Committee's recommendations was passed in 1981.[20] The extent to which the provisions of this Act are put into effect will depend upon the resources made available.

While the school dental service was in an administrative sense unaffected by the introduction of the national health arrangements, it did in fact have a drastic impact. The rewards and opportunities it opened in the new general dental service drew many school dental officers away in order to enter private practice within the new scheme. At the end of 1947 there were the equivalent of 921 full-time school dental officers. By the end of 1949 this figure had fallen to 732. Three local authorities were by then without any dental officers. In 18 months the service had lost one-fifth of its effective strength. The problems associated with staffing the school dental service were to prove very difficult to overcome.[21]

The school health service came to an end as part of the administrative reorganization of the national health service in 1974. The political decision to hand over responsibility for any health provision in the schools to the Department of Health and Social Security and the national health service organization was made known in parliamentary written answers in July

1972 by Margaret Thatcher and Keith Joseph, respectively Secretaries of State for Education and for the Social Services. The professional staff concerned with school health were to be employed in future by a reorganized national health service. It was explained that there would be for each area a doctor and a dentist on the staff of the area health authority with the function of advising the LEA 'in the same way as do the principal school medical officer and the principal school dental officer now'. A working party of officials from the Departments and the local authority associations prepared a report on the detailed arrangements. Some of the education representatives appended a note of dissent in which they indicated their fears. They doubted whether the NHS would be able to accord the necessary degree of priority to a school health service and whether it would be possible to achieve the high degree of cooperation between LEA and area health authority that would be needed. All the local authority associations regretted the government's decision to unify the administration of the health service outside local government. The AEC and the Society of Education Officers particularly regretted the way the school health service was caught up in the application of this general tidying-up principle at the time. Apart from the AEC's representations, the Society of Education Officers emphasized in correspondence with the DES its regret at the decision which would 'remove the health service almost entirely from sensitive and democratic local control'.[22]

The National Health Service Reorganization Act of 1973 transferred responsibility from LEAs to the Secretary of State for Health and Social Security for health service matters in the schools. Under the Act he is required to provide medical and dental inspection at regular intervals of children in maintained schools and for the treatment of such pupils. This responsibility is in fact discharged by the Area Health Authority and the necessary arrangements are coordinated through local joint consultative committees which include representatives from both the LEA and the Area Health Authority.

THE YOUTH SERVICE

Various national voluntary organizations concerned with the service of youth dated from the mid-19th century – among them the YMCA (1844) and the YWCA (1855), but in many ways this service's major contribution came in the course of the Second World War. Right at the beginning of the war the Board of Education undertook direct responsibility for youth welfare, set up a National Youth Committee and called on local authorities to set up their own youth committees. As the war proceeded, the registration of young people was made compulsory and all who were not engaged in full-time education were interviewed with a view to their joining some form of youth organization in the years before they became liable for military service at 18. It was thought particularly important to make provision for the young in their leisure time in the circumstances of wartime. The government came to think of the youth service as a permanent part of education and this was reflected in the White Paper on *Educational Reconstruction* and in the provision made for it in the 1944 Act. The McNair Report (1944) on teacher training also encouraged the idea of youth leadership as a profession which ought to have proper training and conditions of service.

In the immediate post-war years the service continued to make some progress. Although the McNair recommendations were not accepted, the courses of training for youth leaders which some voluntary organizations and universities were offering attracted entrants from among those leaving the armed forces. But by 1950 there were signs of decline and along with non-vocational further education as a whole it was held back as the Ministry felt obliged to put what financial resources it could win into providing more school places and into the expansion of vocational further education. The AEC took the view that since the youth service was part of further education, little could be done to determine the pattern it should follow until county colleges were established. The second report of the NACTST dealt with the recruitment and training of youth leaders in 1951 but it was never put into effect.[23]

Quite apart from the lack of priority which the Ministry felt able to give the youth service, its disparate nature made any move towards establishing national salary scales and a career pattern for youth leaders difficult if not impossible. There was no single national body to represent the various organizations involved. The Ministry was quite prepared to assist in setting up 'a quasi Burnham Committee' for full-time youth leaders. In 1952 Gilbert Flemming, Permanent Secretary at the Ministry, consulted all the bodies involved but while the local authorities supported the proposal and the voluntary organizations which replied would have gone along with it, he confessed that none of the parties showed any 'marked enthusiasm' for the proposal and therefore wondered whether there was any point in persisting with it 'when our financial prospects look as bleak as they do at present'. Within the Ministry it was thought that since national voluntary bodies had no power to commit their management committees to pay a given rate of salary, it would be difficult for them to act as part of an employers' panel. Moreover the employees themselves were scattered over various unions and associations and the YMCA employees declined to separate themselves from their employers and to appear on a youth leaders panel constituted on the Burnham model.[24]

The Ministry made more positive efforts to review the whole position when David Eccles was in office and in 1957 his Parliamentary Secretary, Edward Boyle, met representatives from local authority associations and from the Standing Conference of National Voluntary Youth Organizations to discuss the training and status of youth leaders and the use of public funds on the youth service. The need for more youth leaders was generally accepted and the difficulties were very clear. The local authorities were prepared to consider salary scales if the Ministry made clear what qualifications were expected but the voluntary organizations feared that they would not be able to pay negotiated scales unless public subsidy for this purpose were available.[25]

In 1957 the Commons Select Committee on the Estimates complained that the Ministry of Education was not exercising its responsibility properly for the money voted in aid of the youth service. The Committee accused the Ministry of having little interest in the service and of being apathetic about its future. 'Your Committee consider that this apathy is having a deeply discouraging effect on the valuable work done for the service.'[26] The interest that was stimulated at this time, partly by the Report, led to the appointment of a committee of inquiry in 1958 under the chairmanship of the Countess of Albemarle.

It reported in 1960 and began by noting that it had been appointed at a crucial time, partly because some aspects of national life to which the youth service was relevant were causing concern such as the 'bulge' in the adolescent population and elements of social change to which adolescents were responding sharply and often in ways which adults found puzzling or shocking. Furthermore it was only too obvious that the youth service itself was in a critical condition.[27]

The Albemarle Committee was wise to dwell upon the need for action if its recommendations were not to be ignored. The recommendations requiring action by central government which were acted upon included setting up a Youth Service Development Council to advise the Minister, the increase of government grants, the provision of better accommodation and training facilities for more full-time youth leaders. The Youth Service Development Council was set up and it appointed a review committee to keep under review the objectives of the report and to make recommendations on future developments. A considerable building programme was undertaken with authorization for new buildings amounting to £23 million by 1967 and covering about 3,000 projects, some in the voluntary sector. More money was made available. Ministry grants under the Social and Physical Training Grant Regulations rose from about £300,000 in 1959 to £1,800,000 in 1965. This was to support the training of youth leaders, to assist voluntary organizations with running costs and for local voluntary capital projects. In addition to this, LEA spending doubled to £6,500,000 in the five years following publication of the Report.[28]

The committee accorded first priority to the training of professional leaders and added that recruits of quality would be attracted 'only if the Minister appoints a negotiating committee for salaries and conditions of service'. Conditions for recognition as a qualified youth leader were worked out, the Ministry established a National College for the Training of Youth Leaders at Leicester which admitted its first intake in 1961. Existing training courses at Westhill College of Education, at the Swansea University Education Department, that in Liverpool run by the National Association of Boys Clubs and the YMCA courses in London were all recognized for qualifying purposes.[29] The Committee strongly recommended that the existing 700 full-time youth leader force should be increased to 1,300 by 1966 and by the end of 1965 the number of full-time youth leaders on the Ministry's register stood at 1,287. A Joint Negotiating Committee for Youth Leaders had been set up to determine salaries and to recommend conditions of service. In addition to the training of full-time staff, part-time youth leaders were increasingly expected to take training courses provided by local authorities which awarded certificates to successful candidates who had undertaken courses of instruction and supervised practical work in clubs.

The raising of the school leaving age to 16 reinforced the inclination of authorities in a number of areas to regard their youth service work as an integral part of the provision they were making through their secondary schools for adolescents. Since the large comprehensive schools were themselves developing in some places into institutions which endeavoured to meet some of the cultural and social needs of their surrounding communities it was desirable for the heads of such institutions to have direct responsibility for all that went on. In parts of Yorkshire, for instance, youth tutors were made answerable to the heads of schools with area youth officers acting in an advisory capacity and with the school governors accepting responsibility for youth work in their establishment.

The way in which provision has been made, the degree of cooperation between voluntary organizations and LEAs varies greatly in different districts depending largely on the degree of interest and enthusiasm shown by the local authority. The central government's direct contribution to the voluntary organizations has remained static in real terms for some years. Since the burst of development which was launched in the late 1950s and early 1960s the service has come to provide wider and better opportunities for the more purposeful young people but it is not at all clear that the more anti-social and apathetic are any more attracted by the activities provided than they were in the past.

CHAPTER 5

The Universities

THE POST-WAR SITUATION

The most significant development for the universities in the decades following the Second World War was the extent to which they faced an unprecedented demand for their services, their consequent expansion and the way in which their affairs became the concern of politicians and administrators in a manner hitherto not experienced. Table 5.1 gives an indication of the dimensions of the expansion. The increased demand for places which did so much to dominate the scene during the third quarter of the twentieth century was no doubt due in an immediate sense to the increase in the number of pupils completing a full secondary education and therefore qualifying to go on to a university but this was in itself part of the general rise in the level of expectations dating from the middle years of the war. More and more people sought home ownership, motor cars, more health care, more education and a higher level in all sorts of services. It is against this background that the deliberations of official committees and the pronouncements of ministers on university development need to be considered.

Indeed, in its first post-war Report, that for 1935 to 1947, the University Grants Committee suggested that 'two independent trains of thought pointed directly to a policy of expansion'. The war had shown the country the value to the community of university-trained people and a far smaller proportion of our population was so trained than in many other countries. Secondly the general equality of sacrifice in wartime which the nation had demanded ought to be matched by a much greater measure of social and educational equality than had existed before the war.[1]

During the war the conscription of most university staff up to

136

the age of 40,the conscription of male students from the age of 17½ – except where their courses qualified them to help the war economy in the most direct sense in such areas as science or engineering where shortened, two-year, degree courses were permitted – and the requisitioning of some university premises – particularly in London, Oxford and Cambridge, all meant that a considerable effort would be needed even to get back to the pre-war position. In 1943 the UGC began to consider the steps needed to retrieve the situation and it passed a resolution early in 1944 that 'in the interests of the nation' universities should be able to resume their normal activities in October 1944, 'irrespective of the duration of the war'. In February a meeting was held with the Committee of Vice-Chancellors and Principals to discuss such matters as release of

Table 5.1   Total number of full-time university students in Great Britain, 1938–39 to 1980–81

Year	Students
1938–9	50,246
1946–7	68,452
1948–9	83,690
1950–1	85,314
1952–3	81,474
1954–5	81,705
1956–7	89,866
1958–9	100,204
1960–1	107,699
1962–3	119,004
1964–5	138,711
1966–7	184,203
1968–9	211,294
1970–1	227,956
1972–3	239,366
1974–5	250,565
1976–7	271,779
1978–9	288,389
1980–1	297,200

Sources: UGC Quinquennial Report, 1947–52 (Cmd 8875), 1953; UGC Quinquennial Report, 1957–62 (Cmd 2267). 1963; Statistics of Education, DES, 1967, 1977 and 1979; Statistical Bulletin 3/81, DES, 1981.

premises and release of staff and students from those duties to which they had been conscripted.[2]

While it was obviously not possible to revert to normal university life in October 1944, the preparations and discussions set in train did lead to a quick recovery after the end of the war in Europe in 1945. Release of buildings and of staff generally went ahead at a reasonable pace. The release or deferment of arts students was likely to prove politically a difficult issue for the government. Deferment had been granted each year to about 3,000 young men seeking to read science and engineering. In 1945 this total was redistributed so as to include 600 arts students leaving 2,400 science and engineering deferments. The Ministry of Labour felt it could not increase the total number of deferments. The Minister – by this time R. A. Butler who had moved from Education – argued in a paper to the Cabinet that there had been a loss of 30,000 graduations on the arts side as a result of the war. This shortage was serious for the professions, for many of the higher posts in industry and for the public service. Accordingly he recommended the Cabinet to agree to the early release of 3,000 arts students who had served in the forces for at least three years and who had already won scholarships which circumstances had prevented them from taking up. There was general agreement in the Cabinet on the urgency of increasing the number of arts students in universities and the scheme was authorized at its meeting on 28 July.[3] The arrival at universities by October of the students thus eligible for release represented a very energetic administrative approach both in the services and in the universities.

Discussions on the future size and growth of the universities had been going on inside the government machine for about two years before university activities were resumed on a normal scale in the autumn of 1945. The UGC had its first discussion of postwar policy on 29 December 1943. Informal soundings of the attitudes of universities to expansion were undertaken at this time. A strong impetus to these deliberations was given by a confidential report from an interdepartmental committee under Lord Hankey on the further education and training of those who had been engaged in war service. This report was presented to the Lord President in the spring of 1944 and one of its most important features was a forecast of a 50 per cent increase in the demand for university education after the war. The Hankey Committee's report was clearly a helpful influence in securing from the Treasury the necessary support for university expansion. The UGC recommended that the Treasury should be asked to provide 75 per cent of the additional funds that would be needed. It is perhaps of interest to notice that the need for rapid expansion on a larger scale than some universities themselves seemed to believe possible came to be widely accepted in political circles. Clement Attlee, for instance, who was Deputy Prime Minister in the wartime Coalition Government, fully accepted the need for an increase in the student body of at least 50 per cent. The fact that the universities as a whole did not appear to be planning increases of at least this size was 'a very serious matter, as we cannot hope to solve our post-war problems unless we can increase the supply of trained men and women in the various departments of our national life' he wrote to Bevin in January 1945 and they made these views clear to Anderson and Butler, the ministers then responsible for the UGC and the Ministry of Education.[4] Thus the UGC's request for additional grants met with a favourable response and the Chancellor of the Exchequer told the Commons in February that the annual grant would increase from £2,149,000 to £5,900,000 for the next two years. He also announced that the Treasury accepted the need for a large contribution towards capital development costs of £18,750,000 over the next decade.[5] The pre-war position had been that there had been no state aid for capital costs; universities had had to find these from their own resources.

These decisions, taken while the war was still being fought, led to a permanent change in the financial support for universities. Before the war the state had never contributed more than one-third of their total recurrent income. As a result of these decisions it would in future contribute more than half by way of direct Treasury grants payable through the UGC. The change in the position is illustrated in Table 5.2.

The pressure for university expansion came largely from outside the universities themselves and was expressed by politicians who began to make far more resources available.

Table 5.2   University income, 1935–36, 1946–47 (main sources)

Year	Gifts and endowments, etc. (%)	LEA Grants (%)	Fees (%)	Parliamentary grants (%)
1935–6	17.0	8.7	32.5	34.3
1946–7	11.5	5.6	23.2	52.7

Source: UGC, *University Development from 1935 to 1947*, p. 79.

It was inevitable in these circumstances that the position of the UGC and the formal relationship between the state and universities should be modified to reflect the increasing interest and investment of the former. In July 1946 the terms of reference of the UGC were extended so as to define the position of the Committee more explicitly. The terms of reference employed since 1919 had been to inquire into the financial needs of university education in the United Kingdom and to advise the government as to the application of any grants that may be made by Parliament towards meeting them. The new terms were

To inquire into the financial needs of university education in Great Britain; to advise the government as to the application of any grants made by Parliament towards meeting them; to collect, examine and make available information on matters relating to university education at home and abroad; and to assist, in consultation with the universities and other bodies concerned, the preparation and execution of such plans for the development of the universities as may from time to time be required in order to ensure that they are fully adequate to national needs.

Two months before the augmentation of the UGC's terms of reference, the report was published of a committee appointed by the Lord President, Herbert Morrison, entitled *Scientific Manpower*.[6] In retrospect, this report may be viewed as playing an important part in forwarding the Government's expansionary policy for the university system in the years leading up to the Robbins Report. Sir Alan Barlow, joint second secretary at the Treasury, was chairman of this committee. The committee was set up because of the realization that industrial growth required more highly trained scientific and technological manpower. It asserted that never before had the importance of science been more widely recognized or so many hopes of future progress and welfare been founded upon the scientist. The Report recommended a doubling of the number of graduates in science as soon as possible and added the suggestion that concurrent with the expansion in science and technology there should be a substantial expansion in the number of students studying the humanities. It pointed out that even if the number of students were doubled Britain would still fall far short of a number of other European countries and of the USA in the relative provision it made for higher education. The need to recognize formally the new and closer relationship between the state and the university system as set out for the universities should be assured of 'adequate and continuing assistance from the Exchequer'. Moreover the Government's part in any expansion programme should be the responsibility of the UGC 'which ought to be put in a position to concern itself more positively with university policy than it has done in the past'.

EXPANSION BEFORE ROBBINS

The number of students increased rapidly to 85,000 in 1950 after which there was a slight decline as the number of ex-service students whose studies had been delayed by the war completed their courses. The increase in the number of staff (from about 4,000 in 1939 to 9,000 in 1951) came rather later since in the immediate post-war years there were not enough suitably qualified staff to meet the demand. The provision of new buildings had lagged badly. University building was as much affected as the schools and other areas of activity by the shortages of necessary materials, economic problems generally and by the particular difficulties which beset the building industry and which were noticed in chapter 1. By 1952 the UGC apparently imagined that the major period of expansion was over. The universities were filled beyond capacity and the Committee commented in its Quinquennial Report that they were unlikely to tolerate this as a long-term situation. In fact non-recurrent grants for the purchase of sites, erection of buildings and provision of equipment amounted to £35 million for the quinquennium 1947 to 1952. During this period the Parliamentary grant as a proportion of university recurrent income increased from 52.7 to 66.5 per cent.[7]

The pressure for an increase in the number of scientists and technologists to meet manpower needs continued however. The Committee on Scientific Manpower expressed the fear that if higher education institutions failed to grow they would be unable to keep pace with the growth in demand for scientists necessary to promote increased industrial efficiency and productivity.[8] The needs of higher scientific and technological education received important support from two members of Churchill's Cabinet at this time. Lord Cherwell and Lord Woolton both pressed for the establishment of a number of higher technological colleges with independence of the local authorities. Cherwell was ministerial 'overlord' responsible for the co-ordination of scientific research and development and was therefore in a position to press for a new type of institution after the manner of the German technical hockschule. The Cabinet accepted the principle in 1952 on the basis of a paper from Woolton but both the Treasury and the Ministry of Education were strongly opposed to these new institutions. The Ministry was anxious to develop local authority technical institutions. The impetus behind this move was eventually translated into action through the UGC to double the size of the Imperial College of Science and Technology (from 1,650 to 3,000 students) and to work out plans for the development of higher technological education in consultation with the universities in Leeds, Birmingham, Bristol, Cambridge and Sheffield and universities and colleges in Glasgow and Manchester.[9]

It was not surprising that in the years following the Second World War there was a tendency to look back to the developments that followed the end of the First and to expect something similar to happen again. To some extent this also occurred in considering likely demographic patterns and in producing erroneous population forecasts. In the universities, too, there was some expectation that numbers of students would fall considerably once the ex-servicemen had left just as had been the case a quarter of a century earlier. After the

1914–18 war the number of students in 1920 reached 48,000, by 1925 it had fallen to 41,000 and did not bounce up again. By 1949 there were 85,000 students and the lowest subsequent figure was 80,000 in 1953 – a decline of about 5½ per cent against a decline of 14 per cent earlier in the century. By 1957 the number had risen to 94,000. The decline from 1949 to 1953 had been the net result of a fall of 24,000 in ex-service students holding resettlement awards and an increase of 19,000 in other groups of students. Essentially this was the consequence of the increase in the number of pupils staying in the secondary schools beyond the compulsory school age and of the increase in the number of pupils achieving passes in the GCE examinations. The principal increases in the number of entrants were in science and technology with a considerable growth in the arts subjects – as may be seen from Table 5.3

The increase in the proportion of the 17–18 year age group which was staying at school and qualifying for admission to universities (the 'trend') continued to rise markedly in the later 1950s and into the 1960s when the actual size of the 17–18 age group itself began to increase following the rise in the birthrate at the end of and after the war (the 'bulge'). In 1950 the

Table 5.3   Full-time undergraduate students entering university for the first time

Faculties	Academic years		Increase (+) Decrease (−)	
	1953/54 No.	*1956/57* No.	No.	%
Arts	9,937	11,626	+1,689	+16.8
Pure Science	4,538	6,079	+1,541	+33.9
Technology	2,796	3,835	+1,039	+34.6
Medicine	2,614	2,472	− 142	− 5.4
Dentistry	477	736	+ 259	+54.3
Agric/Forestry	570	587	+ 17	+ 3.0
Veterinary Science	221	230	+ 9	+ 2.1
Total	21,153	25,565	+4,412	+20.9

Source: UGC, University Development, 1952–57, (Cmnd 534), 1958.

Treasury accepted that a considerable increase in the recurrent and capital grants would be necessary in order to permit a further modest increase in the number of places. The Financial Secretary to the Treasury told the Commons that the 84,000 students of 1955–6 would increase to 106,000 by the mid-1960s and that this would involve building much more accommodation. The rate of new building was to be more than doubled for the next three years. Even so, the Government felt that yet further expansion would be needed and was 'giving further thought to this' in consultation with the UGC.[10] In January 1957 the Chancellor of the Exchequer announced acceptance of a target of 135,000 places by 1966 and a larger programme of building projects in the 1960s. In a subsequent detailed statement at the beginning of 1958, Heathcote Amory, then Chancellor, announced a programme of £60 million of new building for the early 1960s and referred also to the possibility of larger ultimate expansion. He also made public the fact that the building programme envisaged building a University College of Sussex – the first of the new universities.[11]

In the first decade following the war the expansion had taken place in existing universities and university colleges. The university colleges at Nottingham, Southampton, Hull, Exeter and Leicester had all received their charters as full universities by 1957 – hitherto their students had taken external degrees of London University. The University College of North Staffordshire, which was set up in 1949, granted its own bachelors' degrees under the surveillance of an academic council which included representatives of the universities of Oxford, Birmingham and Manchester until it gained its Charter in 1962 as the University of Keele. The acceptability of the argument for the new university college in North Staffordshire had lain in the need for educational experiments – not in the expansion of student numbers. In 1946 the UGC considered the case for new universities as a way of handling the limited expansion that then seemed necessary. Among other places, Brighton, Bury St Edmunds, Kent, Carlisle, Coventry, Lancaster, Norwich, Salisbury and York were suggested as suitable sites. The claims of Norwich, York and Brighton were strongly pushed and deputations from these were received by the UGC early in 1947 but they were not successful. Nine of the existing university establishments still had fewer than one thousand students and the extreme shortages of building materials and scientific equipment – even of books – influenced the UGC in its decision. However, Brighton, Norwich and York were invited to maintain an interest in case conditions should change in the future.

With the increasing pressure for places and the need for further expansion conditions did begin to change in the years following 1955. W. G. Stone, Director of Education for the former County Borough of Brighton, had been a keen advocate of establishing a new university institution. In February 1956 he put forward a reasoned case for a Brighton foundation. In June the borough council recommended that a site at Stanmer be made available and promised financial support. In July the UGC received representatives from the five Sussex LEAs – East and West Sussex, Brighton, Eastbourne, and Hastings – who backed the proposal. At this stage the UGC decided that at least one new foundation would be required and that the Sussex plans were the only ones sufficiently advanced to make an early start possible. No further steps could be taken without Treasury agreement and that was forthcoming in February 1957 provided that the capital required could be fitted into the general programme and provided that the UGC was satisfied both with the plans as they evolved and with the likely measure of public support for the new university college.[12]

Sussex and other new institutions were given degree-granting powers from the outset. In all of these the establishment and maintenance of academic standards were initially to be the concern of an academic planning board which would also be responsible for drafting the charter, selecting the principal and professors in the main subjects and for considering the range of subjects to be studied. The academic planning board was to include persons of recognized academic standing – the chairman of the Sussex board was Sir James Duff, Warden of the Durham Colleges.[13] The UGC felt that the initial academic thrust in the new institutions should be in the fields of arts, social studies and pure science. Existing institutions could provide sufficient doctors, dentists, agriculturalists

and other strictly vocational student places. Extensive developments in the colleges of advanced technology as well as those in
engineering departments of existing universities led the UGC
to have reservations about the introduction of technology in the
new institutions.

When Keith Murray, Chairman of the UGC, met the
Committee of Vice-Chancellors and Principals towards the end
of 1959 he explained that given both the 'trend' and the
continuing high birthrate, the potential number of students
might be between 200,000 and 250,000 by the late 1970s. These
figures were based on about the same proportion of the
estimated 17–18 school leaver age group being regarded as
competent to undertake university studies; the Ministry of
Education saw no reason to expect that it would be a lower
proportion. The UGC had now concluded that there would
have to be more new institutions and had established a sub-
committee to consider the question of their whereabouts.
Active consideration was being given to Coventry, Gloucester/
Cheltenham, Thanet/Kent, York and Norwich.[14] The factors
which were considered in determining location were varied. In
view of the increasing importance of residence away from
home, lodgings and rail and road facilities became important
while proximity to a large population no longer mattered. The
adequacy of available sites – of at least 200 acres – was an
important factor, as was the extent of probable local financial
support from councils, industry and the like, the likely effects
on existing institutions and the availability of good lay
members for governing bodies.[15] In March 1960 the UGC
advised the Government to approve proposals in respect of
Norwich and York and in April the Government's approval
of these places was announced. Early in 1961 the Committee
advised acceptance of proposals in respect of Essex, Kent and
Warwick. The seventh recommendation was made a little later
and the government announced in November the foundation of
Lancaster University. An important factor in deciding to set up
a university at Lancaster was the argument that once students
had moved southwards they tended to stay in the south. This
was creating difficulties for industries and some professions in
the north.

A very important consideration in the decision to set up new universities instead of expanding existing institutions received no publicity. The need to provide for increased numbers could have been met by expanding the institutions already in existence. The additional stated reason for setting up new institutions was said to be the need for more experiment in the structure of degree courses, in teaching methods and in university organization. No doubt this was important but it is hardly adequate to explain the positive enthusiasm within the official side of the Treasury for expansion through setting up new institutions. The Financial Secretary at the time has since explained that officials believed that if you had to provide for an additional 2,000 students it would probably be cheaper to do so by setting up a new university than to expand an existing one – at least in capital terms. Certainly the cost of buying land in the central districts of large cities, demolishing existing build-ings and then building anew was a good deal greater than building on cheaper greenfield sites. But apart from this, officials argued that if an existing university were asked to move from, say, 3,000 to 5,000 students it would seek to build an entirely new library not just for the two thousand extra students but for all five thousand and the same could happen with other facilities.[16] In the event most of the additional students in the earlier 1960s had to be accommodated through expanding existing universities since the students needed places before the new universities could be built.

The growth in the total number of students was closely related to increasingly generous provision of student awards for undergraduates. At the end of the war the awards available to those who were not ex-servicemen remained much as they had been in 1939. About 300 state scholarships were awarded on the basis of Higher School Certificate results while LEAs each had their own schemes. Many of the awards they offered covered fees but often only part or even none of the cost of maintenance. The undergraduate was still expected to live at home with his parents and to attend a university within daily travelling distance. Many LEAs only paid part of an award in the form of a grant, the remainder – typically up to 50 per cent – was available as a loan to be repaid once the student had completed his course and started work. Entrance scholarships were also available on a competitive basis from universities and

colleges. In 1946 the state introduced university sup-
plemental awards which enabled students who won entrance
scholarships and exhibitions to have the value of their award
brought up to the level of state scholarships – which met fees
and full residential maintenance.[17] These new awards were a
great help for the endowed entrance awards offered by university bodies had not been increased in line with the fall in
the value of the currency and had in any case often been
inadequate.

Under pressure from the Ministry of Education most LEAs
undertook revisions of their award schemes in 1946 and the
outcome was to make much fuller provision for those who
gained the awards. This process of improvement with a certain
amount of persuasion of the more laggardly authorities by the
Ministry continued for the next 15 years. By 1951 about ⅕ of
their awards were calculated on a full maintenance basis. By
the end of the decade virtually all of their awards were on this
basis although some still advanced part of the sum involved as a
loan not a grant. As late as 1957 the Ministry had to approach
one of the largest LEAs, the West Riding, about its practice of
making loans to students and charging interest thereon.
Although this authority still did not drop loans at that time it
did cease from charging interest on loans granted after July
1957.[18] Thus the total number of awards from public sources at
universities rose steadily so that by 1960/61 21,500 new awards
were taken up. Within this total the great increase in provision
for residential maintenance led to a rapid decline in the
proportion living at home and even greater pressure for
residential places than the overall increase in student numbers
might suggest. At Leeds University, for instance, in 1938/39,
56.5 per cent of students lived at home, in 1950/51, 41.4 per
cent did so. The UGC commented in 1958 that the greater
mobility might eventually have one harmful effect in that the
best students would tend to be 'creamed off to a small number
of institutions'.[19] In retrospect this does not appear to have
become a problem; if a university is not known for strength in
one area, it usually has a strong reputation in some other which
draws able people to the institution as such.

The student grant position was thoroughly investigated by a
committee under the chairmanship of Colin Anderson which

after two years' work reported in 1960. It recommended that all those accepted for university first degree or comparable courses should receive awards from public funds provided that they had two passes at 'A' level and that a general duty be laid on award-making authorities to make such awards. The separate state scholarship scheme should end but whether central or local government should be the awarding body for the single scheme was left open. After consultation the Ministry announced that a Bill would be introduced placing a duty on LEAs to make awards to students taking first degree courses in accordance with regulations to be made by the Minister.[20] The Education Act of 1962 gave legislative effect to the recommendations of the Report. In introducing the measure's second reading, David Eccles said that 'perhaps nothing in the practice of past years has caused more discontent among students than the feeling that one local authority gave an award more easily than another'. The authorities themselves had accepted that the time had come to make the awards automatic. The real benefit, therefore, would be the certainty that once a student had been accepted for a degree course and had the qualifications, the award would be his 'by right'.[21]

THE ROBBINS REPORT

The decision to undertake rapid expansion of the university system and to set up the new universities had been taken well before the Robbins Report appeared. The sheer pressure of applicants had made itself felt very strongly. The Report of the Crowther Committee, *15 to 18*, was published in 1959 and this served to emphasize and publicize the problems caused for sixth forms of schools by the increasing difference between the number of pupils qualified to enter a university and those actually selected. The impression given by the documentation is that both the UGC and the CVCP fretted over the issue but lacked a sense of urgency. The chairman of the former body told the CVCP that in establishing the expansion target of 135,000 the Committee had considered that there was rather more room in the universities for competition for entry and it had therefore reduced the number of potential places quite substantially. There was now (1959), however, less certainty. Some argued that there should be places enough for the same proportion of sixth-formers in the future as in the past and pointed to the need for more graduates. 'On the other side there were those who felt that there was still a tail to be docked, and that the failure rate in some places was unduly high.'[22] In March 1960 the Commons debated the Crowther Report and an urgent pressure for more places found expression in the words of David Eccles as Minister of Education. The race to get to a university was doing great harm to the schools and 'many more university places must be made available.'[23] The facts which lay behind the Minister's comments are well illustrated by the figures in Table 5.4

Table 5.4 *Applications and admissions to British universities (excluding Oxford and Cambridge colleges), 1955–61*

Year	Applications	Admissions
1955	70,000	18,000
1959	134,000	20,300
1960	151,000	22,650
1961	190,000	25,000

Source: CVCP. Submission to Chancellor of Exchequer. Quinquennium 1962–67 (15 Dec. 1961).

The decisive factors in causing the Macmillan Government to set up the Robbins Committee were both the enormous increase in the number of secondary school pupils achieving the minimum standard or better for university admission and the increasing awareness of the lack of any coherent overall plan for the rapidly exploding higher education scene. A Treasury Minute in February 1961 contained the terms of reference of the Committee on Higher Education. It was to review the pattern of full-time higher education and to advise the government on what principles its long-term development should be based. 'In particular, to advise, in the light of these principles, whether there should be any changes in that pattern, whether any new types of institution are desirable and whether any modifications should be made in the present arrangements for planning and co-ordinating the development of the various types of institution.' The Committee carried out a most thorough review of all aspects of higher education in Great Britain – universities, teacher training institutions and much local authority further education – its report together with supporting volumes of evidence and statistics provides an enormous quarry of fact and opinion on higher education in the early 1960s. In retrospect the main significance of the Robbins Report[24] appears above all to have been the effect it had in securing for higher education a much more prominent position in the public and political consciousness. The Committee met at a time when it was able to take opinion in full flood. The very establishment of new universities stimulated the demand for further expansion. Edward Boyle who was Financial Secretary to the Treasury when the Committee began its work and was Minister of Education when its Report came out, has commented that in 1960 the nation had, possibly for the last time, a sense of stable ground, of increased mastery over circumstances. It seemed the right moment to seize the opportunities of an hour that was 'uniquely full of hope'. Such was the optimism that prevailed when the Robbins Committee started its work. By the time it reported, Britain had undergone the most severe economic set-back it had experienced since the war. The obvious consequence for higher education was that Treasury advice over the future of public expenditure became more cautious.[25]

Even so there was a widespread conviction that investment in higher education could be regarded as a special form of economic investment. In October 1962 the Conservative Party Conference called on the Government 'to invest in the future by a rapid and massive development of university and higher technological education'. In 1961, for the first time the UGC told the universities that they would no longer be expected to find any contribution out of their own resources to the new building programmes, these would be funded entirely out of government money. Thus when the main thrust of the Robbins Report was to increase greatly the number of student places it fitted perfectly with the prevailing mood even if some in the Treasury were already beginning to wonder if unit costs could not be reduced. The Committee believed that 350,000 places would be needed in universities by 1980, 210,000 in colleges of education and LEA institutions. Over the shorter term it recommended that 197,000 university places should be made available by 1967/68 – if necessary by taking emergency action – currently authorized places would have taken universities to 153,000 and Colleges of Advanced Technology (CATs) to a further 17,000 places. The Committee's basic axiom, which has since come to be referred to as the 'Robbins principle', was that courses of higher education should be available 'for all those who are qualified by ability and attainment to pursue them and who wish to do so'. This was not so very different from the statement of the Government's intentions seven years earlier when the Financial Secretary told the Commons that 'it is the Government's desire that all those boys and girls who have the mental and general abilities to profit by a university education shall get that opportunity'.[26] The Government announced its acceptance of the main thrust of the Report within 24 hours of its publication. It formally endorsed the Robbins principle and adopted the targets of places required down to 1973/74. These proposals were almost universally welcomed. The one steady source of public criticism was *The Times* which did not accept the premise that the number of places should be increased in line with the increase in the number of suitably qualified candidates. It feared for the maintenance of academic standards which were 'fated to take their place in subordination to the politically overriding aim of putting up numbers'. The paper continued to adhere firmly to the view that more meant worse.[27] *Education* was rather more perceptive in its comment that in the Report 'the principle of education according to age, ability and aptitude is carried through to its logical conclusion'.[28] By this time the great period of school building so as to provide a secondary education for all was drawing to a close and giving way to a period of higher education building partly to meet the very demand created by the growth of secondary schooling.

Apart from the issue of numbers and size, the Report made important recommendations on the structure of higher education. It recommended that the UGC should take responsibility for the whole teacher training sector, the colleges being funded through the universities to which they were affiliated. As the

Chancellor of the Exchequer was unwilling to continue to act as the spending minister for higher education as expenditure grew, the Committee considered this issue and argued strongly against this responsibility passing to the Ministry of Education – which wanted it – and recommended a Ministry of Arts and Science to which both the UGC and the Research Councils would report. It maintained that the disadvantages of subjection to the Controller and Auditor General were such that universities should continue to be exempted from his ministrations. It proposed the creation of a series of new institutions for scientific and technological education, that six more new universities should be set up – one in Scotland – and that the ten direct grant colleges of advanced technology should become technological universities. In order to facilitate the growth of work at first degree level in the local authority sector it proposed that the National Council for Technological Awards should be replaced by a Council for National Academic Awards (CNAA) with its own charter.

The Government statement accepting the Robbins recommendations on numbers was much more cautious on these structural proposals. The 'lead' ministry in formulating government policy in response to Robbins – apart from the Treasury for some aspects – was the Ministry of Education and some of these recommendations were not acceptable there. The granting of charters to the CATs caused no official difficulty since it had already been thought that these institutions would be encouraged to develop into technological universities. The only new university to be founded was that in Scotland, at Stirling. The need for a CNAA administering degree courses for students in local authority institutions had also come to be accepted and the Government welcomed the recommendation as aiding it along a road it wished to follow. There was no undertaking to do more than consider the more major structural proposals. Two of these met with strong opposition from education interests outside the universities who did not want to see separate ministers handling higher education and school education and many of whom did not wish to see the colleges of education leave the local authority sector. The second of these points has already been discussed in chapter 3. Most of the arguments advanced in favour of one minister rather than two centred on the case for one ministry to be in a position to balance the developments in the education service as a whole. Although it was not usually expressed in this way, a good deal of the fear of the universities at being made subject to the one education ministry lay in the feeling that there were far more voters with a direct interest in seeing as much as possible spent on the schools and on further education than there would ever be with any comparable direct interest in universities. The local authority pressure groups whose influence was well established in the Ministry of Education would also scarcely be supportive of the universities' claim on any available resources when they had their own institutions to think about.

In the event the University Grants Committee (UGC) became constitutionally an advisory committee of the education ministry – the Minister taking the rather grander title of Secretary of State for Education and Science. The pressure of senior civil servants within the Ministry was strongly in favour of this and the permanent secretary of the time, Herbert Andrew, did not hesitate to employ quite a powerful political argument in support of his case in a minute to the Minister. 'To have separate ministries for separate kinds of educational institutions would appear to many people to be recognizing a social division which we no less than the opposition believe must disappear, . . . undergraduates are still overwhelmingly middle class in origin. Whether or not natural ability enters into this, there is no doubt that family and social background still have a very large part to play.'[29] In an effort to allay university concern, the idea of a federal ministry was put to a group of ministers by Lawrence Helsby, by then head of the civil service. The first Secretary of State was Quintin Hogg (Lord Hailsham) while Edward Boyle continued in charge of the traditional ministry business as a Minister of State and kept his seat in the Cabinet. This attempted federal arrangement did not last long and after a few months the DES resumed the unitary pattern which it still has. The views of the first Secretary of State apparently diverged rather from those of his bureaucracy. Hailsham felt that however logically appealing it might be, practically the unification of university responsibility with the rest of education was an error. He described the argument that if this decision were not taken there would be higher and lower education which would operate to the detriment of the schools as 'basically a nonsense argument since the differences between school, further and degree standard education will continue to exist whoever is responsible for their organization'.[30]

The Government's decision to accept the Robbins student targets down to 1973/74 meant there was a need for great urgency in expanding the number of places within four years. The burden of additional and more rapid expansion was bound to fall on existing universities simply because there was no time for any additional foundations to absorb students so quickly. Thus the existing 170,000 target for existing universities by 1973 had to be brought forward to 1967. Emergency measures were taken to speed up the building programme. Even so, much improvisation and overcrowding were inevitable. The provision of living accommodation for the additional students proved to be especially difficult in some cases. Such factors as the relative costs of expansion and the state of readiness of each university's plans for the buildings proposed and the likelihood of their being started and completed on time were important considerations for the UGC in deciding which offer of expansion it should accept. The Secretary of State announced the additions to the capital programme in the Commons in May 1964. The last day of March was estimated as the latest possible time to start any building for additional places in 1967/68. If the target for the CATs is added, the new target for 1967/68 became 197,000 – an expansion of 60 per cent over 6 years. In the autumn term 1967 the total of full-time students had risen to 200,287. The short-term Robbins target, intended to meet the emergency of the 'bulge', had been met.

POLITICAL AND ECONOMIC DIFFICULTIES

From the later 1960s an increasing number of difficulties arose as national expectations appeared likely to outrun any probable increase in the rate of growth of the gross national product. At a meeting held between Shirley Williams, Minister of State for Higher Education, the UGC and some Vice-Chancellors the DES produced statistics which showed that by 1981 the number of university places would have to be increased to 450,000 if 1963 principles regarding the percentage of school leavers gaining admission were still to be adhered to. The four possible measures for bridging the gap that were put forward are worth noticing here since in some form they were to recur either as suggestions or in practice. They were

(1)   to abandon the Robbins 2 'A' level minimum qualification for school leavers – but this was seen as raising massive political problems;
(2)   limiting the scale of government financial support to universities and leaving them to solve the problem;
(3)   imposing cuts in unit costs per student;
(4)   reducing the entry by cutting student support and by a more restrictive policy on overseas students.

Possible ways of reducing costs were also discussed including the reduction of post-graduate support so as to diminish the number of such students, two-year degree courses for able students, more home-based students, the sharing of facilities between adjacent institutions and the reduction of staff/student ratios.

The most significant change has been the large cut imposed at the insistence of the Treasury on unit costs. Since 1972 the unit of resource has been reduced by about 25 per cent in real terms. The technical means of doing this has been by not adjusting fully for inflation and by not reducing the number of students in line with cuts in the real size of grant-aid made available. Those concerned with university finance in the Treasury have remained convinced that staff/student ratios are unjustifiably generous.[31] Economies have also been achieved by reducing the number of post-graduate places. In the White Paper, *Education: A Framework for Expansion*, the quinquennial settlement for 1972–77 was linked to a figure of 306,000 full-time students by 1976/77. This was 10,000 fewer than the working hypothesis of the UGC and was to be achieved by leaving the number of undergraduates envisaged virtually unchanged but by cutting 10,000 from the post-graduate numbers proposed.[32]

The attempt to economize by restricting provision for

overseas students, the issues which this have roused and the conflict which surrounds the matter has been especially marked recently. The phenomenon of rising expectations which played such an important part in stimulating the desire for university education in this country was even more marked in very many overseas countries following the ending of the colonial era. The need for far more qualified professional people in the developing countries led to a considerable increase in the number of overseas students in British universities. The educational, legal, commercial and cultural framework built up in colonial days led the students from the former colonies to seek their higher education in British rather than in any other European universities. During the years 1957 to 1962 there was an increase of 3,000 overseas students, mainly from Commonwealth countries so that in 1961/62 there was a total of 13,000 full-time and 4,000 part-time students. A considerable proportion of these students were post graduates (46.9 per cent). While only 7.4 per cent of the total number of undergraduate students came from overseas, the proportion of overseas students among post graduates was as high as 31.5 per cent. The attraction of the graduate schools was particularly noticeable at certain institutions, at the Imperial College of Science and Technology just over 50 per cent of the post graduates were from overseas while the Postgraduate Medical Federation of London University had just under 3,000 students of whom two-thirds were from overseas. The contemporary official attitude to these students as expressed by the UGC was one of encouragement, the Committee 'welcome the fact that this growth has accompanied the general expansion of the universities'.[33]

In planning the expansion of the universities, the UGC had from the end of the war until the Robbins Report in 1963 made provision for an increase in the number of overseas students proportionate to the total increase. During the emergency period following Robbins, Wolfenden, then chairman of the UGC, asked Vice-Chancellors to restrain the entry of overseas students in order to accommodate the 'bulge' of home undergraduates. At a subsequent meeting with the CVCP, he returned to this issue and asked whether members felt that there should be a restoration of overseas numbers fairly quickly after 1967 and this was strongly welcomed by the Vice-Chancellors.[34] The number of full-time students did in fact continue to grow and by 1975 it had reached 31,000 in spite of differentially higher fees being imposed from 1967. The home fee at the time stood at £70 and was little more than nominal – indeed the Prime Minister, Harold Wilson, had spoken of abolishing it completely. Four days before Christmas, 1966, Anthony Crosland, the Secretary of State, announced in a written answer that 'faced with rising costs of higher and further education', the Government had decided to impose an increase in fees for overseas students from £70 to £250. The Conservatives forced a debate on the issue in the Commons the following February and there were widespread protests, but differential fees remained and the overseas fees increased considerably in real terms during the succeeding twelve years.[35]

The imposition of so-called full-cost fees after the return to office of the Conservative Party in the 1979 election has had a much more drastic effect on the admission of overseas students – especially those from the poorer developing countries. In its search for economies the Treasury has withdrawn all grant aid for university places occupied by overseas students. So as to ensure that the general unit of resource for home students is maintained the DES has enforced minimum full-cost fees related to the average – not the marginal – cost of providing a place for a student. Thus the minimum annual tuition fee for an arts-based course has risen to £2,700 and for a science-based course to £3,600 while the medical student's fee has reached £6,600. This is not the place nor is it yet the time to examine in detail the origins of these policies or to estimate their total effect. In 1962 the UGC had stated that 'the presence of these students in our universities is of mutual benefit; we are confident it is to our advantage' and there can be no doubt that the universities are now considerable losers. The extent to which the nation will lose in commercial and cultural terms will become clearer in due course – presumably the estimates of this made in the Foreign Office and in the Treasury are very different.

The world-wide economic crisis which was triggered by the OPEC increase in the price of oil at the end of 1973 has helped to intensify the mood of doubt, disillusion and questioning which has beset the nation for the last decade. At a time when the established institutions are all suffering from public lack of confidence – the political, financial and commercial systems as much as the educational – it is inevitable that institutions as rapid to reflect the current mood as universities should themselves be the objects of criticism and experience a lack of public support.

Although it may seem less significant in retrospect, one of the issues which did play an important part in changing the public attitudes from being generally supportive and benign to a more critical view was undoubtedly the brief phase of student militancy in 1968 and 1969. In Britain this was nothing like as severe or widespread as in the United States and some other European countries, but it did undoubtedly cause feelings of bewilderment and even of outrage among the general public. The causes of this outburst of student revolt were very mixed. In most of the countries concerned there was a 'bulge' in the age group, much larger numbers were coming through the universities, accommodation and facilities had too often become overcrowded and even squalid in spite of efforts to provide more. The university – and higher education systems generally – had not fully adjusted to accept the idea of the student estate becoming as much involved as many students now wished it to be involved in the operation and management of their colleges and universities.

In their study, *The Rise of the Student Estate in Britain,* Sir Eric Ashby and Mary Anderson suggested that in an empirical sense this phase of student militancy was due to a confluence of three circumstances. Firstly, the presence of students' organizations which mobilized and media which publicized corporate opinion; secondly, the presence of issues worth protesting about, some of which were outside the universities, and thirdly the emergence and use of 'novel and effective techniques of protest'. This latter proved especially important in attracting public attention and in upsetting persons in senior positions who found it outrageous that students who were supported by the state should devote their time and energy to disruption. The Committee of Vice-Chancellors and Principals (CVCP) held a two-day meeting at Cambridge in June 1968 to deliberate on the matter and the first session was devoted to hearing rather dismal accounts from some members of what had happened in their institutions. In one university the council meeting had been blockaded and several members had been held by the ankles by 'liers-in' when they tried to leave the meeting, the occupation of administrative buildings was apparently fairly common. A Maoist group was reported to be causing trouble in another university; the Vice-Chancellor had held two secret meetings with them but had got nowhere and feared continuing difficulty. The police seemed generally reluctant to intervene and in one university there was a demand to participate in the choice of the next Vice-Chancellor; other sessions were devoted to inconclusive discussions on discipline and participation.

The discussion showed that the field of student participation was being widened. There was a clear division on the issue of student membership of Senate. The majority opposed to it felt that some other universities had already sold the pass by accepting it.[36]

The degree of public interest and concern which the militant outbreak aroused may be judged from the attention which a Commons Select Committee gave it. This carried out extensive inquiries and travelled to various universities and colleges gathering evidence. The recommendations of the Select Committee were generally sensible and practical. Those which were concerned with student participation and representation on the Council and Senate of universities soon came to be implemented – really because of the pressure of events themselves. On the other hand the rather grand proposal for a Higher Education Commission with statutory powers to provide guidance and coordination for all institutions of higher education came to nothing.[37] The two main consequences of this episode of student turbulence were to weaken the public and political standing of the universities and to bring the student body more participation in the internal affairs of universities.

The quinquennial system of announcing grant aid for five-year periods with some subsequent adjustment for inflation was ended by the state after 1973 under the impact of the first oil price crisis. Since then long-term planning has been difficult. Although there was steady pressure on their unit costs the universities managed more or less to maintain their position until the end of the 1970s. The professed desire of the new government to reduce public expenditure led it to follow a policy of actually reducing the number of places in the universities at a time when the number of qualified 18-year-old students was still rising. The grant to universities has been reduced over a period of three years to 1984. The intention is that this lower level of grant provision should then be maintained in 1984/85.[38] The degree of loss of political and public support for universities may perhaps be judged by setting this reduction in government finance against the considerable increase in public expenditure in real terms since 1979. As a proportion of the gross domestic product public expenditure increased in the three years (1979–82) from 36 to 44 per cent.

One development with which the UGC was not concerned was the foundation of the Open University. It owes its origins partly to the circumstances of the early 1960s – developments in the provision of educational broadcasting and in adult education as well as the current enthusiasm for university level education. It was really Harold Wilson who saw the technical possibility of offering a form of instruction at university level to all those who had missed out for some reason. The political objective of promoting the spread of egalitarianism in education was particularly enticing and the whole project fitted in with the invocation at the time of the 1964 election of the white hot technological revolution which was going to speed up economic development and make everyone much better off. Jennie Lee took responsibility for the project in the Labour administration and a White Paper issued in February 1966 outlined the appeal and suggested the way and means of setting up the University of the Air, as it was then called. Quite apart from television and radio lectures, there were to be correspondence courses 'of a quality unsurpassed anywhere in the world'. The university would provide higher and further education 'without requiring vast capital sums to be spent on bricks and mortar'. Departmental responsibility for the University of the Air should rest with the DES rather than with the UGC.[39]

The first programmes to be set up were undergraduate ones with the general pattern of a multidisciplinary foundation course followed by a further six credits for an ordinary or eight for an honours degree. Two credits per year are regarded as the equivalent of full-time study. By 1981 of some 150,000 students admitted, 45,000 had graduated, 45,000 had left without graduating and 60,000 were still in the University. More than half are thought to have studied simply for the sake of studying and not with any vocational purpose. In recent years the number of graduations has been stable at about 6,000. In the last few years the Open University has also been developing courses in continuing education sometimes lasting only eight weeks with titles such as 'Energy in the home', 'Consumer Choices' and the like.[40] The Open University has been unique and imaginative in the lines of development that it has employed and has undoubtedly brought opportunities to very many who would otherwise have been denied them.

CHAPTER 6

Further Education

The term further education is very broad indeed and can cover both classes to improve literacy and elementary arithmetic in school leavers and post-graduate work. The institutions are extremely varied and staff are needed with a wide range of differing qualifications. Further education is always post-school and outside the universities; it is usually, but not always, provided by LEAs. Before 1944 LEAs had had the power to supply various forms of further education usually under such descriptive terms as technical education, day continuation schools and evening institutes. The 1944 Act laid down the duty of every LEA to secure the provision for its area of adequate facilities for further education, 'that is to say:

(1)   full-time and part-time education for persons over compulsory school age; and
(2)   leisure-time occupation, in such organized training and recreative activities as are suited to their requirements, for any persons over compulsory school age who are able and willing to profit by the facilities provided for that purpose.'[1]

The main priority in developing the wartime plans for reconstructing the educational system was inevitably given to reorganizing and reshaping the schools. In some ways the lower priority therefore accorded in fact – though not by conscious intent – to further education was a carry-over from the pre-war period when the President of the Board described facilities for technical education as 'a matter of serious concern both from the industrial and social points of view' in a Cabinet memorandum.[2] The reference to further education in the White Paper *Educational Reconstruction* in 1943 produced

163

complaints of inadequacy both internally from HMIs in the Board and from the press and public. The criticism had some impact as may be seen by comparing financial provision for technical education in the financial memorandum which accompanied the education bill on publication with that in the 1943 White Paper. The additional funds to be spent in the seven years following the war are now shown as £35,000,000 against the earlier figure of £2,490,000. In 1946 less than one-twentieth of LEA expenditure was on further education, but a quarter of a century later this had increased to one-fifth.

THE PERCY COMMITTEE AND THE HIVES COUNCIL

When the war in Europe ended a major inquiry into the future shape of higher technological education was still incomplete. It fell to Lord Percy to present the findings and recommendations of his committee to Ellen Wilkinson by then Minister in September 1945. The committee's report was written largely in terms of the requirements of engineering rather than of any other industry. Percy felt that, given the composition of his committee, it would not have commanded confidence if it had ventured much beyond the field of engineering. The recommendations foreshadowed the developments of the next decade and included the setting up of regional advisory councils to bring together the LEAs and other parties concerned with technical education in each region and the selection of a limited number of colleges in which technological courses of degree standard should be developed. There were serious differences of opinion within the committee on the question of whether a proposed National Council of Technology should have power to award a bachelor of technology degree or a diploma in technology.[3]

The Ministry believed that if the planning of technical education facilities was to take place on a reasonable basis it was essential to bring LEAs together for this purpose. It would be quite impossible for each authority to make provision for its own needs independently. The Percy Committee's proposal for regional advisory councils on the general lines of those that had grown up between the wars in a few regions – the earliest of which was that in Yorkshire – were incorporated with little alteration in a circular issued in February 1946. Ten of these were proposed including one for Wales. Representation on the councils should include LEAs, universities, technical colleges, industry and commerce. There would need to be one or more executive or subcommittees for handling the day-to-day work of a council as well as industrial advisory committees. The regional councils' functions were to include contact with industry, planning new developments and any expansion of existing facilities, reviewing courses and curricula, advising on financial arrangements for 'out-county' students and arranging for the use of specialist staff and facilities.[4]

The need for adequate regional machinery and many of the other shortcomings in the existing provision – as well as some of the problems likely to be met in overcoming them – may be illustrated from the report of a meeting in Newcastle which Bray, the Under Secretary in charge of the F.E. Branch, had with chief education officers of the Northern Region in the spring of 1948. Bray pointed out that many felt that advanced technical education should be taken away from LEAs and left entirely to the universities. The Ministry did not share that view but it could only defend the authorities if they had sound schemes of further education. Currently facilities were 'pretty poor'. The Ministry found it impossible to seek resources if authorities didn't put forward schemes. It had sought £6 million for F.E. priorities but authorities had only taken up £4 million. On organization, the big regional colleges should concentrate on advanced courses and the local colleges on more elementary work and on preparing students to go on to the regional colleges. Bray emphasized that if the region had had 'free trade' (i.e. free movement of students for courses from one LEA to another) it would have greatly facilitated planning. The clash between larger and smaller authorities came out clearly in the discussion where education officers from smaller authorities spoke of their fears that they would lose their good advanced courses to the bigger centres. Bray seems to have been pushed into suggesting that even if the regional council had on one occasion decided to withdraw a course from an authority it would have to replan after about five years to keep up with fluctuating situations so there would be the hope that the loss would not be permanent.[5] The issues which arose at Bray's meeting no doubt helped to explain the lateness of some authorities in submitting the schemes of further education required under the 1944 Act. The latest date set for these was 31 March 1948. Even by the end of 1948 only 59 out of 146 schemes had been received at the Ministry. By the end of 1949 the majority had arrived, 119, with only another 37 still outstanding.

In 1948 the Minister set up the National Advisory Council on Education for Industry and Commerce (NACEIC). Two years later it submitted a report on *The Future Development of Higher Technological Education*. A good deal of the early part of the report was devoted to attempting to discover and define differences between the functions of higher technological education in Ministry of Education supported institutions and the Treasury supported universities but without any clear difference emerging. It was clear that the technical colleges would need to produce more technologists at about the graduate level to meet the requirements of industry. The Council repeated many of the Percy Committee's recommendations – the need for a national body of high standing to validate courses leading to prestigious awards, also for radical improvements in the staffing, financing and housing of the colleges to enable them to develop such courses. The main conclusions were that the Minister should consider more generous financial aid to authorities running colleges with advanced work and that a 'Royal College of Technologists' should be set up to validate courses and to make awards. The principal award should not be a degree 'which would not receive the support of the universities' but an Associateship at the first level with a Mastership at the second level and a Fellowship at the highest level.[6]

The Ministry undertook the usual round of consultations and by August 1951 had decided to implement immediately the main recommendations of the National Advisory Council. In September it issued a White Paper promising details of higher grants for advanced work 'very shortly' and to arrange for the establishment of a College of Technologists. The Ministry had already had a hard fight to get agreement to these from the Treasury. As early as 1 August Bray wrote from the Ministry to

Alexander that there had been 'a bit of a struggle with the Treasury on the question of percentage grant'. The final decision was 75 per cent for advanced courses, not the 80 per cent 'you asked for'. Further resistance developed at the last minute and the White Paper had to omit the precise percentage. The new grant was in fact offered from 1952.[7]

There was a much more extended interval before any progress was made towards setting up a validating and award-granting body and the change of political control did not help. In his letter of August Bray had said that the term 'Royal' would have to be omitted from College of Technologists and its functions would have to be more limited than had been suggested by NACEIC. Bray himself was disappointed at having to modify the recommendations of the Advisory Council, but the College would have a royal charter and 'if we are careful in drafting the Charter, we might eventually get everything that the Council recommended'. The attitude of Lord Cherwell as ministerial 'Overlord' for technological education in the Churchill ministry strengthened the hands of those opposed to the development of higher level work in the colleges. There was increasing concern among local authorities over the delay. Authorities had feared that they would see advanced work removed from them to the university sector. The 1951 White Paper assuaged this fear, but delay brought back doubts once more. Moreover as the London County Council Education Officer explained, while government might increase grants and LEAs might try to establish advanced courses, 'we shall never attract students into these courses until we are in a position to award academic qualifications . . . at least comparable to a degree'.[8]

Early in 1953 most of the local authority and teachers' associations sought to send a deputation to the minister to express their misgivings and regret that the proposals in the White Paper had not all been implemented and it appeared that the establishment of a Royal College had been abandoned. The National Advisory Council had itself sought an interview to express similar sentiments at about this time and in replying to Alexander's letter seeking a ministerial interview, Gilbert Flemming – the new Permanent Secretary – sent a copy of the notes of the NACEIC's meeting with Kenneth Pickthorn, the

Parliamentary Secretary (substituting for Florence Horsburgh, the Minister). Pickthorn made it clear that while the Ministry had no doubt as to the urgent need for a suitable validating body and a prestigious award, there was opposition to setting up a Royal College of Technologists with the constitution and functions suggested. He asked the NACEIC to look at their proposal again in the light of the difficulties that had arisen and bring forward alternative suggestions. On being pressed the Ministry's representatives agreed that 'something must be done and done within the next six months or so'. Since there was no hope of reconciling opponents to the idea of a Royal College, the only way was to consider some alternative and *'in doing so make it very clear that whatever was proposed was related solely to the Technical Colleges'*. In his letter to Alexander, Flemming suggested that the associations should await the outcome of this new effort rather than send a deputation themselves. If the NACEIC could come up with some suitable alternative to the existing proposal, 'we here will certainly do our best to get it accepted'.[9]

The task of the NACEIC was therefore to narrow their proposal sufficiently to prevent it from upsetting other governmental, university and professional associations of various groups of engineers. The debate over the proposal from Lords Woolton and Cherwell to set up technological institutes at university level which the Cabinet had accepted was being fought to a standstill in the official mechanism during succeeding months – as discussed in chapter 5 – and by early 1955 the Ministry was ready to begin consultations on the NACEIC's new and narrower proposals. By September 1954 the National Advisory Council had submitted proposals for a National Council for Awards in Technology at Technical Colleges. It was merely to create awards and to administer them. The change of ministers apparently helped in further education as in the schools and the impression of struggling merely to stand still which was perhaps typical of the Ministry in Florence Horsburgh's period of office gave way to a greater purposefulness. By July 1955 Bray was able to write to Alexander telling him that 'at last we have found a chairman for the new award making body'. Lord Hives, chairman and joint managing director of Rolls-Royce, undertook the duties and the forerunner of the CNAA did indeed come to be known familiarly as the Hives Council. The establishment of this Council – its title was soon shortened to National Council for Technological Awards – marked the end of the main battle between those who felt the nation's need for technologists would only be met by upgrading certain colleges into technological universities and those who wanted to keep some of this provision in the local authority sector, even though some of the issues involved were to reappear at the time of the Robbins Report and in the enthusiasm of some Ministry officials for the binary policy in higher education.

Outside the area of higher technological education some progress had been made. Although the number of full-time students in 1956 was still only 76,000 at least that was a considerable increase on the 45,000 of 1946. The number of part-time day, evening and evening institute students had increased over the same period from 1,550,000 to 2,173,000. Although the requirement to set up county colleges on a compulsory day continuation basis for all who left school before the age of 18 was never put into effect, the growth in the number of students meant that many further education facilities were fully stretched. While there was pressure from the Ministry encouraging authorities to plan their provision on the basis of concentrating advanced work in regional colleges with area and local colleges dealing with more elementary courses, individual authorities, anxious to exercise their autonomy tended to make their own plans with too little regard to the availability of similar courses nearby. Thus while a good deal had been done by the mid-1950s, it did not necessarily form a coherent overall pattern.

THE WHITE PAPER, 1956

Early in 1956 the Government issued a White Paper on *Technical Education* which set out a pattern and a programme of development for the next five years with a capital investment of £70 million over the years 1956 to 1961. The first objective was to be to increase output from advanced courses from 9,500 to 15,000 each year. Twenty-four colleges were receiving grant at the enhanced 75 per cent rate and most of the expansion was expected in these. The second main objective was to double the number of day-release students which was then about 355,000 and to this end the Minister of Labour was pressing forward with apprenticeship schemes. The need for inter-authority cooperation and planning was stressed and the White Paper also discussed a number of other issues including the supply of teachers and the need for every college to have a library. The comparatively small proportion of girls continuing in technical eduation beyond the age of 18 led the White Paper to scotch the notion that by 'aiming at a certificate they may miss a husband' and agreed that 'far more often than not the knowledge and experience that come from studying for a better job help her to build her own family on foundations of common interests and understanding'.[10]

More detail of the new pattern was given in a subsequent circular. Local colleges were then offering vocational courses, mainly part-time, up to Ordinary National Certificate. Area colleges also offered some work above ONC standard, mainly of a part-time nature. Regional colleges were those doing a substantial amount of advanced work, especially full-time and sandwich courses. Finally the circular went on to describe the new class of colleges of advanced technology. These would provide a broad range and substantial volume of work at advanced level including some post-graduate and research work. An appendix set out conditions that had to be met before recognition as a CAT would be given and included a governing body representative of industry, the universities and professional interests as well as of those LEAs which regularly contributed students; the governors had to have freedom to spend within the agreed heads of annual estimates, the staff should include those suitable for work of university standard while accommodation would have to include adequate library provision, staff work rooms, private study and union facilities for students and enough residential accommodation for each student to spend at least one year in residence. In a debate in the Commons on the day the circular was issued, Michael Stewart for the Labour opposition argued that CATs should not be under local authority control but be supported by the UGC. Eccles admitted this issue was finely balanced, but felt the LEAs should be given the chance to see whether they could make a success of building these colleges up to something like university status. The Minister went on to name eight colleges which were to become CATs – the colleges of technology of Birmingham, Bradford, Cardiff and Loughborough; the Royal Technical College at Salford; and Battersea, Chelsea and Northampton Polytechnics in London. He added that two more were 'on the horizon' one in the North-East and one in Bristol.[11]

If the new CATs and advanced technological education generally were to remain with LEAs the Minister made it clear that much more regional coordination would be necessary. Consent should be given automatically to students attending courses outside their own authority for attendance at any course except in special cases where an authority still felt it desirable that a student should obtain prior consent and the regional advisory council should be informed of the exceptions.[12] Among the other steps taken at this time to give a new impetus to further education and to bring nearer the fulfilment of the developments the White Paper had envisaged was the improvement of salary scales and of general conditions of teachers. The Burnham Technical Committee duly responded with a very considerable increase from 1 October 1956. A committee was appointed under the chairmanship of Dr Willis Jackson to report on the supply and training of teachers for technical colleges. The Ministry's building development group undertook work on the design of further education colleges. The number of technical state scholarships was increased from 120 to 150 and negotiations were undertaken with the Federation of British Industries with a view to settling financial arrangements so as to encourage a large increase in the number of sandwich courses.

By the autumn of 1957 Bristol College of Technology and the Rutherford Technical College, Newcastle upon Tyne, had also been promised designation as CATs as soon as their volume of full-time and sandwich work had been built up to an adequate level. By this time five more institutions had been recognized for the higher rate of grant and had come within the description of 'regional colleges'. Building programmes for four years had been approved which contained 320 projects – 17 relating to

CATs, 35 to regional colleges, 146 to area colleges and 118 to local colleges. About half of the LEAs had put into force the recommendation for free movement of students to courses in other areas without prior consent of their home authority. Applications for recognition of 123 courses leading to the Diploma in Technology had been made to the Hives Council; 49 had been recognized, 34 had been rejected while the remaining courses were still under consideration.[13]

The publication of the Crowther Report, *15 to 18,* in 1959 had a considerable influence on developments in further education. Its recommendations derived from the principle that there should be an alternative road open for all young people who wished to continue their education outside the traditional academic approach through grammar schools and higher education. After the compulsory school age had been raised between 1966 and 1969, county college attendance should be made compulsory in one or two areas with compulsion then being made general gradually, region by region. The Crowther Committee put forward as a long-term aim that 50 per cent of the 16 to 18 age group should be in full-time education by 1979 – against only 12 per cent in 1959. In future there should be more consistent provision for the technician, craftsman and operative grades, a closer relationship between apprenticeship and further education, more day release for girls and the use of block release wherever possible with less dependence on evening classes.

These recommendations produced a quick response from the Ministry which undertook immediate consultations and then put forward its proposals in a White Paper, *Better Opportunities in Technical Education.*[14] The main proposals were that students should start at a technical college immediately after leaving school instead of taking preliminary courses in evening institutes with a frequently heavy drop-out rate; more care should be taken in the selection of students for courses, and colleges should experiment with full-time induction courses and more tutorial work. The Ordinary National Certificate (ONC) course should last two, instead of three, years with a higher standard of entry. There were to be new courses for technicians, designed specifically for their needs and with an entry requirement of the satisfactory completion of a five year course in a secondary school. There were to be more and better courses for operatives and for craft apprentices. The White Paper urged that more time should be provided under day release schemes and that no student should have to rely exclusively on evening study.

The very complexity of the further education system and of the problems facing it were fully recognized by the Crowther Committee. It followed that there could be no clear-cut solutions and the White Paper's proposals confirmed this. The most that the Ministry could really do was to urge and press others to follow along the paths suggested and to see that the resources were available to do so. The NACEIC established a special committee on the Crowther Report to examine the practical consequences of carrying out the recommendations. To give its conclusions wide circulation and to emphasize the main points the Ministry issued a circular early in 1963 summarizing these and giving its comments on them. The NACEIC's report was attached.

In retrospect it is clear that the efforts made to press forward the development of further education from the time of the White Paper in 1956 to the Robbins Report did have a major impact on the nature of further education. The number of full-time and sandwich course students rose from 76,000 to 184,000 and the number of part-time day students rose from 469,000 to 613,000 – increases of 142 and 30 per cent respectively. On the other hand the number of part-time evening students in both colleges and evening institutes only rose from 1,704,000 to 1,854,000, or by 8.8 per cent. The number of full-time teaching staff employed increased from 12,000 to 28,000.

The introduction of the general or block grant system after 1958 under which education grants from the Government to local authorities ended and local authority activities received any support only through Ministry of Housing and Local Government grants meant that the former definition of regional colleges as those receiving advanced technology grant was no longer applicable. The Ministry therefore undertook a review of the existing list of regional colleges in order to designate a revised list. The criteria for admission to the list were specified under four headings.

(1)   The college had to have a sufficient volume of advanced work as judged by the range and number of courses and students along with adequate facilities for research.
(2)   There had to be sufficient staff with high qualifications for teaching advanced courses.
(3)   The premises had to be suitable for advanced technical education and for dealing with full-time and sandwich course students.
(4)   The arrangements for the government of the college had to conform with the minister's recommendations regarding the composition and powers of governing bodies and there ought also to be advisory committees for the major departments of the college.

Before drawing up the revised list the Ministry circulated to each regional advisory council particulars of existing regional and other colleges which might appear to have had a *prima facie* case to be put on the list and sought their comments thereon.[15]

CATs

These steps to prepare a revised list of regional colleges were taken in the spring of 1961. By that time these colleges were on the point of becoming the most senior institutions in the local authority sector for the CATs were shortly to be removed and given direct grant status. When he addressed the AEC conference the Minister, David Eccles, set out his thoughts on this – having taken care to send the draft of his speech to the Association's Secretary a week earlier. His speech reviewed the success of further education policy since 1956 and the extent of the achievement of the LEAs. He went on to speak of the 'unstinting' support LEAs had given to the CATs, all of which made him sure that his decision to leave the CATs with the authorities in 1956 had been right. But the very success of the colleges had raised new problems. Good standards at undergraduate level had been established. The development of postgraduate work required close coordination with universities. Moreover there was an urgent need for suitable staff, especially in the senior posts and this was a question of status as well as of pay. Possibly, too, the time had come for the CATs to give their own degrees instead of the externally-validated Dip. Tech. Eccles thought most of these were matters for the Robbins Committee but one step the Government did propose to take at once – to give the CATs a new status under independent governing bodies receiving direct grant from the Ministry. This would give recognition to the way in which they had grown from local into national institutions and therefore their governing bodies should reflect this by being fully independent.[16]

There had already been private discussions with LEAs that maintained the CATs and those in membership of the AEC did not object. But if the AEC had no objection, the County Councils Association did and sought a meeting of local authority associations to organize joint opposition. At the meeting – which also included representatives from each LEA with a CAT – the only opposition came from London County Council whose doubts the CCA representatives said they shared. The maintaining authorities other than London all believed that the arguments outlined by the Minister were decisive. Special reference was made to the impossibility of the colleges acquiring status equal to that of the universities so long as their governing bodies were sub-committees of an authority. Special reference was also made to the difficulties of these authorities in meeting the initial capital investment necessary to carry out the large extension programme for the colleges. With the exception of London, which reserved its position, it was agreed by all parties that the Minister's proposal be accepted.[17]

The new status was in fact to last only four or five years but they formed an important stage in the development of the CATs since these were the years when resources were relatively freely available and the institutions had direct access to their sponsoring ministry. In some ways it might have been more logical to await the recommendations of the Robbins Committee – as the LCC argued – but if that committee recommended no further change then the CATs would remain as a group of direct grant institutions, if it recommended that they become universities, then they were half-way there. This was an important point for the governing body of a direct grant institution had vested in it final responsibility for the institution. It was the owner of the property and the employer of the staff. The governing body of a local authority institution could only be a sub-committee of a committee of the local authority. The local authority remained the owner of the property and plant and employed the staff. There is one further significant point about the change being made when it was. The Ministry of Education had had little responsibility for higher education hitherto in spite of the ambitions of some of its ministers from the time of R. A. Butler.[18] The appearance of direct grant institutions really served to give it much closer involvement and responsibility for at least a part of higher education when the time was rapidly approaching for a decision as to which government department would become responsible for the whole of higher education.

In accordance with the main thrust of its organizational recommendations which was to provide most higher education through a greatly expanded university system, the Robbins Committee recommended that the CATs should become technological universities. The committee apparently felt that some of the colleges were already achieving standards as good as or even better than those of some universities in their undergraduate work. The lack of prestige which accompanied their inability to award their own degrees or to style themselves as universities meant that they were less attractive to students and staff. Since the new universities had been guided away from technology as it was already the preserve of the CATs, it would have been odd, to say the least, to then leave the higher study of technology in institutions which in some sense had an impaired appeal for able students by comparison with the new institutions providing additional places for pure science. This recommendation was accepted by the Government and responsibility for them was given to UGC. Advisory committees were appointed in the CATs to advise on the changes necessary to achieve chartered status and most of them became universities in 1967. Two achieved university status as constituents of existing universities, the Welsh College of Advanced Technology became a constituent college of the University of Wales while Chelsea College of Advanced Technology became a constituent college of London University in 1971.

BINARY POLICY AND THE POLYTECHNICS

The Robbins Committee's proposals would have produced by 1980 560,000 students in university-type institutions under the Ministry of Arts and Science and funded through grants committees and 65,000 in local authority further education institutions whose students were to be eligible for CNAA degrees. The recommendation to establish the Council for National Academic Awards was vital for the development of the Ministry/ local authority sector and very rapid progress was made in implementing this. Plans for it had been worked out between the National Council for Technological Awards (NCTA) and the Ministry of Education before the actual publication of the Robbins Report and its rapid creation was largely the work of John Pimlott, under-secretary of the FE branch in the Ministry.[19] Discussions on the membership of the new body began in the last few months of 1963. The last chairman of the NCTA became chairman of the new CNAA, Sir Harold Roxbee-Cox. Five of the other members were drawn from industry and commerce, seven from universities, seven from further education colleges and two from LEAs. The CNAA had a much broader field than the body it replaced for it was to handle cases in the arts, social sciences and various professional areas as well as science and technology. Since there was less experience in the technical colleges in teaching at degree level in the arts and social sciences it was not surprising that the CNAA found it more difficult to approve courses here in the early years than in disciplines where colleges already had experience of working successfully for the Diploma in Technology.[20] The Robbins recommendations for the creation of the CNAA had finally ended the universities' monopoly of awarding degrees which had constituted an obstacle to the development of local authority higher education since the end of the Second World War.

The extent to which government and organization of higher education proposed by the Robbins Committee had been rejected by the Government has already been noticed.[21] In March 1964 the Government announced that there was not to be a Minister of Arts and Science but that universities were to become the responsibility of the DES. Soon after the Wilson government came into office later that year, the DES announced that the colleges of education were to remain in the local authority sector and were not to go over to the grant-aided area – although it agreed to permit the development of a Bachelor of Education degree. Early in 1965 Anthony Crosland, now Secretary of State at the DES, announced that no more new universities were to be created and no more leading local authority sector colleges were to be permitted to transfer to the university sector for the next ten years. Thus although the principle of a place in higher education for qualified entrants survived, the Robbins structure had been rejected and the way was clear for the DES to put forward its own preferred policy. According to Toby Weaver, sometime Deputy Secretary of the DES, there was at this time, 'urgent need for an alternative policy'.[22]

That policy was essentially to continue the existing arrangements for higher education consisting of three main elements – that aided through a grants committee, local authority further education and colleges of education. The main change which some in the Ministry of Education had sought was that expressed by Butler 20 years earlier, namely that the UGC should be transferred to the Ministry from the Treasury, and that had now been achieved. The so-called binary policy was an attempt to provide a doctrine for the new situation so that it could be explained and defended. The speech which is generally thought of as setting out the DES's doctrine was delivered at a dinner at Woolwich Polytechnic on 22 April 1965. Crosland spoke of a 'dual' system made up of an 'autonomous' sector, by which he meant the universities, and a public sector represented by 'the leading technical colleges and the colleges of education'. The Government accepted this dual system as being fundamentally the right one. Crosland gave four reasons why the Government's policy was based on the binary system. Firstly an ever-increasing need for vocational, professional and industrially based courses could not be met by universities. Secondly a unitary system based on the 'ladder' concept must inevitably depress and degrade morale and standards in the non-university sector. Thirdly, it was desirable that a substantial part of the higher education system 'should be under social control and directly responsive to social needs' and that local government should maintain a reasonable stake in higher education. The fourth point was somewhat oratorical, that Britain would not survive in a competitive world if it downgraded its non-university professional and technical sector, 'let us now move away from our snobbish caste-ridden hierarchical obsession with university-status'. The three functions of the public sector colleges were to provide degree level courses for students of university ability, to provide full-time and sandwich courses of a somewhat less rigorous standard than degree-level courses and finally to provide part-time advanced courses for the 'tens of thousands' of students who sought them. His Department was now going to find 'a clearer and more national pattern of senior colleges and advanced courses'.[23]

The binary policy received a very mixed reception. The universities, for instance, were hardly likely to agree that they were not responsive to social needs, as Crosland clearly implied. The CVCP feared that the cost of building up the local authority sector would lead to a denial of funds to universities. The larger regional colleges which in terms of the Robbins policy might have hoped to join the ex-CATs as universities were clearly disappointed. The majority of technical college people, on the other hand, welcomed the speech – as did the AEC although William Alexander warned that LEAs would have to allow more independence to college governing bodies.[24] Crosland himself later admitted that the speech was the wrong way of launching the binary policy. He had made 'an appalling blunder' and 'I got the whole thing off on the wrong foot . . !' 'It came out in a manner calculated to infuriate almost everybody you can think of, and in public relations terms it did consider-able harm to the policy.' Crosland remained convinced that the policy itself was right.[25] Certainly it did not become a matter of party political controversy for the Conservative shadow secre-tary, Edward Boyle, assured the Government that his party did not support a unitary system of higher education in the course of a debate in the Commons at the end of April 1965. Subsequently he explained that he had put a paper to the Cabinet in March 1964 containing a rather similar policy. He believed that the record of the contribution which had already been made by the local authority sector to higher education entitled the sector 'to a more optimistic future than the very low proportion – only 12 per cent by 1980 – which Robbins proposed'.[26]

In order to help consider the organizational pattern for public sector colleges Crosland set up a small advisory group under Reg Prentice, Minister of State for Higher Education. The group consisted of persons from technical colleges and local authorities and included among others Alexander (from the AEC), A. Clegg (West Riding), L. Russell (Birmingham), E. Britton and E. E. Robinson (ATTI), and C. A. Hornby (NACEIC). The precise function of the group seems to have been to discuss and offer criticism of DES memoranda. The first paper circulated to the group brought out the disparity of the senior technical college institutions. Six had 500 or more full-time degree and Dip. Tech. students. At the other extreme there were twelve colleges with fewer than 50 full-time degree and Dip. Tech. students including five with fewer than 20. This paper suggested that a limited number of what it called 'polytechnic institutes' might be developed from colleges which appeared to have the greatest potential in higher education. If 30 institutes were created – embracing a considerably larger number of existing institutions – it would form a strong network covering the whole country. These would be given priority in the allocation of resources so as to build up their standards and reputation. The actual contribution of the group to government policy seems to have been to modify and make more practical some of the plans put forward. The DES papers proposed, for instance, to merge colleges from different LEAs under joint committees such as Leeds College of Technology, Leeds College of Commerce and Huddersfield College of Technology. A later redraft noted that it was becoming increasingly doubtful whether this would be an acceptable method of concentrating economic and academic resources in coherent academic communities. Some of the proposed marriages would be 'violently opposed' by authorities and colleges which would have to accept subordination to another authority or college. Thus institutional amalgamations were to be confined normally to those within one authority. Paper 5 noted that considerable importance attached to the actual description of major centres. 'No entirely satisfactory suggestion has been made, but the best is perhaps simply "polytechnic".'[27]

By May 1966 the DES was able to issue a White Paper, *A Plan for Polytechnics and Other Colleges*, in which it set out the pattern for local authority sector higher education. The reasons for concentrating resources were fully given. An avowed object was to reduce substantially the number of colleges engaged in full-time higher education but colleges already offering this and not designated as Polytechnics were to be permitted to continue offering it as long as they satisfied the criteria for course approval. Only in exceptional circumstances would colleges not already involved in higher education courses be allowed to embark on them. In 1967 the Secretary of State indicated 29 of the proposed polytechnics, the last nomination being delayed. The final designation of the 30 was completed by 1974. One condition of the designation of a polytechnic was that the Secretary of State should have approved the Instruments and Articles of Government. In this way the DES sought to ensure that the governmental arrangements were appropriate for an institution serving national as well as local needs and that the governing body should itself have the widest autonomy consistent with the responsibilities of the monitoring local authorities. Not more than one-third of the governors were to be drawn from the LEA, others were to be drawn from among those with experience in industry, commerce, the professions, trade unions, academic staff, students and other persons with relevant experience.[28] The cost of maintaining a polytechnic is the immediate responsibility of its own LEA but since all or nearly all the courses are at the higher education level, all or nearly all of the net cost can be charged against a 'pool' and the LEA in this way secures reimbursement. This arrangement was set up under the Local Government Act of 1966 and obliged every LEA to contribute its share.

The DES described polytechnics as 'primarily teaching institutions'. Their efforts were to be concentrated not on 'the origination of new knowledge' but on the development and application of what was known. The size of the polytechnics increased through the 1970s partly because of the growth of student demand for places in higher education and partly as a consequence of the incorporation of former free-standing colleges of education in polytechnics as a consequence of

Table 6.1   Polytechnics – student numbers and subject groups (groups as % of total enrolment in parentheses), 1970–78

Subject group	1970	1972	1974	1976	1978
Education	2,675 (2.1)	4,466 (3.1)	5,106 (3.5)	18,595 (9.6)	17,794 (8.6)
Medical health, welfare	3,613 (2.8)	5,404 (3.8)	5,913 (4.1)	7,462 (3.9)	7,455 (3.6)
Engineering and technology	43,628 (34.4)	42,488 (29.8)	37,744 (26.1)	40,885 (21.2)	43,593 (21.2)
Agriculture	18 (–)	– (–)	1 (–)	1 (–)	– (–)
Science	14,194 (11.2)	16,666 (11.7)	16,304 (11.3)	19,110 (9.9)	21,845 (10.6)
Social, administrative and business studies	42,326 (33.3)	48,959 (34.3)	54,882 (37.9)	64,673 (33.6)	68,557 (33.3)
Professional and vocational subjects*	10,531 (8.3)	11,480 (8.0)	11,863 (8.2)	12,733 (6.6)	14,098 (6.8)
Languages, literature and area studies	2,252 (1.8)	3,261 (2.3)	3,364 (2.3)	4,113 (2.1)	5,112 (2.5)
Arts (other than above)	1,427 (1.1)	1,877 (1.3)	1,202 (–)	1,103 (–)	4,692 (2.3)
Music, drama, art, design	5,498 (4.3)	7,237 (5.1)	8,095 (5.6)	9,471 (4.9)	10,557 (5.1)
GCE & CSE	655 (–)	892 (–)	169 (–)	298 (–)	310 (–)
Unclassified	– (–)	– (–)	– (–)	14,253 (7.4)	11,983 (5.8)

*Architecture, catering and institutional management, home economics, librarianship, nautical subjects, transport, wholesale and retail trades etc.
Source: DES, *Statistics of Education*, 1970–1978.

government policy on teacher training. Both of these features are apparent from Table 6.1 as is the somewhat static position in engineering and technology by comparison with the buoyant expansion in numbers in social, administrative and business studies.

OTHER FURTHER EDUCATION AND INDUSTRIAL
TRAINING LEGISLATION

The efforts made by the Government and local authorities following the Crowther Report included setting up a committee under the chairmanship of Henniker-Heaton to inquire into the constraints on day-release and to suggest ways in which more young people could be drawn into further education by this means. The failure to meet the Government's aim in this respect as set out in the White Paper of 1956 was admitted by the Minister and said to be due to the fact that too few employers had been prepared to allow students to attend part-time day as opposed to evening classes. He thought that other factors were a lack of interest among some young people and in some areas there was an inadequate range of courses.[29] The Minister (David Eccles) had been having talks with representatives of employers, trade unions and local authorities on the proposal that young employees up to the age of 18 should be given the right to claim release on one day each week to attend a further education course. Before proceeding further, the Minister set up a working party to study the practical and financial consequences of this proposal under the chairmanship of John Pimlott of FE Branch. Their report was considered at a meeting called by Edward Boyle, by then Minister, in 1962. The Minister accepted the general view that the right to day release could not be granted without holding back the prospects for other urgent educational developments. It was at this point that the Henniker-Heaton Committee was set up to see what could be done to encourage more day release short of giving young people a legal right. In these circumstances the report which the committee produced could not amount to very much. Public authority employers ought to give a lead in granting day release, other employers were urged to do their best and to grant release to girls as well as boys – girls appeared to be particularly badly provided for. The report noted that day release had only grown from 185,000 in 1956 to 200,000 by 1960 and estimated that the number needed to rather more than double by 1970.[30]

During the last 20 years legislation concerned with improving training facilities has had an impact on further education. Late in 1962 the Government published a White Paper on industrial training which set out the need to improve the overall quality of training, to establish minimum standards and to spread the cost more fairly. The subsequent legislation empowered the Minister of Labour to set up industrial training boards responsible for all aspects of training in certain industries. The boards themselves were to provide or secure the provision of training, to make recommendations on its length and content and on the further education to be associated with the training, to raise a levy on their industry and to give the Minister such information as he might require. There was provision for education members to be appointed to the boards.[31] By 1970 27 boards covered industries employing 15 million people with a levy income of £200 million. The greater part of the levy was spent on grants to employers for the training they provided and was largely offset against the levy due from them. One aim was to stimulate laggardly employers into providing training by causing them to pay the levy without reimbursement if they failed to do so.

Further education was affected in two ways, firstly by providing courses to meet the education component needed. These were sometimes new but sometimes existing courses were revived – as happened with some engineering craft practice courses. There was also a development of full-time courses in the colleges to meet the needs of some trades. Secondly in 1965 the Minister of Labour decided that he would not normally accept a board's grant scheme unless it made provision for day release for all young people in occupations requiring 'substantial' training – a year or more. Part of the grant paid by the boards was for education and training activities in further education colleges. Some of these were sandwich and full-time, some day release and some for courses for managers or supervisors.

The position was reviewed in the early 1970s and the Employment and Training Act of 1973 made important changes in the organization. The Act established the Manpower Services Commission responsible to the Secretary of State for Employment which included representatives of employers, employees and education. The Commission was to take over training and employment services previously run by the Department of Employment with the Training Services Agency and the Employment Service Agency to operate as executive branches. The training facilities were subsequently reviewed and developed and extensive use has been made under the Training Services Agency of the further education colleges.

It should perhaps be noted that the Ministry of Labour (later

Table 6.2 Course enrolments in maintained, assisted and grant-aided major establishments of further education (thousands) 1949–77

	Full-time and sandwich	Part-time day	Evening only
1949	54	284	761
1951	46	298	550
1953	52	333	550
1955	58	391	634
1957	80	437	633
1959	108	452	687
1961	132	556	784
1963	175	613	779
1965	186	680	796
1967	221	741	811
1969	260	756	713
1971	285	718	746
1973	300	700	783
1975	387	743	802
1977	434	706	687

Note: By 1977 there were approximately 620 major establishments of further education varying from local colleges offering mainly part-time courses for students of 16 to 18 along with some full-time GCE and similar courses to polytechnics dealing with advanced work.

In addition to enrolments shown here, there were a further 1,708,000 in 1977 in adult, recreational, vocational etc. classes held in evening institutes or centres, often housed in schools.

Source: DES, *Statistics of Education.*

Department of Employment) was responsible for the administration of these measures which involved further education. The continued growth in the numbers of students enrolling in major further education establishments as shown in Table 6.2 seems to have been due at least in part to the efforts of this Department.

TECHNICAL TEACHER TRAINING

Since further education includes virtually all forms of post-school education with the exception of universities, the qualifications and experience required of those who are to teach in it must be very varied indeed. The McNair Committee in 1943 accepted that training could not be made compulsory and believed it to be desirable that part of the training of the technical teacher should be undertaken after he had started to teach. Many of the posts in further education required teachers with qualifications similar to those in schools and many further education teachers were so qualified. But a considerable number would always need to be recruited from industry and elsewhere to fill satisfactorily posts requiring particular industrial or craft skills. In order to meet the immediate shortage of technical teachers after the war, four colleges were established, initially on an emergency basis but they became a regular part of the system of teacher supply. These colleges were in Huddersfield, Bolton, Wolverhampton and London.

Faced with the expansion envisaged in 1956 a committee was set up under Sir Willis Jackson to inquire into the supply and training of teachers for technical colleges. It suggested various ways of attracting teachers with the necessary skills and experience so as to achieve its estimated increase in the full-time staff from 11,500 in 1956 to an envisaged 18,600 in 1960–61. It proposed that a period of training should be encouraged, particularly for teachers concerned with less advanced levels of work. The one year pre-service courses such as were being provided at the four technical teachers' training colleges were commended. One year full-time courses should also be introduced for those already teaching and one-term courses were recommended for those who could not take the full year's course. An addition to salary was proposed as an incentive for those who undertook training. The demands which were forecast here for additional teachers were met by 1960, but additional demands which had not been foreseen had arisen. Indeed this tended to be typical of the teacher supply position in the 1960s and efforts had to be made constantly to attract more staff.[32]

In 1966 the sub-committee on teachers for further education of the National Advisory Council on the Training and Supply of Teachers under Sir Lionel Russell reviewed the training position. It noted that under the existing voluntary methods less than a third of the total teaching force in further education and less than a fifth of new entrants to technical teaching were trained. On this basis there was little prospect of improving the quality of the teaching force in parallel with the necessary expansion of further education. In order to introduce compulsory training without causing disruption or a temporary famine of entrants, the committee put forward a careful scheme under which new entrant assistant lecturers were to be seconded to a course of training within the first five years of service (five being reduced to three years later). The costs of the arrangement were to be chargeable to the teacher training pool. It was proposed that the training requirement be introduced in 1969 and that an immediate announcement be made to prepare for it.

The DES did not accept the recommendations. The *Guardian* reported next day that the Russell Report held 'the record for the shortness of the interval between its publication at noon on Monday and its rejection later that afternoon'. The Government felt the cost was too great and on those grounds declined to act. This point was made clearly by Goronwy Roberts, then Minister of State, at a meeting with local authority representatives who were pressing for action in July 1966 and who asked why there had not been the usual consultation before an announcement had been made. In reply to this question the Minister said this was 'simply because implementation was thought to be impossible . . . on grounds of finance' and because the supply of teachers might have been affected: 'this being the Government's view there was, therefore, really nothing to consult about'.[33]

When Alexander, under pressure from Bolton LEA, wrote to Sir Herbert Andrew (then Permanent Under Secretary of the DES) in 1969 complaining that the recommendations had been ignored, Andrew replied that the numbers attending certificate courses had increased by nearly 50 per cent to 1,700 in the current year and that the situation had changed since the Russell Committee had reported. In a later letter he wrote that there were two difficulties about the proposals. 'The first is that they would undoubtedly cost something and as things are this means that we should have to squeeze out something else, which is pretty difficult.' Moreover the teacher supply situation was changing from one of overall shortage to one of pockets of shortage.[34] In fact training for teaching in institutions which operate under the further education regulations has remained voluntary, although additional courses and modifications in their organization have been introduced recently.

CHAPTER 7

The Government and Administration of the Education System

THE CENTRAL EDUCATION DEPARTMENT

The legislative basis of the administrative framework remains the Education Act of 1944. This Act confirmed the traditional position that it was the function of the central government to determine national education policy while the function of local government bodies was to provide services in their areas in accordance with statutory requirements. In the years immediately before the war there had been a marked tendency on the part of the Board of Education to leave the initiative to local authorities, to wait for points to be raised instead of anticipating them. To some extent this had been a consequence of the policy of Lord Eustace Percy, President of the Board of Education from 1924 to 1929. Some senior officials saw the prospect of major legislation as an opportunity to re-establish the position of the Board as the body which would lead and direct the educational system of the country.[1]

The surprising degree of unevenness in provision between LEAs became strikingly apparent to many as a consequence of the wartime evacuation. In rural counties the facilities provided by their home city authorities for evacuees were often manifestly superior to the service offered by the county council to permanent local residents. The upsurge of ideas expressing a desire for social improvements became very marked during the war and the view was widespread that disparity of provision was no longer acceptable and that far more emphasis needed to be placed on national policy and on national levels of provision. Greater centralization was essential if there were to be purposeful national planning. These sentiments found their most obvious expression in Section 1 of the Act which was quite deliberately assertive. 'It shall be the duty of the Minister of Education to promote the education of the people of England and Wales and the progressive development of institutions devoted to that purpose, and to secure the effective execution by local authorities, under his control and direction, of national policy for providing a comprehensive educational service in every area.'

The replacement of the terms 'President' and 'Board' by 'Minister' and 'Ministry' was a further expression of this feeling. Butler had originally proposed the change to the Lord President's Committee of the Cabinet in November 1943, but the opposition of some members – particularly Herbert Morrison, then Home Secretary – led to the proposal being dropped for the time being. But the matter came up in the Commons when an amendment to the Bill to delete 'President of the Board' and to insert 'Minister' was widely supported. The general view was that in the past the Board had been the Cinderella of ministries and the change would be helpful in ending this. Butler took the matter back to the Lord President's Committee and, although Morrison maintained his opposition, the other members accepted the change in the face of this forthright expression of public expectation.[2] Post-war ministers certainly took a much more purposeful and energetic attitude than their pre-war predecessors. Ellen Wilkinson, David Eccles, Edward Boyle and Anthony Crosland, to name only some, will be remembered for the strong and positive leadership they gave to the education service.

The Ministry did not acquire substantial executive functions. This work has fallen on local authorities for most of the education service. At the same time the formation of national policy itself has involved a good deal of administration and various regulatory duties have been laid on the central department by education statutes. Thus the Ministry (or from 1964 the Department) has had to:

(1)　set minimum standards of educational provision;
(2)　control the rate, distribution, nature and cost of educational building;

(3)   support by direct grant a number of institutions of a special kind;

(4)   determine the number and balance of teachers admitted to training and decide the principles governing the recognition of teachers as qualified;

(5)   administer the superannuation scheme for teachers;

(6)   settle disputes within the education service such as those between a parent and a local education authority or between an authority and the governors of a school;

(7)   support educational research undertaken by such bodies as the National Foundation for Educational Research or university departments;

(8)   since 1958 to forecast, after consultation, the level of local authority expenditure on education to be taken into account in determining the size of Exchequer grant to local authorities.

Thus the policy-making functions might be said to comprehend establishing a general framework governing the direction, scale and rate of development of the education service. From time to time it has been necessary to define specific policies to meet particular situations. The Department gives effect to its policies either by means of regulations and orders under the authority of the education Acts or by offering guidance through circulars, pamphlets, handbooks and the inspectorate.[3]

The transfer of responsibility for the UGC to the ministry in 1964 has already been referred to above.[4] Responsibility for the research councils and for civil science was transferred at the same time and the Minister of Education became Secretary of State for Education and Science. This enlargement of ministerial responsibility was in line with what Butler personally would have liked in 1944. He told the Permanent Secretary that he did not think 'one can be a successful Minister of Education and have no contact at all with the universities'. When he was eventually persuaded by his civil servants that it would be unwise to seek to change the existing relationship by which the UGC was directly responsible to the Treasury, he forecast that 'the time will come when a responsible Minister of Education – though shunned by those he desires to help – will wish to discuss with his colleagues the question of the future of the universities, for whom he is so busily supplying candidates'.[5]

The fulfilment of Butler's prophecy 20 years later was the outcome of a situation in which the size and therefore the cost of the universities had increased to the point where the Chancellor of the Exchequer was unwilling to accept direct responsibility. Most other educational interests saw the teaching aspect in universities as predominant – rather than learning or scholarship – and therefore pressed for unification of governmental responsibility for all aspects of education in the one ministry. Lord Boyle has told of how the scheme that was accepted attempted to offer some comfort to university interests through setting up a federal Department of Education and Science with a single Secretary of State but with two subordinate units, one concerned with higher education and the other with the schools and further education. This compromise was originally put to a group of ministers by Sir Lawrence Helsby of the Treasury who was then head of the civil service. The Treasury – which at that time advised on the machinery of government – strongly favoured the unitary solution and undoubtedly civil service advice was important in the outcome.[6] The federal department very soon became a unitary department with a single accounting officer.

In retrospect the absorption of universities within the field of responsibility of the education department appears to have been an entirely natural development and one might almost wonder at it not having happened earlier. Yet it has had its price so far as the universities are concerned. The main strength of the universities–UGC–Treasury arrangement was that the broad policy for university development was produced by a primarily academic body in close contact both with individual universities and with the chief paymaster. Into this relationship there came an additional party, an education minister and a staff of permanent officials all anxious to exercise their authority over higher education. *The Times Educational Supplement* was entirely accurate in its comment that the universities had been saddled with an additional bureaucracy on the other side of the UGC. 'It can only mean that after their plans have been sifted by the UGC they will go through the mincer again inside the ministry.'[7] With the passage of time it has also become apparent that there is now rather more direct political influence over the policies universities are obliged to follow than used to be the case. The number of students studying subjects disapproved of has had to be reduced while more places have had to be provided for the study of subjects which are thought well of by temporary political masters.

The degree of influence and control which the DES has built up over the universities is in some ways exercised more immediately and directly than can possibly be the case with schools and further education. The position of the Ministry and later Department with regard to local authority institutions has been weakened partly as a consequence of the abolition in 1958 of the education grant which was accounted for by the Ministry and was earned largely as a percentage of their total educational expenditure by LEAs. The substitution of various forms of general grant accounted for by the Ministry of Housing and Local Government and subsequently by the Department of the Environment has served to weaken the position of the DES over the years. This has become more obvious with the increasing disparity and unevenness of provision made by LEAs during very recent years when the central government has been trying to enforce retrenchment while seeking to maintain sound standards.

The heavy cost of the education service has always made it impossible for localities to manage without central government assistance. A considerable proportion of the volume of expenditure is not directly under the control of an individual authority. Salary scales for teachers and wage rates for other grades of school staff are fixed nationally and by far the greater part of educational expenditure goes on salaries and wages. LEAs have some discretion over the numbers of staff they employ, otherwise the area for local financial discretion is limited to such essentials as the supply of books, equipment and stationery for schools and the maintenance of buildings. In the 1950s the education grant payable by the Ministry to LEAs on a percentage basis had met about 60 per cent of their expenditure. The main advantage to the Ministry of this form of grant was that it enabled it to encourage the national policies for which it was responsible by introducing any adjustments to encourage certain developments or to discourage others. At the local level this arrangement gave statutory education committees a measure of support in their dealings with other interests inside local government.

Pressure to end the system of a separate education grant had been exerted by the Treasury at different times. Between the two world wars at the time of the Geddes Axe it had tried to move to a general aid grant for local authorities but the Board of Education had resisted this proposal and the difficulties of working such an arrangement when Part III education authorities still supported only elementary schools in their boroughs and urban districts while the county councils provided everything else would have been very great. After the Second World War the Treasury continued to regard the education grant as unsatisfactory since the obligation to meet a certain percentage of total expenditure decided and undertaken by local authorities led it to feel that it did not have sufficient control over the sums it was required to find to meet the government's obligations. The need to increase and sustain at an increased level the building programme during David Eccles' first period as Minister meant that the Ministry of Education had to get the agreement of the Treasury to a high level of capital investment in the schools over a period of some years if there was ever to be a secondary school place for every child over the age of 11. An understanding was arrived at between the Treasury and the Ministry by which the Treasury undertook to see that the capital programme would be sustained if the Ministry did not oppose the Treasury's plan for a block grant system.

The proposed grant system was very strongly opposed by the AEC, by the NUT and by other education groups and a public campaign was mounted, but the outcome was never in doubt.[8] David Nenk, who was Under Secretary for finance and Accountant General in the Ministry, and his senior colleagues were vindicated in their policy of supporting the new arrangements in that the school building programme was sustained even through the financial crises of the period and by 1964 there was a secondary school place for every pupil of secondary age. Moreover, in its early years the new grant system did not unduly restrict the continued growth of recurrent expenditure on the education service. The service had to grow to cope with the increased number of pupils and students. Indeed there was a strong general political will to continue its expansion. One of the foremost opponents of the new system in 1958, William Alexander, wrote in 1976 that what he had feared 'did not occur until recent years. Prior to that monies were fairly readily available and I do not think education suffered.'[9] On the other hand the failure of the British economy and the breakdown of much of manufacturing industry in recent years combined with the effects of local government reorganization have produced increasing strain which might better have been dealt with had there been an education grant. In other words the amount of cuts required from the education committees' estimates in some authorities has been proportionately higher than the cuts applied in certain other services.

The block or rate support grant is decided each year after the government has determined the needs – including the educational needs – of different areas and the DES is fully involved with the Department of the Environment and the local authority associations in discussions concerning this. But it has become impossible for the Secretary of State for Education and Science to ensure that any additional funds put into the grant for some educational purpose will not be spent on a quite different local authority activity. This was in fact what happened when Mrs Shirley Williams provided additional funds in this way in an attempt to increase provision for the in-service training of teachers. Both the Association of Metropolitan Authorities (AMA) and the ACC have opposed any attempt to introduce specific grant on the grounds that it would undermine the power of a local authority to deploy its total resources in the way that it wishes, claiming that only its local authority can really judge an area's needs. This standpoint has also been supported by the Department of the Environment which has apparently viewed its own interests and authority as being threatened by any specific grant. The attempt made by the DES in the summer of 1982 to pay education grant as a separate block grant was reported to have failed in Cabinet Committee by the *Financial Times* which explained that 'Civil Servants in the Environment Department argued the scheme would break up their controversial system of allocating block grants to councils. . . . Control of education spending would pass out of their hands into the Education Department.'[10] It is clear that there have been significant administrative and political changes in the relationship between the Central Education Department and LEAs since the Butler Act and the years following the Second World War – changes occasioned by developments in local government as well as in the growth in power and influence of the Department of the Environment.

LOCAL EDUCATION AUTHORITIES

The principal change in the local education authority structure in 1944 was the abolition of the Part III authorities and the restriction of education powers to counties and county boroughs. Part III authorities were so called because they had been set up under Part III of the Education Act of 1902 to administer elementary schools only in non-county boroughs with a minimum population of 10,000 and in urban districts with at least 20,000 inhabitants. Secondary schools and all other educational provision in these towns had been provided by the county council. The administrative awkwardness of this arrangement had led to its abolition in 1944. Pressure from the Federation of Part III authorities led to the incorporation in the 1944 Act of provisions permitting county education authorities to prepare schemes for the delegation of certain functions to local subcommittees or divisional executives composed of representatives of the district councils in an area, members of the county authority and coopted persons. Any district in which there was an elementary school population of 7,000 children or more had the right to a committee of its own and was known as an excepted district.

The main concentrations of divisional executives were in the West Riding, Lancashire and the suburban districts around London, all of which had had many Part III authorities. The Local Government Act of 1958 provided for the creation of new excepted districts as of right in towns whose populations had grown to 60,000 since the end of the war and in special circumstances in smaller towns. Fourteen new excepted districts were created under this Act, six as of right and eight on the basis of special local circumstances.[11] The divisional executive and the excepted district represented an attempt to reconcile the desire of civic leaders in medium sized towns to run their own education service with the increasing demand for more specialized techniques and functional efficiency which it was thought could only be supplied economically by large authorities. It is probably right to conclude that favourable comment was based upon the system's theoretical possibilities while most of the criticism of divisional administration was directed towards the system as it actually operated. In practice everything depended on the degree and quality of the cooperation between county authorities and executives and this was not always adequate.[12] In the London area divisional executives were abolished when the London Government Act of 1963 came into force in 1965. In the rest of the country they were abolished by the Local Government Act of 1972 which made no provision for the delegation by LEAs of any of their functions to a lower level of administration.

During the two decades immediately following the Education Act of 1944 the education committees of all counties and county boroughs in England and Wales with the exception of London County Council were drawn into membership of the AEC. This Association with its energetic general secretary enabled LEAs jointly to exercise a positive influence over the creation of national educational policy which they could never have exercised individually or, indeed, if they had simply been represented by the general local authority associations – one for the counties and one for the municipalities. It is not too much to claim that one of the reasons why the 1944 Act was not as ineffective and neglected as those of 1918 and 1921 was the influence of the AEC. The Association came to be recognized as the 'lead' organization on educational issues among local authority associations and provided the secretariat for the employers' panel of the Burnham Committee.

A joint letter from the CCA and the Association of Municipal Corporations (AMC) to the Permanent Secretary in 1946 complained that their associations had not been consulted before a circular was issued. This led to an exchange of minutes within the Ministry which indicated the degree of confidence Alexander had built up with civil servants. At the time the Ministry had a number of working parties on issues ranging from planning buildings and acquiring sites to the licensing of theatrical children. It was thought that even if the views of the AMC and CCA could be obtained and reconciled 'without intolerable delay', they would be of little assistance on what was workable and practical.

If for these working parties we frequently call upon Dr Alexander, that is because his wider experience and interest are specially valuable, and not because he represents the AEC rather than the AMC or any other body. Also his extensive and constant contacts with Education Officers all over the country put him in a specially good position to offer informed advice and to explain to them the procedures which are the outcome of the working policies.[13]

It was the confidence and special relationship shown here which enabled the AEC and its general secretary to play such an influential role in such areas as school building policy, external examinations and the establishment of the Schools Council.

The first major change in the pattern of local government was brought about by the London Government Act of 1963. The Report of the Royal Commission on Local Government in Greater London was published in October 1960. The main recommendations involved abolishing the London County Council (LCC), and establishing the Greater London Council (GLC) within whose area the main units of local government would be London boroughs as they were called. Education would be the responsibility of the Greater London Council which would devolve much of the executive work of educational administration on to the 52 boroughs. The Ministry of Education was alarmed by these proposals and in a telephone message to Alexander urged that the AEC – which had not given evidence to the Royal Commission – should now express its views. The Ministry feared that education would be the only service which the proposed reorganization would not fit. Officials were particularly concerned lest the pattern of a large conglomerate authority with executive authorities working under it would set a pattern for the reorganization of local government across the whole country. Any expression of views, however arranged, would be welcomed by the Ministry. The Ministry also contacted such other educational organizations as the NUT, Joint Four, ATTI, NADEE to suggest that they should also submit their comments on the Royal Commission's proposals from the education viewpoint.[14]

The AEC then submitted a memorandum on the unsatisfactory nature of the proposals for the education service. The weakness which the Commission had found in Middlesex where large excepted areas were said to have created major problems would become typical of the whole of the London area. The idea that one authority should appoint teaching staff while others would have the right of dismissal was unreasonable. The difficulties of administering a building programme to be settled overall by the GLC and then to be allocated equitably among 52 boroughs were described as 'very great'. The Association concluded by urging that the government should not apply the Royal Commission's proposals to the education service.[15]

The Government's White Paper published in November 1961 differed from the Commission's recommendations in two respects. The boroughs were to be fewer and larger with populations of 200,000 or so. Given the larger boroughs, education could and should become a borough service over the greater part of the London area. In the centre of London, however, there would need to be a large education authority for an area comprising several boroughs.[16] The Government hesitated as to how to handle central London. The LCC education committee had been dominated by the Labour Party for nearly 30 years and its policies were politically often in conflict with those of Conservative ministers. At the same time the attempt to divide central London would have meant massive daily migration by pupils and students across the boundaries of any new LEAs which might be set up since the education services had grown upon a unified basis. David Eccles admitted in the Commons that this would create a situation which would overwhelm any extra-district payments transfer scheme. In the event the LCC education apparatus was to be kept in being at least until 1970 and the Inner London Education Authority was set up. This was a special committee of the GLC to administer the former LCC area. Membership has consisted of councillors of the GLC representing the inner London boroughs together with one representative of each inner London borough council and of the Common Council. By 1967 the decision was taken not to review the future of the Inner London Education Authority (ILEA) in 1970 but the return to office of Margaret Thatcher's administration in 1979 served to re-open the question of whether to continue this unique arrangement; however, no change has been proposed.

The reform of the structure of local government over the rest of the country followed only after another decade. The position of education within the local government framework inevitably came to be examined. The AEC was invited by the Royal Commission on local government to submit evidence and there is some evidence of disapproval of the Association's giving evidence on the part of both the CCA and the AMC.[17] There was quite a strong thrust by this time towards reorganizing local government on a corporate management basis in which emphasis would be placed on giving each local council the maximum amount of discretion in judging the needs of its area, in switching resources between the different services it offered and in general getting away from the traditional concept of a local authority as a provider of various different services, all operating their own way, possibly without paying sufficient heed to each other. Thus in its evidence the AEC was out of step with other local authority associations in that it emphasized that 'the independence which was established in the last century between education and other local government functions . . . is wholly desirable'.[18]

The Royal Commission recommended that around Manchester, Liverpool and Birmingham there should be an overall county comparable to the GLC with district councils for certain local functions. Elsewhere the single main authority was recommended although 'local' councils were suggested to provide a voice for smaller units even though they would not themselves have executive functions. The report was accepted by the Wilson government just before its defeat in the 1970 election. The Heath administration was pledged to introduce a two-tier system and after consultation Peter Walker, by now the Minister responsible, produced a new model for reorganization preserving the historic shire counties and extending the Commission's concept of metropolitan county to three more industrialized areas, West Yorkshire, South Yorkshire and

Tyne and Wear.[19] In the shire counties education was to be a county function, in the metropolitan counties it became a function of the district councils. The Government stated that it accepted the view that units appropriate to the provision of education should have populations broadly within the range 250,000 to 1,000,000. Thus there was a good deal of criticism of the decision to make some districts with populations well below the minimum education authorities.

A number of education officers and the AEC made representations to the Permanent Secretary, William Pile, on this point. In a letter to Alec Clegg in the West Riding, Alexander reported that Pile shared their views entirely about the 11 smallest metropolitan districts. The DES had done its best to move the Secretary of State for the Environment, Peter Walker, 'but Walker was adamant'.[20] Since some of these small authorities were in impoverished and declining industrial areas they have indeed had more of a struggle than better endowed areas to maintain a reasonable education service.

In accordance with the corporate management style which then appealed strongly, the Department of the Environment proposed to dispense with statutory requirements to appoint particular committees. It stated that 'this power should remain unfettered in order to enable the new authorities to apply the advice ultimately to emerge from the Management Exercise in whatever manner each authority think most suitable to their needs'. While police and national parks committees would remain statutory the government saw no need to retain the requirement to establish an education committee indefinitely. Ministerial controls over the appointment of chief education officers were to be repealed.[21] The AEC made strong representations to the Department of the Environment on the need to continue statutory provision for education committees and education officers indefinitely. It pointed out that education remained a national service locally administered and stressed the need for statutory committees which enabled the churches and teachers to be brought into the local governing pattern for education. It was also imperative that all powers relating to the education service should be delegated to the education committee by the parent county or district council. Copies of the

AEC's representations were also sent to the Permanent Secretary at the DES for information.

The Department of the Environment's working group on local authority management then pressed for virtually all statutory requirements on local authorities to appoint particular committees or officers to be withdrawn on the grounds that they 'would be likely to hinder the new authorities from being good managers'. The most important objection to such statutory provision was said to be that it encouraged 'departmentalism'. Committees failed to bear in mind that it was the local authority as a whole, not its committees or departments that were responsible for the provision of services. This group in its report disagreed with the Environment Department's paper and in the interests of corporate management pressed for the abolition of all statutory requirements to appoint certain specified committees.[22] This report produced an explosion of feeling among education bodies. The various teachers' associations wrote to the Environment Department for, as Alexander wrote to Fred Jarvis of the NUT, if there were no statutory requirement to appoint an education committee or education officer 'there will be no bar to the appointment of a retired Master Gunner to rule the local roost and to dictate on professional matters to the teachers'. The DES regarded the whole business as a most extraordinary chain of events and took care to ensure that ministers heard other views besides those expressed by the working group on local authority management while church organizations also wrote to the Environment Department to object to the removal of statutory requirements which gave them an opportunity to be represented on education committees.[23]

Among local authority associations, the County Councils Association accepted the case for a statutory committee. When the Local Government Reorganization Bill was published in November 1971 it was clear that this battle had been won. Alexander sent a letter of congratulation to Margaret Thatcher, Secretary of State, for her efforts and to Pile, the Permanent Secretary, who replied that 'no one will deny that it was quite a battle – and a nice one to win'.[24]

The old pattern of counties and county boroughs disappeared and the new arrangement of shire counties and metropolitan districts took their place as LEAs on 1 April 1974. In the event the Local Government Act required that each of these authorities should appoint an education committee which must include persons of experience in education and that councillors themselves must form a majority of the members. The Secretary of State in a circular which indicated the nature of the constitution that she would feel able to approve for such committees, indicated that between a quarter and a third of the members should be non-councillors. They should be chosen from among serving teachers, from nominees of the churches and from persons with knowledge and experience of industry and commerce, agriculture and the universities. The circular suggested that church nominees should be sought from the diocesan education committee, the bishop of the local Roman Catholic diocese and from the local Free Church Federal Council. While the Act required the appointment of a chief education officer it no longer required each authority to submit the short-list of candidates for appointment to the Secretary of State for approval before making an appointment. This latter requirement had been inserted in the Education Act of 1944 largely on the initiative of Chuter Ede, then Parliamentary Secretary, who sought to introduce this practice on the basis of his local authority experience in dealing with the appointment of chief constables where the Home Secretary did possess the right of veto over names of possible appointees. In fact there is no record of the Minister or later Secretary of State for Education actually forbidding the appointment of an individual. Thus, dropping this provision did not change actual practice.[25]

The reorganization of local government in 1974 did not result in the ending of the statutory system of LEAs and their chief education officers as seemed probable at one time, but it did mark an important step in the decline of the influence of the education interest as distinct from the party political interest in local government. In some ways the decline and ending of the Association of Education Committees provided an index of this change. The squabbles over the form of secondary organization from the mid-1960s made it increasingly difficult for both parties to accept the continued existence of a body which tried to protect the rights and interests of education committees as such. Circulars 10/65 and 10/66 and the national political drive for comprehensive schools made any defence of the right of an individual LEA to determine the structure of its own secondary provision appear increasingly hostile to the Labour Party in the eyes of some of its supporters. It was therefore understandable that the active campaign to prevent education committees from having their own organization after April 1974 centred on the efforts of the urban oriented and Labour-controlled AMA. There is no space here to relate this story and it has in any case been chronicled in detail in a very full article in *The Times Educational Supplement.*[26] The Conservatives and the ACC certainly did not strive to keep alive the AEC even if they did not actively seek its end in quite the way that some of their opponents did.

A significant official step in the ending of the AEC was taken by Reg Prentice as Secretary of State in May 1974 when he wrote to state that the Association would lose its membership of any Burnham Committee from September of that year. The grounds for this were that 'it cannot be disputed that responsibility for education within local government resides with local authorities in their capacity as local education authorities and not with particular committees of those authorities'. This had, of course, been the legal position since 1902 but at this point the AMA and the ACC had pressed their claims to the exclusion of the AEC. In his letter Prentice added that he had decided that the DES would continue to consult the AEC on matters of general educational concern and went on to acknowledge the great benefit derived from consulting it on a multiplicity of such matters in the past. But once out of the Burnham fold, the AEC could not survive and it was formally wound up in 1977.

In the course of the controversy over the AEC in 1975, a letter from Lord Boyle provided a useful indicator of the extent of the influence of the Association in the decades following 1945. He pointed out that although in a formal sense the AEC had not taken any part in Rate Support Grant negotiations 'it would be quite false to suppose that the AEC doesn't therefore *influence the outcome* of such negotiations'. The minutes of the AEC executive had been of the greatest value to him as a minister when arguing education's case with ministerial colleagues. 'The three men who did most to launch the notable era of educational expansion, which lasted from 1954 to 1973 were

Eccles, Gould and Alexander.' It was vital that there should continue to be 'an effective, unified voice for the education service with a sufficient degree of independence'.[27]

The increased influence of the Department of the Environment centrally, and of the AMA and ACC locally, are both products of the greater emphasis on party political considerations in recent years. It is very difficult to conceive now of any positive sort of initiative from the local authority area such as that which produced the national curricular and examinations arrangements in the post-war years even in the face of Ministry opposition although the new organizations can undoubtedly exercise very considerable negative influence over DES initiatives. The AMA and ACC do join in the Council for Local Education Authorities which meets annually but control over their education policy decisions remains firmly with the separate associations.

Notes and References

CHAPTER I *Pupils and Schools*

1. *The Economist,* 1 and 15 Sept. 1945.
2. PRO, ED 136/336, War Cabinet, Memorandum R(44)67, Post-war Building Programme, 30 Mar. 1944.
3. Ibid., Reconstruction Committee Minutes, 24 Apr. 1944.
4. *The Economist,* 6 July 1946.
5. AEC, C56(a), Report of the Committee on School Sites and Buildings Procedure, 1946.
6. Ministry of Education, Circular 48, 24 May 1945.
7. AEC, 103, Director of Education, Northumberland, to Ministry, 28 July 1945; Ministry to Northumberland LEA, 10 Aug. 1945.
8. Ibid., John Maud to W. P. Alexander, 4 Jan. 1946.
9. Reports in *The Times, Manchester Guardian, News Chronicle, Yorkshire Post* on 15 Jan. 1947; AEC Minutes, 16 Jan. 1947.
10. PRO, CAB 128, Cabinet conclusions, 16 Jan.1947.
11. Ministry of Education, Annual Reports for 1947, 1948, 1949.
12. Ministry of Education, Circular 64, 27 Sept. 1945.
13. AEC, A266, Correspondence between W. Cleary, R.N. Heaton and W. P. Alexander, 29 June to 28 Sept. 1949.
14. Ibid., A361, School Buildings, Memorandum by the Association of Chief Education Officers, 18 Jan. 1961.
15. Ibid., B112a, G.G. Williams to Percival Sharp, 8 July 1944; Ministry of Education, Circular 10, 14 Nov. 1944 and Memorandum on Building Regulations, S.R. and O. No. 345, 1945.
16. Ibid., W. Cleary to W. P. Alexander, 27 May 1946.
17. Ibid., A. A. Part to W. P. Alexander, 13 Apr. 1949.
18. Ministry of Education, Statutory Instruments, 1949, No. 2279 and Circular 222, 13 Dec. 1949.
19. Ibid., Building Bulletin No. 2, *New Secondary Schools,* 1950, p. 2.
20. AEC, B 89(a), W. P. Alexander to S. A. W. J. Marshall, 21 Mar. 1950.
21. Ibid., B 89(b), Conference Papers, Sept. 1951.

22. Ibid., A 361, School Building, Memorandum by the Association of Chief Education Officers, 18 Jan. 1961.
23. *Economist*, 19 Mar. 1949; *TES*, 28 Oct. 1949.
24. Ministry of Education, Circular 245, 4 Feb. 1952.
25. *The Times*, 5 Feb. 1952, Report of speech by R. A. Butler and leading article.
26. AEC, B 111 (b), D.M. Nenk (Ministry) to Alexander, 14 Mar. 1952.
27. Ibid., Nenk to Alexander, 25 and 28 Nov. 1952.
28. P.P. 1952–53, Eighth Report from the Select Committee on Estimates, 20 May 1953.
29. Edward Boyle, 'Parliament's views on responsibility for Education Policy since 1944', a lecture delivered on 7 May 1976 at the Institute of Local Government Studies, p. 3.
30. AEC, B 126 (a), F. Barraclough to Alexander, 3 Nov. 1954.
31. AEC B 157 (a), Alexander to Eccles, 2 Mar. 1956.
32. Ibid., A 361, School Building, Memorandum by the A.C.E.O., 18 Jan. 1961; P.P. 1960–61, Eighth Report from the Select Committee on Estimates, 21 Aug. 1961.
33. AEC, A 19 c, Morrell to Alexander, 23 June 1961.
34. DES, *The Schools Building Survey, 1962*, 1965.
35. P. H. J. H. Gosden, *Education in the Second World War*, 1976, pp. 271–91, 325–6.
36. PRO, Cabinet 26(50), 22 Apr. 1950; Cabinet 27(50), 1 May 1950; Cabinet 28(50), 4 May 1950; Cabinet Paper (50) 87 dated 27 Apr. 1950, 'The Churches and the Education Act, 1944'.
37. Hansard, H C, vol. 474, cols 1914 and 1919; *Education*, 10 Feb. and 19 May 1950.
38. Education Act 1953.
39. AEC A528, Canon Leonard [Secretary, Schools Council of the Church of England Board of Education] to Alexander, 21 Jan. 1959.
40. Ibid., Braithwaite to Alexander, 30 June 1958; Alexander to Braithwaite, 4 July 1958.
41. Ibid., W. K. Reid (Ministry of Education) to Alexander, 27 Jan. 1959; R. N. Heaton to Alexander, 9 Jan. 1959.
42. Hansard, H C, vol. 735, cols 902–3 (Sir Edward Boyle).
43. AEC, E20, D. H. Leadbetter to Alexander, 28 Sept.1966; DES Circular 3/67 explains fully provisions of the Act.
44. Hansard, H C, vol. 735, col. 866 where Tom Driberg read from a letter from Canon Wild, Secretary to the Schools Council of the Church of England Board of Education.
45. PRO, ED 46/155, Postwar social development and its effects on schools. W. Cleary, 13 Jan. 1941.

46. PRO, ED 136/212, Williams to Holmes, 3 Mar. 1941; ED 136/217, Holmes to R. S. Wood, 3 Mar. 1941.
47. AEC, A266, Ministry to Middlesex County Council, 7 Jan. 1949.
48. Lord Boyle, 'The politics of secondary school reorganization: some reflections.' *Journal of Educational Administration and History*, IV, 2, p. 31.
49. Ibid., p. 32.
50. West Riding Education Committee, SG605, Clegg to Fletcher, 3 and 15 May 1963.
51. AEC, A1097, H.F. Rossetti (DES) to Alexander, 9 Nov. 1965; Note of a meeting between officers of the DES and the local authority associations, 2 Dec. 1965.
52. Ibid., A699, Correspondence from 9 to 21 Jan. 1969; *Guardian*, 22 Jan. 1969.
53. Ibid., A1113, Correspondence between Robinson (Southport) and Alexander, 17 and 20 Mar. and 20 and 27 Oct. 1969.
54. Ibid., AMC to its Vice-President in the Commons, Education Bill, 11 Feb. 1970; Short to Alexander, 26 Mar.; Alexander to Short, 28 April; Short to Alexander, 4 May 1970.
55. Roger Woods, 'Margaret Thatcher and Secondary Reorganization, 1970–74', *Journal of Educational Administration and History*, XIII, 2, p. 53. This article gives a careful account of the way in which Mrs Thatcher's policies developed.
56. *Times Educational Supplement*, 29 Jan. 1971.
57. Lord Boyle, op. cit., p. 36.
58. *Guardian*, 4 Sept. 1973, 'Mrs Thatcher's long delays'; Roger Woods, op. cit., p. 59; *Education*, 16 June 1972.
59. AEC, E74, Brown (ACC) to Lord Amory, 30 Sept. 1976; Alexander to Mulley, 27 Feb. 1976; Mulley to Alexander, 17 Mar. 1976.
60. Secretary of State for Education and Science *v* Metropolitan Borough of Tameside (1977) A.C. 1014.
61. DES, Press Notice, Direct Grant Grammar Schools to be phased out, 11 Mar. 1975.
62. DES, *Education: A Framework for Expansion*, Dec.1972, Cmnd 5174; *Education*, 22 Dec. 1972.
63. *Education*, 21 Dec.1973, pp. 625–6; Hansard, H C, vol. 866, col. 964, Chancellor of the Exchequer.

CHAPTER 2   *Curriculum and Examinations*

1. Sheila Browne, 'Curriculum: an HMI view', *Trends in Education*, 1977, 3, pp. 38–9; DES, Report of the Central Advisory Council

for Education (England), *Children and their Primary Schools,* 1967, vol. 1, p. 189; DES, *Primary Education in England, a survey by H.M. Inspectors of Schools,* 1978, chs 5 and 6.

2. P. H. J. H. Gosden, *Education in the Second World War,* 1976, pp. 370–1.

3. Board of Education, *Curriculum and Examinations in Secondary Schools,* 1943, pp. 140–1.

4. PRO, ED 12/480, Barrow to Williams, 16 Dec. 1943 and 5 Jan. 1944; Williams to Barrow, 12 Jan. 1944; Norwood to Williams, 11 May 1944.

5. Ministry of Education, Circular 103, 16 May 1946.

6. AEC, B74(c), Williams to Alexander, 15 Feb. 1946, enclosing draft circular; Alexander to Maud, 15 Apr. 1946; Ministry of Education, Circular 113, 26 June 1946.

7. Ibid., SSEC Minutes no. 1, 9 Oct. 1946; no. 2, 23 Jan. 1947; no. 3, 6 Mar. 1947; no. 4, 17 Apr. 1947; no. 5, 22 May 1947; no. 6, 4 July 1947; no. 7, 21 July 1947; no. 8, 19 Nov. 1947.

8. Ibid., Alexander to Alderman Jackson, 27 May 1947; Professor G. B. Jeffery to Alexander, 14 Feb. 1947; Ministry of Education, *Examinations in Secondary Schools,* Report of the SSEC, 1947.

9. AEC, A103(b), Verbatim copy of Minister's speech to IAHM, 31 Dec. 1948.

10. Ibid., E. B. H. Baker (M of Ed) to D. N. Bungey (Essex), 12 Apr. 1949; Cleary to Alexander, 6 July 1949.

11. Ibid., K. A. Kennedy (M of Ed) to E. Woodhead (Kent), 12 Sept. 1950; AEC Discussion Paper, Examinations in Secondary Schools.

12. Ministry of Education, *Education in 1951,* 1952, pp. 31–5.

13. AEC, C56(a), Beloe to Alexander, 8 Apr. 1952; Alexander to Beloe, 6 May 1952; G. G. [Williams] to My Dear Bill [Alexander], 30 July 1952.

14. Ibid., Alexander to My dear G.G.[Williams], 28 May 1952.

15. Ibid., Alexander to Odgers, 11 July 1952; Odgers to Alexander, 15 Sept. 1952; Alexander to Odgers, 22 July 1952; Ministry of Education, Circular 256, 4 Sept. 1952.

16. AEC, B74(c), Hirst to Alexander, 26 Apr. 1949; Odgers to Alexander, 29 Apr. 1949; SSEC, Sub-Cttee, Discussion with Standing Conference of Regional Examining Unions, Minutes, 1 Mar. 1949; Cyril Lloyd to Philip Morris, 27 Nov. 1950; GCE, Second Memorandum by the bodies sponsoring the proposal for a Ninth Examining Body, 20 Nov. 1950.

17. Report of the Local Examinations Syndicate, Cambridge University Reporter, 2 June 1954.

18. P. Fisher, 'The influence of the AEC upon the development of

secondary school examinations in England, 1943–1964', unpublished PhD thesis, Leeds, 1979, p. 197.

19. AEC, C56(a), Stephenson (Nottingham) to Ministry, 28 Dec. 1955.

20. Ibid., Alexander to Fletcher (Ministry), 11 June 1954 and subsequent correspondence on this file.

21. Ministry of Education, Circular 289, 9 July 1955, AEC, C56(a), Memorandum of observations on Circular 289 for submission to the Minister of Education, 22 Dec. 1955.

22. Ministry of Education, Circular 326, 3 July 1957; Fisher, op. cit., p. 281.

23. AEC, B153(a), Lockwood to Minister, 3 Apr. 1958; Minister to Lockwood, 17 June 1958.

24. Ibid., SSEC-S-Cttee on Secondary School Examinations, Minutes, 30 Sept. 1958. For Beloe's own view of his attitude see Robert Beloe, 'Looking Back on the CSE' in *Secondary Education*, vol. 1, no. 2 (1971) pp. 11–13.

25. AEC, B166(a), S.T. Broad to S-Cttee on Secondary School Examinations, 13 Mar. 1959; Minutes of S-Cttee, 16 Mar., 21 Apr. and 25 May 1959; J. Wilkinson (Ealing) to Alexander, 10 June 1959.

26. Ministry of Education, *Secondary School Examinations other than the GCE, Report of a Committee appointed by the SSEC in July 1958*, 1960, pp. 47–8; Ministry of Education, *Examinations in Secondary Schools: The Certificate of Secondary Education. A Proposal for a new School Leaving Certificate, Fourth Report of the SSEC,* 1961.

27. AEC, C57(c), SSEC, Paper no. 219, Secondary School Examinations other than the GCE, Committee's Observations on Comments Received, Mar. 1961.

28. Hansard, H.C. DCXLIV, 909–912 (17 July 1960); Ministry of Education, *Education in 1960*, 1961, p. 25 and *Education in 1961*, 1962, pp. 16–18.

29. Ministry of Education, *The Certificate of Secondary Education: Notes for the Guidance of Regional Examining Bodies*, SSEC Fifth Report, 1962; R. Beloe, op. cit.

30. Ibid., *Scope and Standards of the CSE*, SSEC Seventh Report, 1962.

31. Boyle Papers, 'The Work of Schools Branch: A New Look', Oct. 1961.

32. AEC, A511, Mary Smieton to Alexander, 9 Mar. 1962.

33. Ibid., Alexander to Smieton, 12 March 1962; *Education*, 23 March 1962; *Times Educational Supplement*, 31 Aug. 1962.

34. *Education*, 9 Oct. 1962; AEC Executive Committee Minutes, 255, 29 Nov. 1962.

35. AEC, A31a, Morrell to Alexander, 21 Feb. 1962 and accompanying draft memorandum.
36. Hansard, H.C., vol. 678, cols 155–6. (Written answer Boyle to Thompson, 29 May 1963.)
37. AEC, A31a, Note by Mrs Marjorie McIntosh (LCC) on the Ministry's Memorandum: 'Proposed Schools Council'; The School Curriculum and Examinations, Proposal to establish cooperative machinery, Minutes of 19 July 1963.
38. Ibid., County Councils Assn., Proposed Schools Council, Note of Meeting, 3 Sept. 1963.
39. Ibid., CEWP, Papers 1, 2, 3, 4 and 5.
40. Ibid., CEWP, Paper 12a; Morrell's secretary to Alexander's secretary, 19 November 1963; CEWP, Minutes 3, 27 Nov. 1963, paras 8 to 14.
41. AEC, A347a, Morrell to Alexander, 28 Nov. 1963; Alexander to Morrell, 29 Nov. 1963.
42. AEC, A31b, Correspondence from many organizations seeking the right to nominate to the Schools Council. Decisions on applications in Schools Council Minutes (64) 1 (b).
43. Schools Council, *Raising the School Leaving Age*, Working Paper no. 2, 1965.
44. AEC, A962, Sibson (Schools Council) to Alexander, 6 Feb. 1973.
45. Ibid., Parker to Alexander, 11 Feb. 1971 and 19 Feb. 1973; Warren to Alexander, 29 Mar. 1972.
46. Ibid., Alexander to Sibson, 8 Feb. 1973.
47. *Proposals for a Certificate in Extended Education*, Report of the Study Group (Chairman, K.W. Keohane), Cmnd 7755 (1979).
48. *Education*, 30 Nov. 1979.
49. *Secondary Examinations Post-16: A Programme of Improvement*, Report of the Working Party, Schools Council, London, Mar. 1980; Hansard, H.C. vol. 982, col. 300 (written answer Boyson to Short 3 April 1980); DES, *Examinations 16–18*, Consultative Paper, Oct. 1980.
50. *Times Educational Supplement*, 'Edited extracts from the Yellow Book, the DES memorandum to the Prime Minister', 15 Oct.1976.
51. Ibid., 15 Oct. 1976.
52. *Education*, 10 Mar. 1978.
53. Eric Briault and Frances Smith, *Falling Rolls in Secondary Schools*, 1980.

CHAPTER 3 *The Supply and Training of Teachers*

1. PRO, ED 143/1, Board of Education, Report of the office

committee on the immediate post-war supply and training of teachers, n.d. [1943].

2. Board of Education Circular 1652 (15 May 1944).

3. Ministry of Education, *Challenge and Response. An account of the emergency training scheme for the training of teachers*, Pamphlet no. 17, 1950.

4. NUT, *Annual Report*, 1945, p. xliii; AEC, B25(a) R. S. Wood to Alexander, 4 Apr. 1946; G. N. Flemming to Alexander, 2 Mar. 1950.

5. PRO, ED 86/94, Committee on the Training of Teachers, Paper 102, Memorandum by S. H. Wood embodying a proposal for a major constitutional reform 12 Mar.1943; Wood to G. Savage, 31 May 1943.

6. PRO, ED 86/109, R. S. Wood to R. A. Butler, 4 Aug. 1944.

7. Ibid., Notes on interview and deputation from CVCP, 9 Aug. 1944; Minute S. H. Wood to Sir Robert Wood; Chuter Ede to R. A. Butler, 12 Sept. 1944.

8. Ibid., R. S. Wood to Ellen Wilkinson, 25 July 1945; Wilkinson to Wood, 19 Aug. 1945; Wood to Wilkinson, 21 Aug. and 21 Sept. 1945.

9. Ibid., A Note on the outcome of a meeting of officers of the Ministry, S. H. Wood, 21 Nov. 1945; Memorandum, Universities and the training of teachers, the McNair recommendations, 18 Mar. 1946.

10. AEC, B25(b), G. G. Williams to Alexander, 4 Nov. 1946.

11. Ibid., Ministry of Education, R. N. Heaton to Williams, Flemming and Howlett, 14 Apr. 1947; Interview Cttee Paper 11, 2 Feb. 1948.

12. Ibid., Working Party on the Distribution of Teachers, Minutes 13 Feb. and 10 Mar. 1948.

13. AEC, B26(a), Williams to Alexander, 30 Aug. 1948.

14. NACTST, Standing Cttee A, Minutes, 14 Feb. 1950.

15. *Three Year Training for Teachers*, Fifth Report of the NACTST, 1956, para. 24.

16. Ministry of Education, Circular 325, 17 June 1957; *The Scope and Content of the Three Year Course of Teacher Training*, Sixth Report of the NACTST, 1957.

17. *The Economist*, 24 May 1958, p. 677.

18. AEC, A278, Miss H. M. Simpson (ATCDE) to Alexander, 10 Nov. 1960; 'The training of teachers in relation to the expansion of higher education', ATCDE memorandum to the Committee on Higher Education, July 1961; AEC Evidence submitted to the Robbins Committee, 29 Sept. 1961; Alexander to H. Oldman, 22 Nov. 1961.

19. AEC, A278, 'Jack' [Wolfenden], Chmn UGC, to 'Maurice' [Dean], Treasury, 24 June 1964.
20. AEC, A1133, Alexander to Dacey, 8 Jan. 1964; Dacey to Alexander, 9 Jan. 1964; DES, Note of meeting with representatives of the LEAs to discuss the future of the training colleges, 30 Nov. 1964; DES, Statement by the Secretary of State on the future of teacher training colleges in England and Wales, 11 Dec. 1964.
21. Ministry of Education, *Staffing the Schools*, Reports on Education no. 6, Dec. 1963.
22. DES, *Colleges of Education*, Reports on Education no. 49, Oct. 1968.
23. DES, *Report of the Study Group on the Government of Colleges of Education*, 1966; DES, *Education and Science in 1969*, 1970, p. 65.
24. DES, *Teacher Education and Training*, 1972.
25. This matter has been explored fully by David Hencke, *Colleges in Crisis*, 1978, pp. 42–7.
26. Hansard, HC, vol. 888, cols. 471–2 (20 Mar. 1975), Written Answers, Prentice to Clemitson.
27. Hansard, HC, vol. 919, cols 133–4 (9 Nov. 1976), Written Answers, Williams to Price, ibid., vol. 913, cols 528–9 (23 June 1976), Written Answers, Mulley to Bennett.
28. AEC, G25, Criteria for restructuring the teacher training system, ACSTT, 1977.
29. DES, *Education and Science in 1969*, 1970, pp. 31–2.

CHAPTER 4 *Social and Welfare Provisions*

1. 6 Edw VII, C.57.
2. PRO, ED 50/234, Note of meeting with Children's Nutrition Council, 18 Mar. 1940.
3. PRO, ED 50/233, War Cabinet. Lord President's Committee, LP (43), 100, 4 May 1943, joint memorandum by President of Board of Education and Minister of Food; ibid., LP (43) 31st meeting, 7 May 1943; Ministry of Education, *Statistics Relating to Education for the Years 1935–46*, 1948, p. 13.
4. PRO, ED 138/60, E. D. Marris, War history of school meals and milk, 1944: Hansard, HC, 386, cols 1665–6 (16 Feb. 1943).
5. Ministry of Reconstruction, *Social Insurance, Part I*, Cmd. 6550, Sep. 1944; Hansard, HC, 406, col. 986 (2 Nov. 1944).
6. Ministry of Education, Circular 21 (4 Jan. 1945).
7. Ibid., S.R. & O. 1945, no. 698, Reg. 10(3)(a) and S.I. 1951, no. 1320, Reg. 3.
8. AEC, C54(a), Alexander to Lawrence (Essex), 16 Mar. 1959.

9.   DES, Circular 25/66 (15 Dec. 1966).
10.   AEC, B132(b), G. G. Williams (Ministry) to Alexander, 12 July 1951.
11.   AEC, B132(b), Ministry to all CEOs, 16 Oct.1954: Longland (Derbyshire) to Alexander, 18 Mar. 1955; C40(c), correspondence between Alexander and Thornton (Ministry) 7 Feb. to 14 Mar. 1956.
12.   Hansard, HC, 756, cols 708–9, Gordon Walker (19 Jan. 1968).
13.   AEC E73, Taylor (Somerset) to Alexander, 6 Jan. 1976; *Public Expenditure to 1979–80*, Cmd 6393, Feb. 1976.
14.   1980, c20.
15.   DES, *Annual Report 1981*, p. 16.
16.   Ministry of Education, Circular 29 (12 Mar. 1945).
17.   PRO, Ed 50/287, Bevan to Wilkinson, 8 Sep. 1945; Bosworth-Smith to Cleary, 11 Sept. 1945; Ministry of Health, *A National Health Service*, Cmd 6502, 1944, p. 39.
18.   Ministry of Education, Circular 179 (4 Aug. 1948); AEC, B18(b) contains correspondence, notes of meetings with Ministry officials and between local authority associations concerned with the implementation of these new arrangements in 1948.
19.   Ministry of Education, *The Health of the School Child*, Report of the Chief Medical Officer of the DES for the years 1962 and 1963, HMSO, 1964.
20.   DES, *Special Educational Needs*, Report of the Committee of Enquiry into the Education of Handicapped Children and Young People, Cmnd 7212, 1978.
21.   Ministry of Education, *The Health of the School Child*, Report of the Chief Medical Officer for the years 1948 and 1949, 1952, p. 46.
22.   Hansard, HC, vol. 840, cols 400–1, 445–6 (13 July 1972); AEC, A1115, Report of School Health service sub-committee of the working-party on collaboration; AEC, AMC, CCA, ILEA, WJEC, School Health Service; C. Read (Society of Education Officers) to DES, 26 Oct. 1972.
23.   AEC, B136 (a), Alexander to Wilson (King George's Jubilee Trust), 15 Feb. 1950; Ministry of Education, *Recruitment and Training of Youth Leaders and Community Centre Wardens*, Second Report of the NACTST, 1951.
24.   AEC, B190(a), Flemming to Alexander and reply, 14 and 22 Feb. 1952; Bray (Ministry) to Alexander, 9 Feb. 1955.
25.   Ibid., Kennedy to Alexander, 1 Jan. 1957; Note of discussion between parliamentary secretary and representatives of local authority associations and the SCNVYO, 6 Mar. 1957.

26. *Seventh Report from the Select Committee on Estimates*, The Youth Employment Service and Youth Service Grants, H.C. 240, 24 July 1957, p. x.
27. Ministry of Education, *The Youth Service in England and Wales*, Report of the Committee appointed by the Minister of Education in November 1958, Cmnd 929, 1960, p. 1.
28. Ministry of Education/DES, *Annual Reports*; Administrative Memorandum 2/62 (16 Feb. 1962).
29. Ministry of Education, Circular 11/60 (17 Aug. 1960).

CHAPTER 5   *The Universities*

1. UGC, *University Development from 1935 to 1947*, 1948, p. 26.
2. PRO, UGC 2/25, Notes of a meeting between UGC and CVCP held on 10 Feb. 1944.
3. PRO, CAB 65/53, CP(45)80, Release of students from the forces, Memorandum by the Minister of Labour and National Service, 14 July 1945; CM(45)15, Conclusion of a meeting of the Cabinet, 18 July 1945.
4. PRO, E.D.46/295, Attlee to Bevin, 29 Jan. 1945.
5. Hansard, HC, CCCCVIII, 35–7 (13 Feb. 1945). The recurrent grant for the second year was subsequently increased to £9,450,000 – Ibid., CCCCXIX, 319 (22 Feb. 1946).
6. *Scientific Manpower*, Report of a committee appointed by the Lord President of the Council, Cmd 6824, 1946.
7. UGC, *University Development from 1947 to 1952*, Cmd 8875, 1953.
8. Committee on Scientific Manpower, *Fifth Annual Report*, Cmd 8561, 1952.
9. Anthony Seldon. *Churchill's Indian Summer: the Conservative Government 1951–55*, 1981, pp. 280–1; UGC, *University Development 1957–1962*, Cmnd 2267, 1964, p. 154.
10. Hansard, HC 560 col. 1750 (21 Nov. 1956).
11. Ibid., 582, cols 1400–1 (20 Feb. 1958).
12. UGC, *University Development, 1957–1962*, Cmnd 2267, 1964.
13. A full list of the members of academic planning boards is given in *University Development 1957–1962*, Appendix J.
14. The other two places where universities were actually founded, Lancaster and Essex, were on a 'potential' list alongside Hereford, Stevenage, Whitby and Bournemouth.
15. CVCP, Minute 61, 23 Oct.1959.
16. Lord Boyle, *Government, Parliament and the Robbins Report*, Joseph Payne Memorial Lecture, 1979, p. 6.

17. Ministry of Education, *Education in 1947*, Cmd 7426, 1948, p. 59.
18. P. H. J. H. Gosden and P. R. Sharp, *The Development of an Education Service: The West Riding 1889–1974*, 1978, p. 227.
19. UGC, *University Development 1952–1957*, Cmnd 534, 1958, p. 25.
20. Ministry of Education, *Grants to Students*, Cmnd 1051, 1960; Circular 5/61 (28 March 1961).
21. Hansard HC, 649, cols 36–7 (13 Nov. 1961).
22. CVCP, op. cit.
23. Hansard, HC, vol. 620, cols 52–3 (21 Mar. 1960).
24. Committee on Higher Education, Report, Cmnd 2154, 1963.
25. Boyle, op. cit., p. 7.
26. Hansard, HC, 560 col. 1751 (21 Nov. 1956).
27. *The Times*, 24 Oct. 1963.
28. *Education*, 1 Nov. 1963.
29. Minute from Herbert Andrew as Permanent Secretary. Boyle, op. cit., p. 14.
30. Lord Hailsham, *The Door wherein I went*, 1975, p. 143.
31. CVCP, Report of meeting, 17 Oct. 1969; DES Statistical Bulletin 1/81, Jan. 1981–3; personal information.
32. DES, *Education: a Framework for Expansion*, Cmnd 5174, 1972; UGC, *University Development 1967–1972*, Cmnd 5728, 1974, p. 15.
33. UGC, University Development 1957–1962, Cmnd 2247, p. 25.
34. CVCP, Minute 61, 23 Oct.1959; Minute 288, 19 June 1964.
35. Hansard, HC, 738, cols 376–7 (21 Dec. 1966) and 741, cols 1981–2044 (23 Feb. 1967).
36. Notes on the Vice-Chancellors' Committee Meeting at Cambridge, 14–16 June 1968.
37. Select Committee on Education and Science, Session 1968–69, *Student Relations*, 1969.
38. DES Press Notice, 15 July 1982, and open letter from the Secretary of State to the Chairman of the UGC, 14 July.
39. DES, *A University of the Air*, Cmnd 2922, 1966.
40. Australia College of Education, Conference Paper, Lord Percy, 'The Open University', 1981, pp. 4–7, 10–11.

CHAPTER 6   *Further Education*

1. 7 & 8 Geo. 6, c. 31, S 41.
2. PRO, ED 46/226. Development of Technical Education, CP 58 (39), 1 Mar. 1939.
3. PRO, Ed 46/295, Percy to Ellen Wilkinson, 10 Sept. 1945; Ministry of Education, *Higher Technological Education*, 1945.

4. Ministry of Education, Circular 87 (25 Feb. 1946).
5. AEC, B160a, Northern Advisory Council for F.E.., Report of a meeting of F. Bray with Chief Education Officers of the Northern Region, 12 Mar. 1948.
6. Ministry of Education, *The Future Development of Higher Technological Education*, Report of the NACEIC, 1950.
7. Ministry of Education, Higher Technological Education, Cmnd 8357, 1951; AEC, C69(a), F. Bray (Ministry) to Alexander, 1 Aug. 1951 and 13 Sept. 1951; Ministry of Education, Circular 255 (14 July 1952).
8. Supra p. 142 for some discussion of Lord Cherwell's own ideas and position; see also Hansard, HL, 177 no. 72 p. 181 (12 June 1952). AEC, C69(a), Brown (LCC) to Alexander, 14 Oct. 1952; Association of Education Officers, memorandum on the White Paper on Higher Technological Education, 28 Sept. 1951.
9. Ibid., Alexander to Flemming, 13 Feb. 1953; Flemming to Alexander, 23 Feb. 1953; Interview Memorandum, Deputation from NACEIC, 18 Feb. 1953.
10. Ministry of Education, *Technical Education*, Cmnd 9703, 1956.
11. Ministry of Education, Circular 305 (21 June 1956); Hansard, HC, 554, cols 1639–766 (21 June 1956).
12. Hansard, HC, 557, cols 27–8 (24 July 1956). It may be noted that of the 8 designated CATs, 4 were LEA controlled, 3 were Aided, and 1 was Direct Grant.
13. AEC, B154a, NACEIC, Report on developments, Sept. 1957.
14. Ministry of Education, *Better Opportunities in Technical Education*, Cmnd 1254, 1961.
15. Ministry of Education, Circular 3/61 (13 Mar. 1961).
16. AEC. A492, Draft of speech to be given by the Minister to AEC Conference on 23 June 1961, 15 June 1961; Dame Mary Smieton to Alexander 22 June 1961.
17. Ibid., Alexander to Smieton, 27 June 1961; Dacey (CCA) to Alexander, 11 July 1961; Alexander to Dacey, 12 July 1961; CCA Note of meeting held on 27 July 1961 of representatives of Associations and LEAs maintaining CATs, 5 Oct. 1961.
18. PRO, ED 136/560, Butler to the Permanent Secretary, 12 Feb. 1943.
19. Sir Toby Weaver, *Higher Education and the Polytechnics*, The Joseph Payne Memorial Lecture, 1973, p. 6.
20. CNAA, *Report for 1965–66* and *Report for 1966–67*.
21. Supra, pp. 152–4.
22. Weaver, op. cit., p. 7.

23. DES, Admin. Mem. 7/63 (6 May 1965). In this the Secretary of State issued the text of his speech at Woolwich.
24. CVCP, Minute 265, 21 May 1965; *Education*, 7 May 1965, p. 947.
25. M. Kogan, *The Politics of Education*, 1971, p. 193.
26. Lord Boyle, *Government, Parliament and the Robbins Report*, The Joseph Payne Memorial Lecture, 1979, p. 16.
27. AEC, A317, Mr Prentice's advisory group on higher education within the FE system, Paper no. 1, 23 June 1965; Paper no. 1 (first Revise) 14 July 1965; paper no. 5, Nov. 1965.
28. DES, *A plan for polytechnics and other colleges*, Cmnd 3006, May 1966, AEC, A731, DES to AEC enclosing a memorandum, Government and academic organization of polytechnics, 22 Aug.1966, and subsequent correspondence.
29. Ministry of Education, *Technical Education*, Cmd 9703, 1956; Hansard, HC, 642, cols 159–60 (22 June 1961).
30. DES, *Day Release*, Report of a Committee set up by the Minister of Education, 1964.
31. Ministry of Labour, *Industrial Training Government Proposals*, Cmnd 1892, 1962; Industrial Training Act, 1964.
32. Ministry of Education, *The Supply and Training of Teachers for Technical Colleges*, Report of a special committee appointed by the Minister of Education in 1956, 1957; Ministry of Education, *Education in 1960*, 1961.
33. *Guardian*, 8 Mar. 1966; AEC, A501, copy of DES note of meeting between the Minister of State and representatives of the Association of Municipal Corporations, 19 July 1966.
34. AEC, A501, Alexander to Andrew, 24 July and 8 Sept. 1969, Andrew to Alexander, 6 Aug. and 9 Sept. 1969.

CHAPTER 7   *The Government and Administration of the Education System*

1. PRO, ED 136/212, R. S. Wood (Deputy Secretary) to M. Holmes (Permanent Secretary), 8 Nov. 1940. See also Holmes's comments in a note in this file 5 Nov. 1940.
2. PRO, ED 136/520, War Cabinet, Lord President's Committee, LP (44) 35, 1 Mar. 1944; Ibid., LP (44) 11th meeting, 3 Mar. 1944.
3. Select Committee on Expenditure, Tenth Report, 1975–6, *Policy making in the Department of Education and Science*.
4. See chapter 5 of this book.
5. PRO, ED 136/560, Butler to the Permanent Secretary, 12 Feb. and 4 Mar. 1943.
6. Lord Boyle, *Government, Parliament and the Robbins Report*, 1979, pp. 14–15.

7. *Times Educational Supplement*, 14 Feb. 1964, p. 381.
8. Ministry of Housing and Local Government, *Local Government Finance*, Cmnd 209, 1957; W. P. Alexander and R. Gould, *The Threat to Education*, 1957; Interview, Lord Boyle, 7 Mar. 1979.
9. AEC, A1152, Alexander to M. L. Franks, 16 Dec. 1976.
10. *Financial Times*, 2 Aug. 1982, 'Education block grant scheme rejected'.
11. 6 and 7 Eliz. C55, S 52; NADEE Report of 15th Annual Conference, 1961.
12. Divional administration is fully discussed in T. E. Reller, *Divisional Administration in English Education*, 1959 and in E. W. Cohen, *Autonomy and Delegation in County Government*, n.d.
13. PRO, ED 136/807, W.R.L. to Permanent Secretary, 16 Jan. 1947.
14. AEC, A518. Telephone message taken by R. Parsons from M. A. Walker (Ministry of Education) to Alexander, 29 Nov. 1960; also letter confirming message from Walker to Alexander of same date.
15. Ibid., Memorandum on the Report of the Royal Commission on Local Government in Greater London as it affects the Education Service, 27 Jan. 1961.
16. Ministry of Housing and Local Government, *London Government: Government Proposals for Reorganization*, Cmnd 1562, 1961.
17. AEC, A1060. Note from R. P. to Alexander, 6 July 1966; Correspondence between Alexander and Cllr. Mrs Wormald, 25 and 26 Oct. 1966.
18. Ibid., Memorandum on local government reorganization in England to be submitted to the Royal Commission on Local Government, 30 Sept. 1966.
19. Department of the Environment, *Local Government in England: Government Proposals for Reorganization*, Cmnd 4584, 1971.
20. AEC, A1065, Alexander to Clegg, 22 Apr. 1971.
21. Ibid., Department of the Environment to AEC, 26 Aug. 1971 and accompanying paper entitled 'Statutory provisions affecting the internal organization of local authorities in England and Wales'.
22. Ibid., Interim Report of the Working Group on Local Authority Management to the Secretary of State for the Environment, 16 Sept. 1971.
23. Ibid., Alexander to Fred Jarvis, 15 Oct. 1971 and subsequent letters on this file from teachers' organizations, the DES, the Catholic Education Council and the Church of England Board of Education.

24.   AEC, A1065, File to Alexander, 10 Nov. 1971.
25.   DES, Circular 1/73 (16 Jan. 1973) and Circular 8/73 (29 Mar. 1973).
26.   *Times Educational Supplement*, 1 Mar. 1974.
27.   *Education*, 11 Apr. 1975, p. 410.

Index

221